Paddling Our Own Canoe

By

Phil Waterton

ShieldCrest

© Copyright 2024 P Waterton

All rights reserved

This book shall not, by way of trade or otherwise, be lent, re-sold, hired out, or otherwise circulated without the prior consent of the copyright holder or the publisher in any form of binding or cover other than that in which it is published and without a similar condition including this condition being imposed on the subsequent purchaser. The use of its contents in any other media is also subject to the same conditions.

ISBN: 978-1-915657-40-4

MMXXIV

This book is made from materials which have been sourced from sustainably managed forests.

A CIP catalogue record for this is available from the British Library

Published by
ShieldCrest Publishing,
Boston, Lincs, PE20 3BT England
Tel: +44 (0) 333 8000 890
www.shieldcrest.co.uk

My love and thanks to my wife Jan for her support, patience and hard work in the editing of my book. In spite of much water flowing under many bridges, I have yet to send her completely round the bend.

To my old mate Kev.
Looking forward to many more 'Men Behaving Badly'
days to come.

Contents

Chapter

    Preface

1. Do We Know Our Port from Our Starboard?............1
2. The Point of No Return..................................6
3. To Portage or not to Portage? That is the Question 12
4. A Place for Everything and Everything in its Place 25
5. From Small Beginnings...... 29
6. Close Encounters of the Feathered Kind..................35
7. I Name This Ship……. 64
8. Spires, Punts and Pudding 83
9. What Shall We Do with the Drunken Sailors........107
10. Things That Go Bump in the Night 128
11. Stormy Waters..................................147
12. Relics and Rain..............................162
13. Dining Al Fresco.............................183
14. High Society & Affairs of State....................210
15. Soup, Chairs and a Knot 236
16. As Green Turns to Grey 261
17. Parting Is Such Sweet Sorrow 278
    Epilogue 301
    The Author 303

Preface

Sometime during the autumn of 1998, Kevin and I were idling along the south bank of the Thames in London. We may have visited one too many historic ale houses in the course of what we like to call 'a men behaving badly day'. This isn't quite as bad as it sounds. Three or four times a year, the two of us meet up for a day trip to London or anywhere else that takes our fancy. A day to please ourselves. A day of companionship that always includes good food, fine wine and visits to a fair selection of the public houses in the area.

Kevin is Kevin McHale, my best pal since the age of eleven, and co-conspirator in far too many escapades to safely and prudently recount. This occasion, I recall, was dedicated to studying history. We'd started with the London Dungeons in the morning, sampled a couple of bottles of vintage red wine over lunch, and were now researching the old inns and taverns along Southwark that had been frequented by the likes of Pepys, Shakespeare and Dickens.

"I wonder how many pubs there are along the banks of the Thames from its source to London?" one of us asked.

One thing led to another, as these things do between scholars, quizzers and collectors of trivia, and before we knew it, we'd decided to ascertain the exact number personally. Moreover, we needed a good way to celebrate reaching the ripe old age of fifty. So, visiting fifty pubs and having a celebratory drink in every one sounded like a good idea.

As it turned out, fifty proved to be an underestimate, but let's not get ahead of ourselves and spoil a good story....

Route down the Thames

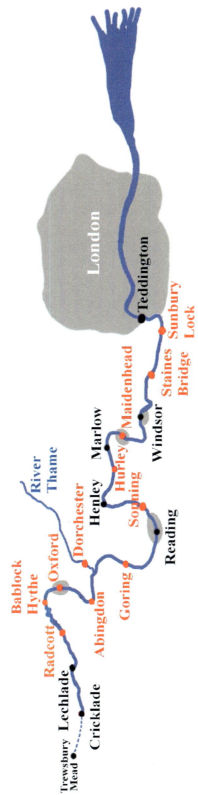

Red Indicates places stayed each night

Not to scale

CHAPTER 1

Do We Know Our Port from Our Starboard?

It's funny how you attract the most attention when you least want it. The crowds at the Longridge Scout Boating Centre at Marlow on the sunny June afternoon we launched our canoe career may indeed have wondered if the spectacle unfolding in front of them was choreographed specially for their benefit. In hindsight, I can understand their amusement. The sight of two robust men in their prime – that would be our description of our fifty-year-old selves – standing chest-deep in the Thames beside an overturned Canadian canoe must have been splendid. I'm surprised nobody called for an action replay.

How we arrived at that pivotal moment is a story that started many long years ago – a story with as many twists and turns as the Thames itself.

Kevin and I met on our second day of secondary school and have remained firm friends, sharing our highs and lows, our ups and downs, good times and bad. Broken engagements, bones and marriages; births, illnesses and deaths – not our own yet, fortunately, a few close calls notwithstanding. We puffed our first cigarette together, pinched from my mother's packet of Craven A. We've skied together, climbed mountains together, walked footpaths, hot-air ballooned, drunk a few bottles of whisky, a few pints of beer and yet a few more bottles of wine. It's a friendship that doesn't need constant conversation, although we usually have plenty to say.

We'd both trained as PE teachers, which somehow compelled us to celebrate our 50th birthdays under our own steam. We would show everyone we weren't ready for the pipe and slippers yet. But how?

Cycling along the Thames path? "Mmm," said Kevin thoughtfully, "your bad back."

Walking? I could see him wince at the memory of the blisters that knocked us off our stride on the Ridgeway Long Distance Path.

"What about canoeing?" one of us said. "Gloves and chamois leather shorts should do the trick to stay free of blisters."

So it was settled. Although we had both flirted with canoeing in the past and had occasionally arranged for pupils to experience the challenge of paddling, our own skills and level of competence in the art of canoeing – for that it proved to be – were as low as a lizard's armpit. These failings would be proved to us and in no uncertain way.

The more we talked it through, the more the idea appealed. Our families humoured us. "Perhaps they'll grow up soon" we heard on more than one occasion. But the seed had been sown.

Using canoes as our mode of transport seemed to be the answer but, I thought, would Kevin be able to keep up with me? "I was just wondering," Kevin said aloud, "if the pace I set will be too much for you?"

What would one do if the other were swept over a weir? What if only one of us was kidnapped by a cruiser full of Amazonian women on a wild weekend party?

"We'll have to stay together," I said firmly.

The answer was a two-man Canadian canoe. But where to find one?

We quickly discovered that new Canadians cost a great deal of money and hiring a boat for anything over a weekend would be difficult and expensive. We bought every canoe and outdoor pursuit magazine on the market, hoping to find a reasonably priced second-hand Canadian for sale. Nothing.

Do We Know Our Port from Our Starboard?

"We'll just have to make one," Kevin suggested. Visions of *Hiawatha*, hollowed-out tree trunks and birch bark came to mind.

It may have been thoughts of evenings in the garage with waterproof glue trying to stick bits of canoe together that the obvious solution suddenly hit me: the Longridge Scout Boating Centre at Marlow. They must have canoes of all shapes and sizes. I phoned and explained our intentions.

The duty manager sounded duly impressed with our plans but unfortunately, they didn't have any canoes for sale or hire. However, he did invite us to come down to the centre when he would gladly lend us a Canadian canoe for a few hours for some practice. We jumped at the chance. We read through our one-star, beginners manual from the British Canoe Union again just to make sure that our skill levels and competence were up to scratch.

The Longridge centre is just below the Marlow lock on the River Thames, separated from the main stream by an island. Scouts and Guides from London and the Southern Counties go on residential visits to participate in water activities. It's a superb facility enjoyed by hundreds of young people each year.

We'd planned a morning visit, but as Kevin had travelled south from Coventry on the Saturday and we'd spent the evening on a 'planning session' in my local, and as this 'planning session' had gone on longer than anticipated, an early morning start was out of the question. So, we arrived at Longridge after lunch full of misplaced confidence and raring to go.

The young instructor who was to look after us seemed somewhat embarrassed to be put in charge of such obviously accomplished canoeists who were intending to canoe the entire length of the Thames non-stop. He was, he explained, only with us this afternoon for insurance purposes and as he had only just passed his canoe coaching award, an award incidentally that only very proficient canoeists can expect to gain, he wouldn't have the effrontery to interfere with our training session but would follow at a discreet distance and try to keep up with us.

"Don't worry," I said modestly, "we're only going to take it easy today."

We adjourned to the changing rooms while he went to find us paddles and a buoyancy aid each.

It was a warm sunny afternoon with a slight breeze. When we emerged from the changing rooms clad in t-shirts, shorts and old trainers, it immediately became apparent that most of Buckinghamshire's Scouts and Guides had been spending the weekend at Longridge. They were everywhere, sitting on the bank, cleaning boats, swimming, canoeing and sailing.

The buoyancy aids our instructor handed us with what seemed a slight bow of the head were rather like padded waistcoats with several dangling straps and buckles all needing adjustment. We nonchalantly put them on as if it were a chore we did every day. I was uncomfortably aware that many pairs of eyes seemed to be scrutinising our every move. "You've got yours on back to front," Kevin uttered quietly through a false smile. I withdrew into the changing rooms as if I'd forgotten something and made the necessary re-adjustments. I re-emerged to see Kevin purposefully striding after our minder who was heading towards the canoe store.

The Canadian canoe we were having for the afternoon was, we were informed, brand new and was yet to get its bottom wet. Kevin and I picked up an end each and carried it proudly down to the jetty while our young friend carried his much smaller kayak and the paddles. All eyes were definitely looking our way.

Our canoe looked elegant and eager as a young thoroughbred as it enjoyed its first feel of water. It had to be restrained from wandering off downstream without its masters. It was at this point that a slight doubt crossed my mind as to what exactly we were doing. I caught Kevin's eye and he looked rather serious. "Jump in and we'll get going," said our instructor.

My moment of doubt past only to be replaced by another: Canadian canoes are pointed at both ends. Which was the front and which was the back?

On the way to Longridge, we'd decided that I would sit in the back of the canoe to begin with and then we'd swap over later. I had to decide quickly. Can you imagine the scene if we'd both got in and sat facing away from each other and had then tried to paddle off in different directions? Of course, the seating arrangements would give me a clue, no problem. I hoped that our large audience hadn't perceived any hesitation or uncertainty.

I stepped in with only a slight wobble, sat down and held onto the jetty with both hands to steady the canoe ready for Kevin's entry. He placed his right foot in the canoe leaving his left foot firmly on the jetty. The gap slowly widened. To compensate, I tried to pull the boat back to the jetty. This resulted in the canoe beginning to tip over towards the bank.

Kevin was now almost in the split position, and I was at arm's length from the jetty lying almost horizontally along the surface of the water. All this seemed to be happening in glorious slow motion. Seconds later we were testing our buoyancy aids.

Kevin surfaced and began to furiously tread water until he realised that I was standing up only chest deep. We looked at each other trying to get our breath back after the sudden shock of being baptised in the cold Thames. We convulsed into laughter until the tears mingled with the river water running down our faces.

Our young instructor looked down from the jetty in quiet disbelief, all his illusions no doubt shattered. When we had eventually calmed down, he said to us with a sigh but with new found authority, "Push it over here and I'll show you how to empty it."

That Sunday afternoon at Longridge was not a complete disaster. In fact, we spent a very pleasant afternoon paddling around the island under the watchful eye of our 'keeper'. He turned out to be a very competent instructor and by the time we left he had instilled in us a new – and this time justified – confidence and taught us the fundamentals of canoeing. We could go forwards and backwards, turn right and left – that would be port and starboard, or is the other way around? – and what's more we now knew the correct method of getting in and out of a canoe without capsizing.

CHAPTER 2

The Point of No Return

Old Father Time, just like Old Father Thames, marches ceaselessly on. We had set a date to start our epic voyage, the 12th of August – the Glorious Twelfth – which gave us plenty of time at the beginning of the school's summer holiday to prepare and, more importantly, a period at the end to recover before we went back.

By now friends and colleagues knew of our plans and several bets and wagers had been made. Would we manage to visit fifty pubs? Would we complete the journey? Would the trip actually take place? Many people had by now agreed to sponsor us.

The excuse of visiting a pub for every year of our lives was undoubtedly the prime motivation for our trip but we both agreed that we should not waste the opportunity to raise some cash for a worthy cause – and we knew plenty.

The Kosovo crisis was at its height at the time. We were particularly impressed by the work of UNICEF and wanted them to be our worthy cause. If our trip was to be a sponsored event, we'd have to collect photographic evidence to prove that fifty pubs had in fact been visited. Each inn, tavern or pub had to either front the Thames or have its own jetty or mooring place.

Kevin volunteered to speak to UNICEF. After UNICEF had sent us information, stickers for the canoe and T-shirts with their logo, we realised how embarrassing it would now be if our bluff were called and our excuse for pulling out was a lack of a suitable craft. 'Up the creek without a paddle' took on a whole new significance.

The Point of No Return

Strange as it may seem, Kev and I are neither fools nor irresponsible (well, we may have had the odd moment) and we knew we had to give the river the respect it deserved. Safety and physical preparation were essential if we were not to embarrass or endanger ourselves. So, we both enrolled in our local fitness clubs. It proved to be a smart move. In due course, we found that paddling a canoe, even downhill all the way, is a lot tougher than it may look.

I say 'enrolled' in clubs, but I was lucky enough to receive six weeks' free membership to a fitness club near my school. I had to pass it twice a day, so there was no excuse for missing a session.

I had called in one evening on my way home to see if they would sponsor us. "Sorry," was the reply, "we already have a charity we support regularly but we'll give you all the help you need to prepare for your trip." This was the first of many offers and acts of kindness which would raise our faith in human nature during the coming weeks and months.

Before I could be let loose on the barbells and machines with their ominous clanks, they had to assess my fitness levels: strength, heart rate, blood pressure, body fat, stamina, lung function and flexibility. It's what they do when you sign up for their brand of blood, sweat and tears.

I was impressed, if I may say so myself, and quietly pleased with the results apart from the flexibility bit. For this assessment, you sit on the floor with your legs stretched out in front of you. You then have to reach forward and push a marker along a bar as far as you can. It is called the 'sit and reach test '. I couldn't even reach the marker, let alone push it forward.

But soon I began to look forward to my daily workout and stuck rigidly to my programme. Not once did I miss out on the sauna and steam room! At the end of six weeks, I'm proud to say I could just about reach the marker.

The end of the spring term signalled the time for the talking to stop and the actual planning to begin. Big questions remained: how long would it take? Would we make the steady walking pace – three miles an hour – that we reckoned on? Reader, these were key considerations.

We decided to begin at Cricklade which is actually fifteen miles from the source of the Thames, but beyond Cricklade the river is not navigable, even for a boat that draws less than an inch of water. The river here is still little more than a stream and the extremely low bridge, too low even for a canoe to pass under, bars the way upstream. Besides, the bridge at Cricklade is the point where the navigational rights of the Thames end. "Navigational rights," I read aloud to Kevin, "means that anyone has the right to use the river as a highway even when it passes through private land." We agreed it would be unwise to tempt fate at the start of the grouse season.

Just below the bridge is an area known as Hatchet's Ford which looked a likely spot for launching. It was decided that this was where we would begin our journey. This reconnoitring trip had taken up yet another very pleasant Sunday and I can report that Cricklade has a very acceptable Indian restaurant and several very agreeable ale houses.

So, we were to start at Cricklade but where was an appropriate place to end our expedition? Teddington lock seemed the obvious choice as from there on the Thames is tidal and we didn't fancy our chances on the tidal reaches. We would either be swept out to sea or be paddling for hours against the tide. So, Teddington it was: a distance of 136 miles from Cricklade with forty-five locks to negotiate.

With the parameters scoped out, serious calculations could begin. At three miles an hour, 136 miles, forty-five locks, fifty pubs, falling in, getting dry, bad back, blisters, places of interest to visit, chatting to folk, that morning-after-the-night-before feeling, comfort stops, divided by the number we first thought of, equals twelve days.

That's an average of about 11.5 miles and 4.5 pubs a day. Naturally we could round the miles down and the pubs up...

So we solemnly ruled off 12th to 23rd of August 1999. The act of marking it down on the calendar seemed like signing a contract. We were committed, we couldn't back out now.

Kev bought the Ordinance Survey Guide to the River Thames, which proved to be a very useful book. As well as the detailed small-scale map of the river, it's full of other information such as planning a cruise, the history of the river, fishing the Thames, how to negotiate locks, how to tie knots and what to do if you have a fire or explosion on board. You can warn other craft to steer clear with signals from your hooter. I quote:

'It is very important to know the basic signals in order to recognise or issue warnings to other craft. Remember that starboard is right and port is left when facing towards the bows (front). One short blast, I'm going to starboard. Two short blasts, I'm going to port. Three short blasts, I'm going astern. Four short blasts, I'm turning round to starboard. Four short blasts followed by two short blasts - I'm turning round to port. Continuous sounding horn indicates distress.'.

It seemed to us quite a bit to remember in an emergency. "Was that three shorts followed by one short, or was it one short followed by three shorts? Is it his left or our left? Sod it! Sound the horn continuously!"

We decided a more direct approach using a megaphone would be much safer: "Move over, get out of the expletive deleted way!"

Joking aside, we found the book extremely beneficial by indicating exactly where we were on the river and what features to expect during the next day's paddling. We needed to cut the 136 miles down into twelve manageable chunks. This sounds fairly easy until you start looking for inns the appropriate distances apart.

"Should we perhaps be thinking of roughing it?" Kev suggested a little too helpfully.

"Certainly not," I replied. It was a celebration, after all. Still...

"Remember climbing Snowdon?" I began. "Rolling back the flap of our tent to that clear, fresh Welsh morning, looking down the Llanberis Pass?" Actually, I wasn't thinking of the camping; it was the breakfast that I vividly remembered. A bacon roll has never tasted so good. Ever since, I've been haunted by that perfect bacon roll. Maybe we could recreate the magic.

I had heard of a tiny island near Hurley lock on which, for a very reasonable fee, you could pitch a tent. I could picture the mist rising off the river as dawn broke, the lonely call of a coot emerging from the reeds, the grass covered in millions of dew-drop diamonds sparkling in the early morning sun, with the smell of freshly cooked bacon in the air.

Kevin, ever the optimist, pictured raindrops bouncing on the river's surface, the cry of Terry Wogan coming from a radio on a small boat nearby, mud oozing through the wet grass covering our trainers and the smell of gas as the camping stove went out yet again.

"One night only?"

"Freshly cooked bacon, mate – can't you just taste it?"

In exchange for indulging my quest for the ultimate bacon roll experience, Kev generously agreed to let me organise the search for the rest of our accommodation. We needed to find ten riverside inns or hotels about eleven miles apart, with a room available on specific days in high season. Once again, the OS Guide to The River Thames proved very useful.

Two weeks and what seemed about a thousand phone calls later, I had assembled an itinerary on the availability of accommodation. "It doesn't work out at exactly eleven and a half miles per day," I warned Kev, "but I think it's the best we can do."

The longest day, unfortunately the first one, was to be an eighteen-mile paddle; the shortest was a mere seven and a half miles. "The fifth day we'll need to include a detour up the River Thame for about two miles to reach Dorchester and the George Inn," I explained. "Otherwise, it would mean a stretch of about twenty-one miles."

To the seasoned canoeist, these distances must seem miniscule in the extreme, but you must remember we carried the added heavy burden of having to visiting on average four and a half pubs a day.

But at this point, burdens aside, things were looking good. Promises of sponsors were coming in thick and fast and our itinerary was finalised. We were well past the point of no return. Families and friends were coming to terms with the fact that the idea was not going to fizzle out and no, 'they are not going to grow up just yet.'

Just one problem remained; still no canoe.

ITINERARY

August

12th	Cricklade to Radcot	18 miles	The Swan
13th	Radcot to Bablock Hythe	13.5 miles	The Ferryman
14th	Bablock Hythe to Oxford	11 miles	The Head of the River
15th	Oxford to Abingdon	7.5 miles	The Old Anchor
16th	Abingdon to Dorchester	12 miles	The George
17th	Dorchester to Goring	13 miles	The Miller of Mansfield
18th	Goring to Sonning	13.5 miles	The Bull
19th	Sonning to Hurley	12.5 miles	Camping
20th	Hurley to Maidenhead	9.5 miles	The Thames Hotel
21st	Maidenhead to Staines Bridge	13.5 miles	The Swan
22nd	Staines to Sunbury Lock	9.5 miles	The Flowerpot
23rd	Sunbury to Teddington Lock	8 miles	

CHAPTER 3

To Portage or not to Portage?
That is the Question

I believe that the air is filled with millions of ideas just floating around looking for somewhere to land. If you're patient, one will alight on your shoulder. It might be a good idea or a bad idea. The skill is to know which ones to keep and nurture and which ones to flick away as you would annoying flies.

It was now nearly the end of June. Pledges at so much per pub visited were landing thick and fast. We had also decided to raise money for our respective schools by asking the staff, parents and children to sponsor us, and this was also going well. The accommodation was arranged. The equipment was bought including state-of-the-art buoyancy aids known by us affectionately as our 'nookies' after their brand name. We had also purchased a pair of handmade paddles, a design known as Sugar Island, which proved to be a very worthwhile expense. They seemed to mould into the hand and kept our hands free of blisters. The equipment also included a supply of insect repellent, films and a camera for the evidence, sun screen lotion, lightweight waterproofs, a bottle opener and various other bits and pieces. With the acquisition of essential equipment plus our pocket money and accommodation, it was not going to be a cheap holiday. What the hell, it was after all a celebration.

Now a celebration requires a certain level of decorum. We needed to carry a supply of clean clothes, washing and shaving gear and other comfort accessories, and we needed to pack them into something compatible with our journey and transport: they had to be waterproof and remain afloat should we capsize. One of those ideas came to rest on Kevin's shoulder.

He persuaded the owner of his local curry house into giving us two blue plastic watertight barrels that were surplus to his requirements. They were perfect for stowing our fresh clothes; almost as perfect as they had been for their previous use, which was storing perishable food items for the restaurant. But in spite of Kevin diligently washing them out several times, my barrel never lost its fragrance of mango chutney and Kevin's clean attire always had the lingering and distinct aroma of curry powder.

Everything seemed to be falling into place except that we still didn't have a canoe. We noticed with alarm the words 'lilos' and 'rubber rings' beginning to creep into the planning meeting conversations.

We knew exactly the type of canoe we wanted – one known as an 'Old Town' – but at this point any make of Canadian would have been acceptable. The situation was beginning to look like an emergency, so we called an emergency planning session.

"Not really an emergency," I suggested as we sat down to a leisurely Saturday lunch at a local pub known to Kevin, "let's think of this as a 'don't panic' meeting."

The upshot of it was we reluctantly decided that the only course of action left to us was to fork out for a new and expensive canoe and hope to sell it on afterwards as long as it was still in reasonable condition, and we hadn't actually lost it.

It was while driving home down the M40 on the Sunday morning that an idea decided to land on my shoulder. At the time, I taught an adult badminton evening class at a local secondary school and I recalled reading an article on the notice board inviting students to join the Marlow Canoeing Club. Surely they would have a Canadian canoe?

"Sure, we can help," replied the canoe club secretary. "All you need to do is to join our club and then you can borrow our Canadian."

The following Sunday morning, the two newest members of the Marlow Canoeing Club drove across to Marlow to be introduced to 'our' canoe. She was perfect – could have been a 'he', I'm not sure how to tell the difference – all watercrafts seem to be called she. The canoe was exactly what we wanted, an Old Town of fine vintage, flat bottomed and stable.

"Take her out for an hour or two," someone suggested. We looked at each other as thoughts of the Longridge fiasco came to mind.

The Marlow Canoe Club is situated beneath the Marlow suspension bridge, on the riverbank opposite the famous Compleat Angler Hotel, a very upmarket establishment. It being a fine, sunny late morning, quite a crowd had assembled on the terrace looking across the river sipping, one supposes, gin and tonics or Pimms. People were walking along the towpath in ones and twos or in family groups, among them were a fair number of dog walkers and joggers. All seemed to be casually gazing in the direction of a dozen or so canoe club members dressed in wet suits and helmets who were preparing to launch their one-man kayaks, obviously intent on testing their skills in and around the slalom gates on the white water in the weir pool opposite. The exceptions were the two older-looking chaps dressed in T-shirts, shorts and old trainers preparing to launch a larger two-man red canoe.

Kitted out in our newly acquired 'nookies', we looked, may I say, extremely smart as we laid our beautiful wooden paddles – which had been admired and handled by several of our new colleagues – into our canoe. Taking position at each end of our canoe, we picked it up and marched down to the small wooden jetty. "Please God keep us dry," I whispered to myself.

Our canoe sat waiting patiently and quietly in the water. "After you," Kevin offered.

"No, after you," I insisted.

Our eyes met and we each took a deep breath. In stepped Kev like a pro, remembering to place both feet squarely in the middle of the canoe and sitting down all in one movement. A perfect manoeuvre, worthy of the fine gymnast he had been, without a suggestion of a wobble. He held on to the jetty looking up at me with a mixture of triumph and pleading in his eyes.

I suddenly felt the need for the toilet and retreated into the club hut. On my return, I was alarmed to see that a small queue had formed at the jetty waiting to launch. "Sorry about that," I said in what I hoped was a confident manner. I repeated the silent prayer, stepped in and sat down and I'm sorry to disappoint but my prayer was answered.

Kev let go of the jetty and we slowly drifted away on the gentle current.

Almost immediately a large 'gin palace' of a cruiser slid past at a rate of knots, setting up a large wash. The waves bore down on us and seemed to grow larger as they approached. They collided with us square on, breaking over the side of our canoe. Somehow, we remained upright but now we had about two inches of water in the bottom of the canoe and we were soaked. "God moves in a mysterious way," I reminded myself.

That was our first lesson. From then on, we always met the wash of a passing boat head on while for some inexplicable reason singing the signature tune of 'Hawaii Five-0', always a source of amusement to passers-by. In fact, the worst washes we found were from small boats with outboard motors rather than from the larger vessels with their inboard motors.

We decided to head upstream through Temple Lock and on to Hurley to reconnoitre the camping island and to experience a lock. Our canoe, for she was our canoe now, seemed to slide over the surface with surprisingly little effort from us even though we were paddling against the current. Our confidence soared. We practiced the various manoeuvres we had learned from our Longridge instructor, turning, stopping, going backwards and using the draw stroke that enables you to go into the bank sideways. All very impressive, for us anyway.

Kev demonstrates the 'Draw Stroke' on terra firma

We even tried the emergency manoeuvre known as 'slapping for support'. This is supposed to stop you from capsizing. In order to practice, we both needed to lean over to one side until we felt that the canoe was going to flip on us, then to reach out as far as possible with our paddles and slap them hard onto the surface of the water which, in theory, is enough to prevent the boat from tipping over.

Our first attempt was a wimpish affair. We can't have leaned over more than two or three degrees before Kevin smashed his paddle down with such force that it sounded like a very loud gun shot. If anyone passing by hadn't noticed the two in the red canoe, they did now. The net results of this effort were three coots and five ducks taking to the wing in fright and – because of the angle of Kev's paddle at the point of impact – we were soaked again.

We had another go, this time creating a list of at least five degrees and managing to smack the surface at the same time. Two loud gun shots. The same fowl, having landed nearby, flew up once more in panic, never to return. We took another self-inflicted soaking.

To the observers, it must have seemed like some kind of canoeists' ritual or a form of floating Morris Dancing. "Perhaps the mad pair are trying to concuss passing fish..."

On our third attempt, my paddle must have twisted slightly in my hand so instead of slapping the surface flat, the blade connected side-on and slipped under the water like a knife through butter. I almost followed it and would have taken Kev and the canoe with me. Somehow, with more luck than judgement and more than a little panic, we remained upright.

"I think we've 'mastered' it," I said. "Let's wait for a genuine emergency before we try it again."

We paddled happily on drying in the sun. Large houses with lawns sweeping down to the water's edge, fringed with willow trees were on one side, their delicate branches dipping into the water like green curtains. On the other side were meadows with grazing cows and the tow path. At one point our canoe inexplicably decided she wanted to explore under the said willow trees which seemed to be the haunt of every flying insect known to man. With an amount of hilarity and questionable language we managed to cajole her back out into the sunshine and mid-stream again.

I can't begin to describe the growing feeling of exhilaration and freedom that I felt as my confidence grew and we became more at ease with this new mode of transport and its environment. With every passing minute, our level of proficiency increased and we became more adept at influencing our will over our craft. Or so it seemed.

About a mile and a half upstream from Marlow, we came upon Temple Lock, just one of the forty-five we were going to encounter during our forthcoming twelve-day trip. There are two ways you can negotiate such an obstacle with a canoe. Well, three if you go headlong over the weir... One way is to carry or 'portage' your canoe around the lock. It's easy and quick if you're travelling with a small one-man kayak but a little more irksome and awkward with a Canadian, fully laden with luggage and especially if there isn't any convenient landing or re-floating spots available adjacent to the lock.

The other way is to sit tight and enter the lock with the other craft, most of which of course would be considerably larger and several tons heavier than a glass fibre canoe.

As we approached Temple Lock, we discussed at length the pros and cons of both methods. Neither seemed to have a lot going for it.

"I think I'd rather ride it out," I said. Perhaps it had more risks attached to it, but it would be easier on the back.

The lock was full of very large cruisers. I heard Kevin mumble something about an egg being crushed in a box. We decided to portage.

Unfortunately, the approach to the lock had a steep bank covered with long grass with a towpath running along the top of it not dissimilar to a railway embankment. People were walking along the path or sitting on benches eating ice creams idly watching the boats entering and leaving the lock.

We paddled as near to the lock gates as we dared, then expertly used the draw stroke to draw us into the bank. Perfect! Kev grabbed a tuft of grass to steady us, I followed suit and grasped a handful of young stinging nettles. I doubt if the young family who quickly vacated their seats on the bench above us remember that day, but if they do, I would like to take this opportunity to for my colourful language.

It also became apparent that this particular area was the favourite haunt of the lock keeper's dog. Undaunted, we alighted from the canoe and proceeded to drag her up the bank.

From being a graceful craft skimming across the surface of the river, she had now become a dead weight. Kev pulled from the top end while I pushed from the bottom. Progress was slow. One of our paddles fell out and rolled down the bank into the water. As I let go of my end to retrieve it, the sudden extra weight took Kevin unawares. The canoe slipped several feet back down the bank, pulling him with it on his backside. Another young family felt the need to move further away.

Kev eventually reached the top with his end of the canoe. He was standing on the path holding the end while the canoe rocked like a seesaw over the edge of the bank. It only needed a good shove from me to complete the task so I pushed as hard as I could and as expected the canoe easily slid over the edge and came to rest across the path. At the same time, Kevin disappeared from view with another outpouring of Anglo-Saxon expletives from him and laughter from the ice-cream brigade.

I found him lying on his back at the bottom of a ditch that ran along the other side of the path. Without a word he climbed out, picked up his end of the canoe, waited patiently for me to stop laughing and pick up my end. We marched purposely through the crowd to the other end of the lock, trying hard to ignore the strong aroma of the lock keeper's dog's calling card which was now smeared along the bottom of our canoe. Thankfully, access to the water at the top end of the lock was much easier. We paddled away without a backward glance.

Ten minutes of steady paddling brought us to Hurley Lock. To portage or not to portage, that was the question. As things worked out, it didn't need answering. Just before the lock, the river branches off to the right. This quiet backwater takes you around to the other side of the lock to several small islands and then on into the weir pool. We decided to explore to find the island on which we hoped to spend the eighth night of our trip, seeking out the Holy Grail of bacon rolls.

It didn't take long to find the island; the few small tents pitched on it was the clue. Their owners turned out to be mostly fishermen spending the weekend fishing around the islands and in the weir pool. Beneath a willow tree, a small sandy beach had formed that looked to us like a promising landing spot. We paddled straight for it at full tilt with a lusty rendering of the 'Hawaii Five-0' tune. It wasn't until we'd run aground and hauled the canoe up out of harm's way that we saw the fisherman who was sitting quietly under the willow minding his own business, enjoying the solitude of this idyllic Thames backwater.

"Any luck?" Kevin enquired in an apologetic and friendly tone.

We weren't quite sure what exactly his reply was but we think the gist of it was that he had not had any luck yet and now wasn't likely to.

The island is only about eighty metres long and about thirty metres wide. The perimeter is fringed with willows with the weir pool at the far end. A footbridge connecting the island to the mainland has a large iron gate topped with barbed wire and secured with a large padlock and chain. Kev said what we were both thinking: "I wonder if that's to keep the public out or the campers in?" The British version of Alcatraz!

It was actually a very pleasant spot with the constant murmur of the water tumbling over the weir in the background. We discovered, hidden by a clump of alders, a clean shower and toilet block with hot and cold water. This, Kevin confessed, was a great relief to him as he had half-expected a hole-and-shovel job at dawn. The one night under canvas seemed less daunting... until, that is, it dawned on us that it meant having to find space in the canoe for a tent and all the camping gear, for a one-night stopover.

On our way back to the beach, we passed a small and secluded tent just as a young couple emerged. "Excuse me," Kevin immediately began. The pair were surprised; it was obvious they weren't there for the fishing. For one anxious moment I thought he was going to ask them if they'd caught anything, but to my relief, he enquired. "Do you happen to know where we can find information about camping here?" he asked. They directed us to the lock keeper.

We relaunched our canoe as unobtrusively as possible so as not to disturb our fisherman friend again. "Good luck!" Kev called cheerfully as we quietly paddled away. Again, his reply was inaudible but by his gesture I took it that his luck had changed and he had caught two fish.

Back in the main stream, we moored the canoe below the lock gates and sauntered up to the lock itself. It was extremely busy with boats of all kinds in the lock or waiting to enter. On a fine sunny day, it's just the place to linger and people-watch. And there were many people doing just that. People on the boats watching the people on the side, who were watching the people on the boats.

The only person doing anything other than watching was the lock keeper. It was his lock; he was in charge and in complete control. A tall but portly gentleman nearing retirement age, he sported well pressed navy-blue trousers and an immaculate white open necked, short sleeved shirt, over which was an orange, fluorescent buoyancy aid, that appeared as if he might have borrowed it from a small child. His trousers were held up precariously with a thick black leather belt with a heavy silver buckle, which sat just below his substantial beer belly. His white, peaked Captain's cap nestled amongst his thick, red curly hair which merged into his full 'Captain Birdseye' style beard. On his feet he wore a pair of well-polished black brogues; It was a one man show and the lock was his stage, and what a performance! We watched in admiration as in a deep, aristocratic accent he ordered the boats to leave the lock; nobody moved until he said so. He would then skilfully select the next set of boats to enter and direct each craft to its exact spot in the lock. The boats came in all shapes and sizes, but time after time he managed to fill the lock without a square foot of wasted space.

In a calm but well projected voice, he then made sure everything was safe and to his liking. "You sir, you sir, you on Lazy Days, take up the slack of your stern rope." "Keep your hands inside the boat sonny." "You lads in the skiff, put the beers down and concentrate." "Keep your dog under control Kittiwake." "Stay back from the gates Off The Hook."

He then strode to the electric control box which resembled a lectern. With the flick of a switch, the gates closed and with the flick of another, the lock would begin to empty. The gushing water escaping through the sluice gates sounded like applause.

He then wandered slowly the length of the lock to the other set of gates, stopping occasionally to speak to members of his audience. Then he repeated the act at the other end of his stage, except that now his majestic flicking of switches filled the lock instead of emptying it. "Watch him closely, Kev," I whispered, "he's going to break into a tap dance on his way between the gates."

"Or at least take a bow between performances," Kev replied.

We needed to speak to the lock keeper. It felt rather like wanting to ask the star of the show for his autograph, but he was obviously busy and his work was important. We watched for a while and tried to imagine what sort of state we might be in the next time we passed that way. A wisp of a cloud of doubt entered my mind. Would we get as far as Hurley? It was the twenty-ninth lock and 95 1/2 miles from our launch spot at Cricklade and we would have visited quite a few pubs by then.

"When you think about it," said Kev thoughtfully, "actually it's all downhill. And besides, the sun always shines on the righteous."

I had to agree. "Of course we'll get as far as Hurley, and we'll manage the rest of the 40 1/2 miles, the fifteen locks and all the pubs between here and Teddington." I hoped I sounded convincing because it was the first time I'd mixed miles, locks, pubs and the weather in one thought.

We were just about to leave when we noticed that an understudy had replaced the principal player so he could take a much-deserved break in his office, which was situated by the side of the lock. I hesitated before knocking, wondering what sort of reception to expect. We felt we were intruding on the poor man's few minutes of peace and quiet. Our concern was unfounded.

"Come in, come in," he commanded, and we did as we were told.

He couldn't have been more helpful, which incidentally was the norm for every other lock keeper we met on our expedition. We explained our intentions and itinerary which, when expounded to somebody for the first time, gives the impression of a twelve-day pub crawl which, on reflection, I suppose is what it was.

The fee for the night's camping was extremely reasonable and we reserved a pitch for the 19th of August. We were about to take our leave when our new-found friend stopped us.

"Why don't you leave your tent and camping gear in the storeroom at the end of the shower block?" he said. "You can stow it there before you begin your trip and collect it later." Genius: no sooner said than done.

"Perhaps we can leave some clean clothes too," Kevin said. This would save us having to cram so much into our watertight barrels.

"Why not?" said our genial lock keeper. "I look forward to your arrival by canoe and hope to join you for a drink at one of the hostelries in the village." He signed a sponsor form and wished us bon voyage as we pushed off.

We paddled back to Marlow in a buoyant mood, another piece of the jigsaw in place. Accommodation was sorted, we had a perfect canoe for the job and state-of-the-art paddles and nookies. The fitness training was going well, and we felt inspired by our improving canoeing skills.

Above Temple Lock, a racing skiff with two rather fit and striking females caught us up. Feeling somewhat overconfident with our ability, I suggested that we keep up with them. Reliant Robin versus Ferrari springs to mind. Within four strokes, they had left us for dead.

As we approached the canoe club and paddled under the Marlow suspension bridge, we both felt an overwhelming desire to keep on going. That afternoon we had experienced a tiny morsel of what we thought to expect, and we liked it. The river and the weather had been kind to us on this occasion and had lulled us into a sense of security. All doubts were forgotten.

We handed 'our' canoe back to the club for safe keeping. I arranged to reclaim her the week before our departure and again I must thank the Marlow Canoe Club for their kindness and cooperation. We were now counting the days to the 12th of August. We drove home in a jubilant mood and couldn't resist stopping off for a planning session on the way.

CHAPTER 4

A Place for Everything and Everything in its Place

On the Saturday morning of August, the 7th I drove the 10 miles to Marlow to collect our canoe. I had arranged for a couple of the club members to meet me and help load her onto the roof of my Mondeo Estate. Upside down and secured with some old rope she looked very undignified. A complete opposite to the sleek craft that had taken us to Hurley and back a few weeks before. She reminded me of a beached whale. Graceful and at home in the water but completely helpless and useless on land.

Back at home she rested patiently on the lawn waiting to be returned to her own environment. Members of the family sat in her and paddled an imaginary course across the lawn whilst several neighbours stopped to make light-hearted comments. More than one seemed quite envious of our impending twelve days of freedom. I ran through some of the paddling techniques we had mastered. Everyone seemed duly impressed especially with the 'slapping for support' demonstration. Somehow all fear and trepidation leave you when you have terra firma beneath you instead of ten feet of cold river water.

Kevin arrived down from Coventry the next morning fully prepared to customise the canoe. After a brief lunch and 'planning session' in the Red Lion we set about our task. UNICEF had sent Kevin several large blue and white stickers. We decided to stick a large circular one depicting their emblem on either side at the front of the canoe and a rectangular one either side at the back portraying the word UNICEF in bold letters.

I should start to use the correct terminology regarding a canoe. Two stickers at the stern, one on the starboard side and one on the portside. A further two stickers, one port and one starboard, at the bow. They were situated on the hull between the waterline and the gunwale. Impressed?

Kevin also brought down the two blue watertight barrels he had acquired from his local Indian restaurant. These in turn were given the treatment and emblazoned with the UNICEF motive. The barrels had a diameter of about thirty centimetres and were approximately 55 centimetres tall into which our spare clothes for the trip were to be stowed. We found the best method was to roll up each individual item of clothing into a sausage shape, thus keeping them fairly crinkle free. The barrels had screw on lids and Kevin assured me that he had tested them for water tightness by submerging them in his garden fishpond. As mentioned before, he had endeavoured to eradicate the aroma of curry powder and mango chutney by washing them out thoroughly several times but to no avail, so the aroma of the Taj Mahal restaurant remained with us throughout the trip. Given the right time and circumstance not an unpleasant odour. But, your head in a barrel at seven thirty in the morning after a few bevvies the night before, trying to locate a clean pair of boxers, is not the right circumstance.

We also adhered to both sides of the hull the names of the dozen or more shops and businesses who had kindly agreed to help sponsor our trip.

We decided it would be a good idea to fasten all our luggage securely in the canoe so that in the case of a capsize our possessions would remain together and not disappear off down the river. We laid the barrels on their sides between the two centre thwarts of the canoe and threaded a nylon strap through their handles and then around the thwarts. A thwart, by the way, is a piece of word running across the width of the canoe at gunwale height which helps keep the boat rigid. We also carried a white plastic bucket with a watertight lid, into which we stored things we would need to get to quickly during the day.

Camera, first aid kit, notebook, map and information, insect repellent, sun screen lotion, corkscrew, bottle opener and hip flask of medicinal whiskey. This, together with a piece of kit call a dry sack, rather like a very tough bin liner with a waterproof seal, was also secured to the thwarts. In the dry sack were packed our wet weather gear and a couple of warm sweatshirts each. Along the inside of the hull, we secured two spare paddles, not a patch on our beautiful wooden ones. We hoped to be well prepared for any eventuality. To finish off the personalisation we attached a good length of mooring rope at either end, and a padlock and chain. One of our main concerns was what to do with our canoe at night and would it still be there, where we left it, in the morning? This was a bridge we would need to cross at the time.

I was able to show Kev the articles which three of my local newspapers had published about our impending nomadic navigation along one of Britain's oldest and best-known landmarks with its abundance of diversity. The Royal River of Kings and Queens. The river of Julius Caesar and the Romans, the Saxons and the Danes. The river of writers, poets and artists. A river which flows through quaint picturesque villages and towns. Through Oxford, the city of dreaming spires and Windsor, steeped in history with its magnificent Castle. A river teeming with flora and fauna. A river with its ever-changing moods and a different breathtaking vista around every meandering bend.

The first article had the headline, 'Teachers 136 Mile Pub Crawl by Canoe'. The second was headed. 'Two Men in A Boat Take on 50 Pubs'. The third headline read, 'Canoe Pub Crawl to Mark Their 50th'.

The local radio station for my area also got wind of our forthcoming campaign and phoned me out of the blue for a taped interview. The interview, or parts of it I was told, would be played over the air waves on the hour throughout the next day as a news item, unless anything more newsworthy cropped up to take its place. I felt it went fairly well although as was becoming the norm, pubs, hangovers and breathalysers seemed to be the main topics of interest of my inquisitor.

The next morning, I duly tuned in for the first news report of the day. The News at Ten programme on ITN a few years back always finished with a, 'and finally' item. It was always something amusing or obscure. Well, we were the 'and finally' item on local radio. Apparently, on the hour throughout the day, a different part of the recording was transmitted, up until 3 o'clock after which a superior item took its place.

The following day I received yet another phone call, this time from BBC Radio Thames Valley no less, whose studio is in Oxford. It was one of their researchers who was very interested in what we were doing. She asked if it would be possible for us to call in to the studio on our way to the launch at Cricklade for a live on- air interview.

After spending the day preparing our canoe Kev returned home. Preparation and planning completed; all boxes ticked. The next time we were to meet would be the penultimate day of our impending expedition.

CHAPTER 5

From Small Beginnings……

After a restless night dreaming of raging weirs, whirlpools, giant pike and aggressive radio presenters I awoke early and lay in bed wondering what fate held in store for us over the next 12 days. It wasn't such a big deal. We weren't about to climb Everest or row across the Atlantic but nevertheless there was an element of the unknown attached to the venture. If we kept well clear of weirs and fisherman, gave swans with signets a wide berth, were polite and submissive to lock keepers, avoided all other craft on the river and kept a wary eye out for boys on bridges, what harm could we come to?

All had been prepared the previous day. Barrels, dry sack and bucket packed and checked for contents. The canoe securely lashed to the roof rack. Paddles and 'nookies' in the back of a car. Money and mobile phone in waterproof wallet. Nurofen and glucose tablets easily accessible.

Kevin had travelled down the day before. In the evening we had one last planning meeting in the Red Lion and luckily just avoided being 'locked in'. The last thing we wanted was to weigh anchor under the cloud of a headache. It was in fact a bright clear morning.

Radio Thames Valley needed us to be at the studio in Oxford in time to go on air at 8:35am which meant leaving home at 7:15 to give us plenty of time. It would only mean a slight detour from our seventy- five miles journey to Cricklade for the launch. As we were to appear on live radio, we thought we ought to dress smart casual rather than turn up in our regulation canoeing gear of old trainers, T-shirt and shorts. As Kev rightly pointed out, you never know who might be listening.

Jan, my understanding and long-suffering partner at the time, (now my wife) accompanied us. She had at last conceded that we were actually going to carry out our "mad idea" and was coming to see us safely on our way. Besides, she had the important task of driving the car back home again from Cricklade. She also needed to be on call in case of an emergency, so she had cancelled her idea of a week away in the Bahamas. Several friends and members of our families had expressed a wish to join us somewhere along the way for a drink and a 'catch up' so we had issued them with our itinerary and Kev's mobile number.

We found the studio with little trouble and with time to spare. The woman who met us at reception immediately greeted us with the words, "Good morning you must be our canoeists." I felt chuffed that she had recognised us as fit, athletic, broad-shouldered canoeists who braved the elements and unforeseen dangers of wild raging rivers. I then realised she had seen us through the large glass double doors of the foyer as we drove into the car park with a large red canoe tied to the top of our car.

We were introduced to the producer of the programme who quickly explained the procedure and then ushered us into the control room to await our allotted time slot on air. He informed us it was from 8:37 to 8:40, to the second. It felt like sitting in the dentist's waiting room, waiting to be called for an interview and sitting outside the headmaster's office when I was ten years old after being caught absent without leave during a particular lunchtime, all rolled into one. Kev was also suffering from the sweaty palms and weak bladder syndrome. It feels strange now that we had both felt so nervous but it seemed such an odd and unreal situation to be in. Jan, who had accompanied us into the control room, found it most amusing that we were in such an agitated state.

During the next quarter of an hour between visits to the toilet, we watched the presenter from the control room through a large glass partition, presenting his program. He was a cross between Terry Wogan and Chris Tarrant. I don't recall his name or the name of the programme, but it seemed very interesting. News items and phone-ins interspersed with popular music. He was lively and witty and we tried desperately to anticipate the kind of questions he might put to us.

Whilst Tina Turner belted out 'River Deep Mountain High', we were ushered into the inner sanctum where the presenter introduced himself and tried to put us at ease. With a large pair of earphones each, we settled behind our microphones. He was good at his job, asking sensible questions and letting us do most of the talking. I wish we could remember exactly what we had said but our conversation with him past in a blur. However, we felt that our brief flirtation with the live media and fame, albeit for all of three minutes, was a minor success. Jan agreed that we hadn't disgraced ourselves and it had sounded very good. On the way out the producer wished us the best of luck and asked if it would be ok if they called us periodically for live on-air updates. We readily agreed and gave him Kev's mobile number. We fully expected to be mobbed for our autographs on our way back to the car but the car park was deserted.

The drive from Oxford through the fringes of the Cotswolds and then down to Wiltshire was pleasant but slow. We were anxious to get to Cricklade as quickly as possible but having the canoe strapped to the roof of the car greatly restricted our speed. More than once I stopped to check the bindings. It had taken us long enough to acquire the canoe, we didn't want to lose her now.

It was well past 10am when we eventually found ourselves driving down the back lanes of Cricklade to our appointed launch site, the ancient Hatchet's Ford, a place of baptisms by complete immersion in the 19th century. Hopefully, it wouldn't be us being baptized today. Morale and anticipation were now at their peak. At last, all the plans, schemes and training were about to be put to the test and we couldn't wait to get started.

At last, the time had arrived to launch our canoe.

The Thames, our highway for the next twelve days, was no more than a twenty-foot-wide stream, crystal clear and looking extremely shallow. Too shallow to float a canoe? Much to our relief, on closer inspection we found that the water was in fact at least four-foot deep. It was the clearness of the water that had fooled us. The river was putting us to the test already.

Although the Thames is still in its infancy at Cricklade, only twelve miles from its source, a tiny spring, it used to be a very prominent place. The name Cricklade is derived from the ancient word Criccagelad meaning 'place of wharves or creeks where the river can be crossed'. The Romans were probably the first to build a bridge here as the Roman road known as Ermine Street, now part of the A 419, crosses at this point.

Cricklade was first established by Alfred the Great, famous for the burning of the cakes, our first celebrity cook. He built a strong point here in AD878 during his battle with the Danes. Before that in AD597 it is believed that Saint Augustine converted the Anglo-Saxons of Wessex to Christianity at Cricklade, perhaps even baptising them at our launch site? King Canute is also said to have passed through Cricklade.

In 1821 William Cobbett described the town as 'a villainous hole' due to its poverty. I hasten to add that this is not the case today. It has, amongst other things of note, a butcher's shop, situated in the high street, which is famous for its award-winning sausages made to a secret recipe handed down from father to son. It also boasts that one of its two churches, Saint Mary's, is the oldest Catholic Church in Britain. The parish church was built in the 12th century and is dedicated to the Celtic Saint, Saint Samson. Its new tower was added in 1552!

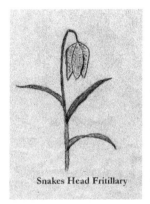
Snakes Head Fritillary

Just upstream from the bridge is North Meadow National Nature Reserve, an area of international importance covering one hundred and eight acres. It's famous for its wildflower communities, in particular the Snakes Head Fritillaries which now can only be found growing wild in just a few places in Europe. Before 1930 they were widespread in lowland England, particularly in meadows along the upper Thames Valley. Now, due mainly to modern agricultural methods, there are very few suitable sites and in fact only twelve such meadows remain. The North Meadow at Cricklade holds a very large proportion of the population of this particular plant. In early April and May when the Fritillaries are in flower the meadow becomes a 'purple haze'. (As well as King Canute and King Alfred I wonder if Jimmy Hendrix ever passed that way?) Later, in June, the meadow becomes a kaleidoscope of colour when a multitude of 'hay meadow flowers' bloom.

North Meadow has become one of the finest uncultivated ancient meadows in Britain because of its special management regime. The Nature Conservancy Council has owned the meadow since 1973 and continues to manage it as it has been for hundreds of years. During the summer an organic hay crop is grown and sold to local farmers who cut it after the 1st of July and have to remove it by the 12th of August. Scattered across the meadow are a number of ancient carved stones which mark out the portions of hay so that each purchaser knows exactly where to harvest their particular part of the crop. On the 12th of August the 'hayward', appointed by the historical Cricklade Court Leet, unpadlocks the gate to allow the inhabitants of the town to graze their cattle and horses on the meadow. Sheep take over in the winter and stay, unless there is flooding before, until the 12th of February. This enables the vegetation to start its growth cycle again without being grazed off.

As mentioned before the bridge at Cricklade marks the boundary of the Authority of The Thames Conservancy, where the official right of navigation begins or ends, depending on which way you're travelling. In the Ordinance Survey Guide to The Thames, it states that 'a few small boats have made it this far upstream, but this is not recommended'. We were about to find out why.

Just downstream from the bridge the River Churn joins the Thames. It's the longest of the forty or so tributaries between the source and Teddington which combine to help the Thames to be the proud waterway it eventually becomes. Looking at it then it was hard to imagine that it was the same River Thames which glides majestically through London, flowing for two hundred and fifteen miles and passing through eight counties until it reaches the North Sea.

We hurriedly changed from our radio celebrities gear into our canoeing attire, the now familiar shorts, T-shirt and trainers. Jan was busy taking photographs as we prepared and loaded the canoe. She had a look of resignation on her face and kept shaking her head and muttering, "boys will be boys" under her breath. We donned our 'nookies' and stood proudly with our paddles by the canoe for a photograph. Jan said we looked like big game hunters posing next to a large red crocodile we had just shot. I don't think she was treating the moment with the seriousness it deserved. Later, she did confess that after we had disappeared around the first bend, she had become quite worried and concerned for our safety. Some people believe we disappeared around the bend quite a few years ago!

CHAPTER 6

Close Encounters of the Feathered Kind

Cricklade to Radcot - 18miles

The river seemed to be beckoning us to follow. The descriptive passage from the Wind in the Willows written by Kenneth Grahame, when the mole first stumbles across the river comes to mind.......

'This sleek, sinuous, full bodied animal, chasing and cheekily gripping things with a gurgle and leaving them with a laugh, to fling itself on fresh playmates that shook themselves free and were caught and held again. All was a shake and a shiver, glints and gleams and sparkle, rustle and swirl, chatter and bubble'.

A quick check in the car to make sure we had everything and at last after all the weeks and months of preparation the time had arrived. Twelve days of freedom from time restraints. Twelve days to do as we pleased. Twelve days of paddling our own canoe.

Some friends of Kev, who own a holiday caravan nearby, had arrived to wish us well and so there was now quite a crowd of three adults and a dog to see us off. I said my goodbyes to Jan and was just about to board our vessel when Kev reminded me of what used to take place at that very spot. "Have you been baptised?" he asked. I told him I had. "So, have I," he said, "So we'll get straight off then."

It had just passed 10:30 when we paddled out into midstream, paused to pose for more photographs and then let the current take us gently downstream. The sun shone reflectively off the crystal-clear water and the way looked gentle and open. After about half a minute we came to a ninety-degree left-hand bend, we turned and waved once more before being swept quite rapidly under a low willow tree and out of sight of human contact.

A last wave goodbye before we were swept backwards round the bend.

Our progress had suddenly increased considerably because the stream had now become somewhat narrower, quickening the current. We weren't used to this fast-flowing water. Up to now the wider and deeper river at Marlow and Hurley had been placid and friendly. Here it now seemed rather irritable and in a hurry. The current took control and we did a complete three-hundred-and-sixty-degree pirouette in mid-stream before we were propelled towards the seemingly impenetrable branches of another willow tree that had fallen across the stream. Perhaps it was time for another baptism after all. Whether it was through the fear of capsize I don't know, but Kevin, sitting in the helmsman's seat at the back, managed to gain control of the canoe. Through sheer skill, (Kevin's words) adrenaline, survival instincts and much ducking and fending off of branches from me sitting in the front, we emerged on the other side of the tree unscathed.

Having to master the current and battle our way through that tree so early in the trip was a blessing in disguise. We had passed our first trial and it felt good. The adrenaline was flowing and confidence was now sky high. It quickly became apparent that no other craft had passed that way for several weeks or even years. More fallen trees seemed to block our way and reed beds seemed to stretch as far as the eye could see. Nevertheless, we paddled on undaunted, around and under branches, picking our way through the reeds.

One tree did succeed in barring our way. As there was no way around the only option was to portage. It was hard work. The bank was steep, all our baggage had to be unloaded and then the canoe needed to be dragged around the obstacle, re-floated and re-packed. After that getting back on board from a steep muddy bank was not an easy task. We managed, but decided there and then that it would be worth the risk sharing the locks with other larger craft, rather than going through that rigmarole again forty-five times.

In places the current was really quite brisk and all we needed to do was steer the canoe and let the stream carry us along. The river twisted and turned, at times almost turning back on itself. We were being propelled quite rapidly around a 'dog leg' bend when I suddenly disappeared from Kevin's view, behind what he described as a green curtain. We abruptly came to a halt. The canoe had been propelled full tilt into a wall of six feet high reeds.

The way is blocked by seemingly impenetrable reed beds.

My half of the canoe had managed to penetrate the foliage which had then closed behind me. During fits of laughter Kevin managed to reverse and extract me from the verdant convert. I emerged coughing and spluttering as thousands of gnats, which after being unexpectedly disturbed, had taken refuge in every available orifice I had to offer. This incident continued to greatly amuse my companion throughout the whole trip and indeed still does to this day.

The reeds at this point had completely choked the river and there was no obvious route to take. We decided to try and force our way through. It proved to be extremely hard work because the reeds seemed to tangle themselves into knots around the bow of the canoe, it was as if they were consciously working together to impede our progress and trap us. They also ominously sprang up again behind us, blocking off our means of retreat. After about ten minutes of struggling, we were stuck. We could neither paddle forwards or backwards. I envisaged, later on in the year when the reeds had died back, a dog walker discovering two skeletons sitting in an old red canoe.

"I think there is a way through."

So, this is why the Ordinance Survey Guide to the River Thames didn't recommend boats to venture this far upstream. Yet again we found laughter was the best form of medicine. We checked our provisions. A bottle of water, a packet of extra strong mints and a hip flask of 'medicinal whiskey'

We sat for a minute or two sharing the 'medicine' and wondering what to do. Then out of the blue Kevin asked me if I had ever seen the film, starring Humphrey Bogart, called The African Queen. I hadn't, so Kev kindly told me the story while he sat in the canoe as I waded ahead up to my ankles in mud and water well above my knees, dragging the canoe through the reeds by the mooring rope. After a good ten or fifteen minutes of heaving and swearing, the reeds began to thin out and I was able to clamber back on board and we both resumed paddling.

Kev kindly tells me the story of the African Queen.

The river continued to twist and turn along its lonely course devoid of any human presence or influences. There are no roads or even farms anywhere near the river between Cricklade and the next settlement of Castle Eaton. The landscape is flat pasture liable to flood during wet periods, so man has left the land to the Thames to do with it as it wishes and only graze their cattle on its water meadows during the dry summer months.

Rounding yet another tight bend we came face to face with one of the most worrying and potentially dangerous situations we were to constantly encounter during our trip. Swans! Worst of all swans with signets! Not, I grant you, anything to be concerned about when you are safely on the bank and they're on the water, but when sitting in a canoe at swan height, eyeball to eyeball, it's a different story. They are large and powerful creatures with a long neck which can easily reach into a canoe. At the end of the neck is a formidable beak with serrated edges. They stare at you with cold unfriendly eyes and the stories told of the damage they can inflict with their wings are best not thought about. What's more, swans can move extremely quickly when aroused.

Mute Swans with Signets

This particular pair of swans had a family of five half- grown signets. The river was still quite narrow, no more than ten feet of open water between the reeds. The problem was that as we suddenly rounded the bend the youngsters somehow got behind us which meant we had separated the family. Mum and dad were not very happy with this situation. The river was not wide enough for the adults to pass us at a safe distance and they became more and more agitated. Remember, I was sitting in the front of the canoe, not the best place to be in this situation unless making an in- depth study of angry swans.

We stopped paddling and sat still hoping the youngsters would have the courage to pass us, but to no avail. The situation was growing uglier by the second and a physical confrontation seemed imminent. At least it did from where I was sitting. Behind me my 'friend' was again in fits of laughter. It was alright for him; he had a human shield between himself and the river's self-appointed guardians.

I tried reasoning with the swans in a quiet calming voice telling them that we meant no harm and please would they let us proceed in peace. This induced a fresh bout of laughter from my companion. The adults came closer with a fixed stare focused directly at me. It was time for a change of tactic. I waved my paddle at them and told them, in a loud voice this time, to 'go away'. No reaction from my adversaries just more laughter from behind.

The way the swans were behaving reminded me unnervingly of the way sharks approach their prey, swimming closer each time before attacking. As far as I was concerned there was only one option left. I paddled as hard as I could into the reeds which again swallowed my half of the canoe leaving enough space for the family to be reunited. Another ten thousand gnats were disrupted and deemed it necessary to take refuge about my person. Kevin was now helpless with hysterical laughter. I will be patient and bide my time I thought. My time will come.

Our progress was gradually becoming easier as the river slowly grew and the chocking reeds began to thin out. A few fallen trees still tried unsuccessfully to block our way. We passed the River Ray's tributary which contributed to the flow of the Thames together with many unnoticed drainage ditches, helping it to grow although it was still no more than about ten metres across at its widest point.

We paddled on enjoying the quiet and the solitude but at the same time I felt as if we were trespassing. We were intruders in an environment that, up till now, had been fortunate to have been rarely visited or tainted by the most selfish of all species, Homo Sapiens. The occasional human had undoubtably passed this way before but had generally left the environment to be managed by the natural flora and fauna. No doubt many unseen pairs of eyes, belonging to the 'residents', anxiously watched us pass by and were relieved when we disappeared from view round the next bend.

As well as our swan family, since leaving Cricklade we had made a passing acquaintance with some of the neighbourhood. Countless numbers of moorhens, coots and ducks, three kingfishers, two herons and a water vole.

Our first human contact was made at about 11:45am when we rounded a bend and suddenly, there he was. A solitary fisherman. I don't know who was more surprised, him or us. As fisherman go, he was quite chatty and proudly showed us the fine catch of seven or eight roach he had in his keep net.

Kevin isn't a fisherman, unlike me who enjoys a spot of angling. I once, and only once, took him fishing one fine Sunday when we were no older than about twelve or thirteen. After sitting quietly for about five minutes he became bored. To relieve his boredom, he took to throwing pebbles at his float and then at mine. I took the sport seriously and told him very politely, of course, to please stop. We were sharing the bank with a herd of cows and Kevin's attention was now drawn to them.

Amongst my equipment was a bright yellow cycling cape carried in case of wet weather. You don't tend to see them around these days. It was like cycling in a tent with your head sticking out of the top. Lethal in windy conditions as it acted like a sail.

Using the cape Kevin decided to be a bullfighter. Unfortunately, one of the cows decided to co-operate and head down charged. Kev dropped the cape; I dropped my rod and we ran. The whole herd then came over to investigate the strange yellow object laying on the ground and proceeded to trample on everything in sight. Not content with trampling on everything they also ate our sandwiches. They were obviously very moved by the experience in every sense of the word. What equipment was salvaged smelt of cow dung for months after.

That was the first and last time Kevin ever went fishing therefore his knowledge on the subject is extremely limited. However, he is a quick learner. Every fisherman we met from then on was asked the same question from my learned friend. "Any luck, caught any Roach?"

A few minutes after meeting the fisherman and passing beneath our first bridge, a rather ugly structure constructed of iron girders, a very welcome sight came into view. The Red Lion at Castle Eaton. It was a momentous occasion for it was our first pub on the banks of the River Thames. It had taken one and three-quarter hours to negotiate the four miles from Cricklade and we felt dearly in need of a pint.

Our first hostelry; The Red Lion at Castle Eaton.

The Red Lion, a Georgian inn, has a large open garden sloping quite steeply to the water's edge. The bank was uneven and crumbling with large clumps of nettles, brambles and roots of trees making landing from a canoe quite an ordeal. Obviously, the landlord didn't expect many river borne customers.

We tied the bow and stern of the canoe to a couple of tree roots and with much hilarity and noises of exertion we scrambled up the bank. It felt good to walk around stretching our legs and straightening our backs, performed in a rather extravagant manner by the pair of us.

A couple sitting on a bench under an apple tree, unnoticed at first by us, must have wondered what on earth was going on. Two men, dressed in shorts and 'blue padded waistcoats' suddenly appearing over the bank with much laughter, dissolving into an impression of a cross between the Wooden Tops and Thunderbirds, performing some weird kind of rain dance?

After apologising we got into conversation. They were a retired couple who had walked from London along the towpath in several stages over a period of just over two years. This was the last stage of their journey and they had, no doubt, some interesting tales to tell. How strange that we should meet on the first leg of our journey and the last stage of theirs. No doubt we would have some stories to tell on our last day.

The Red Lion was full of atmosphere with many old black and white photographs adorning the walls recording Castle Eaton of days gone by. Once upon a time, as the name suggests, Castle Eaton had a fine Norman Castle the remains of which have now long disappeared.

Over a couple of beers, the landlord told us of his two resident ghosts, although he remained sceptical of such phenomenon. The first was in residence when he took over the premises and had been present for many years beforehand. He was told that a previous landlady of the pub, who was in the habit of using rose water as perfume, still walks around the place. The landlord said that quite often when sitting alone upstairs after hours he had smelt the delicate sent of roses. He still remained sceptical!

The other 'happenings' had started quite recently. He had gone on holiday and left a friend in charge of the pub. Unfortunately, while he was away this friend had quite suddenly died in bed. Since then, for no apparent reasons, pictures have fallen off the walls, doors have opened and closed on their own and lights have been switched off. And he still remained sceptical!!

We chatted for a good half an hour but as we still had fourteen miles to cover, we needed to press on. After visiting the gents, no smell of roses there, we bid our host farewell, not before he had taken the important photograph for us as evidence of our visit. Our new wayfaring friends were still sitting under the tree. They wished us good luck and kindly gave a donation to UNICEF. The first pub had been visited, only forty-nine more to go.

The Thames now looked a little more like a river, wider and deeper, but its course was still secretive and in places, as before, overgrown and difficult to negotiate. It twisted and snaked its way through open fields with still only the wildlife for company. It slips unnoticed past the village of Kempsford, where once in Elizabethan times it was said five thousand sheep grazed on the great water meadow by the wide sweeping bend of the river below the village.

The village was once in the heart of the great Cotswold wool industry. An industry in which Dick Whittington, with or without his cat, made his fortune. An industry which was once England's traditional source of wealth, hence the woolsack in the House of Lords, introduced by King Edward III (1327-1377) to celebrate the country's prosperity due to the wool trade.

The Lord Speaker sits upon the woolsack, a large square cushion stuffed with wool and covered in red cloth. Today wool from several countries of the Commonwealth is used to symbolise unity. During the reign of Elizabeth I the woolsack was also adopted as a symbol to commemorate an Act passed against exporting wool.

The wool industry grew in and around this area for several reasons. The riverside water meadows provided lush grazing for the vast flocks of sheep. A kind of clay, called Fullers Earth, is common in this part of the country which possesses highly absorbent qualities capable of absorbing grease and has been used since ancient times for cleaning and felting wool. The many streams in the area were used for washing the fleece and of course the Thames played its part as a trade route to London.

Kempsford, meaning 'ford of the great marsh', was fortified by the Saxons and part of their earthwork is still visible on the north bank of the river. In January 800 a battle was fought here between the two kingdoms off Wessex and Mercier, the river being the frontier between the two kingdoms. A large meadow on the banks of the river named Battlefield is supposed to be where this battle took place. Spearheads have been found on the site which seems to back up this theory.

A Norman castle was built to defend this once important crossing point of the Thames. During its heyday four kings were entertained at the castle, Edwards I, II and III, and Henry 1V. The castle, of which no traces remain, was demolished in the seventeenth century.

Kingfisher

We continued our solitary journey whiling away the time counting Kingfishers. There seemed to be an unusual amount of these brightly coloured birds which despite its colour are usually difficult to spot due to their small size and rapid flight. Because a canoe is such a silent form of transport, they didn't hear us coming and therefore we were fairly close to them before they took to the wing.

We must have counted at least twelve of these shy and elusive birds as we paddled quietly along this wild and untouched part of the Thames. We presumed it was due to the fact that so little alteration to the waterside had been made in this area that these creatures were so prevalent.

In flight the Kingfisher looks like a flash of bright blue light as it skims fast and low over the water. It's one Britain's most beautiful birds, with upper parts of an iridescent cobalt blue or emerald green, depending on the angle at which the light catches them. It has a noticeable paler blue streak stretching from neck to tail. The cheeks and underparts are a warm chestnut colour. There is a patch of white on the throat and sides of the neck. Its legs are red.

As the name suggests, they are expert fishers. Preying on small fish such as minnows, bullheads and sticklebacks which the Kingfisher catches by diving straight down into the water from a convenient perch and seizing them in its open beak. It then returns to its diving point to swallow its meal. The whole operation, from leaving its perch to returning is over in seconds.

Apparently, not having sampled one myself, the kingfisher is seldom preyed upon because of the unpleasant taste of its flesh.

The nest is built at the end of a tunnel, up to a metre in length, which the pair excavate in an exposed bank of a stream, river or lake. When there are young in the nest disgorged fish offal will be seen around the opening as well as dark slime trickling from the hole, the excrement of the young. Not the most pleasant of neighbours to have living next door!

A couple or so miles further on we passed beneath Hannington Bridge built in 1841 on the site of a very much earlier Roman bridge. Here the river is hidden from the road by steep sandy banks and the river is especially swift and shallow which took us unawares. We had an unexpected and exhilarating few seconds as we were accelerated through one of the narrow arches sideways on.

It was another hour before we quietly passed the once great medieval village of Inglesham of which now only a farm and church remain. The tiny 11th century church of Saint John the Baptist stands alone beside the river. It's a haven of peace, restored just over a hundred years ago by William Morris who fought successfully to save it from the elaborate restoration schemes of the Victorians. He founded The Society for the Protection of Ancient Buildings and saving the church at Inglesham in 1880 was one of the societies first triumphs. It's said the 'Society' led indirectly to the forming of the National Trust.

About three quarters of a mile further on the Thames loses its innocence at the 'Round House'. This is the recognised limit of navigation for powered craft travelling upstream. A footbridge across the river seems to act as an indicator to powered boats to turn around. From now on we would be sharing the waterway with other fellow humans.

The 'Round House' marks the entrance, via a lock, to the old Thames and Severn Canal which opened in 1789 and continued in use until 1933. The 'Round House' was the lock keeper's cottage built circular, similar to a lighthouse; an economic style established by the canal designers. Horses were stabled on the ground floor and the lock keeper and his family lived above. The flat lead roof acted as a water tank. Its design is typical of the other lock cottages of this canal. This particular cottage has been converted into a very desirable private riverside residence.

Another ten minutes and we arrived at Lechlade. By now the river had at least trebled in size since we had begun our journey at Cricklade, eleven miles back up stream. It was 3pm when we pulled alongside our second pub aptly named The Riverside Pub.

A Victorian writer, J. E. Vincent, wrote The Story of The Thames and in it he writes that above Lechlade boating is, 'a mere labour of sorrow, penetrating the weeds to pass Castle Eaton and Kempsford to Cricklade'. I partially agree, at times it was a labour and we did our share of weed penetrating, but a sorrow it certainly was not. For a few hours we had been transported from the everyday humdrum existence of clock watching, pleasing others, etiquette and other such irritations that we have to adhere to in our 'civilised' world. It sounds selfish, and I suppose it is, but it's not often that we can truly please ourselves. Kevin said he felt as I did, a feeling of contentment, well-being and mental calmness. In retrospect, I don't think I can honestly say I felt complete mental calmness during the swan encounter. We only had ourselves to please and that feeling remained with us for the rest of the trip. Although, now we were back with society we needed to adhere a little more to the etiquette side of things. Incidentally, it had taken an acquaintance of J.E. Vincent's at the turn of the century, from 10.30am until 5pm to complete this same journey in a canoe. We had bettered his time by two hours.

Lechlade, mentioned in the Domesday book, derives its name from the river Leich which joins the Thames a little further downstream and the word 'lade' meaning to load. Many hundreds of years before the Thames and Severn canal was built, Lechlade was a busy port. Salt from Droitwich, Wiltshire and Gloucester cheeses, Cotswold stone and wool were transported by road to Lechlade then loaded onto barges and sent down river to London.

During its heyday the riverside at Lechlade was a bustling, energetic rendezvous for barges and other freight carrying vessels. Very much an industrial area with wharves and warehouses. Nowadays, it's a sedentary picturesque terminus for the pleasure craft that are resting before heading back downstream.

The Riverside Pub began its existence as a warehouse. We had to moor against the wall of the old wharf and struggled to heave ourselves out of the canoe and up and over onto the pubs' lawn. A small child was taken unawares as we suddenly appeared like a couple of grunting seals rolling over the parapet. It ran away screaming to its parents who were sitting a little way off at a picnic table. Up until then they had been enjoying the peace and quiet of the river. They eyed us suspiciously as they consoled their offspring.

It suddenly dawned on us that we hadn't eaten since breakfast which seemed way back in the past. Kev disappeared into the pub to order sandwiches and a couple of beers whilst I sat on the lawn and admired the old road bridge with its intriguing name of Half Penny Bridge. It was given this name because that was the price one had to pay for crossing. Built in 1793 the old toll house still remains although it's been free to cross since 1875. Up until then even walkers, unless you were on your way to church or a mourner, had to pay the half penny toll to use the bridge.

Every Bank Holiday Monday between the years 1903 and 1935 an extremely popular water carnival was held at Lechlade. At times it was said to have attracted as many as ten thousand visitors. The events; boating, swimming and diving from Half Penny Bridge were very popular competitions. Indeed, the West of England's swimming and diving championships were held at Lechlade for a time. I wonder what those bygone competitors would make of the heated indoor swimming pools and the purpose-built diving pools of today? Those were the days when men were men and swimming costumes were woollen hand knitted affairs.

It was about 3:30pm as we paddled under Half Penny Bridge feeling refreshed after 'refuelling' and a rest. We still had about another eight miles to cover before our first day's paddling was over. The most difficult and physically demanding part of the journey was now behind us. The way was now free of reeds and obstructions and the Thames looked more like a river than a stream. New man-made hazards were awaiting us. Weirs, locks and cruisers. From now on the river is no longer wild and free, it's been tamed to a certain extent. It was now a working river, a highway.

The Thames snakes its way out of Lechlade winding its way through open water meadows in a series of oxbow bends creating the allusion that the elegant spire of the Church of St Lawrence back at Lechlade was on the move, at times appearing on our right and then on the left. At one time it even seemed to be ahead of us. The poet Shelley composed, 'A Summer Evening Churchyard', based on the church of St Lawrence, whilst staying at Lechlade in 1815 after rowing up the Thames from Old Windsor with his mistress, Mary Godwin, and his friend Thomas Peacock.

The constant meandering of the river was very time consuming and energy sapping so we adopted a method of paddling diagonally across the river, cutting the corners thus keeping us on a straight a course as possible and therefore having less distance to paddle. The correct course to take is to follow the right-hand side, opposite to road travel, but as we hadn't seen another craft as yet we decided to risk the manoeuvre in order to save time and energy.

After about a mile we came upon the first man made obstacle, St John's lock. It was the first of the forty-five we were going to have to negotiate over the next twelve days. Another note-worthy occasion, it was 4pm.

Close Encounters of the Feathered Kind

Kev remarked that as we were the only craft in sight and would therefore have the lock to ourselves it would be a good time to experience going through a lock instead of portaging. I agreed. The lock gates were open and we paddled through watched by a friendly looking lock-keeper. "Going far?" he enquired. "Only as far as Teddington," Kev nonchalantly replied.

The gates crashed shut behind us like a trap. The dripping sides of a lock have chains at intervals dangling down into the depths, the purpose of which, we presume, is for the poor souls who fall overboard to cling onto until rescued. Or, for canoeists to grasp whilst the lock fills or empties! In our case, as we were heading down stream, all the locks would be emptying. We held onto the somewhat slimy chains as the water level fell and we slowly descended. The fall of the locks vary a great deal, St John's being a mere two feet ten inches. It all went to plan for us without any problems, but of course on this occasion we hadn't had to share the lock with other craft.

Kev, down in St John's lock with the blue barrels and the rest of our luggage

Sitting on one side of the lock is the statue of Old Father Thames made by Rafaelle Monti for the Great Exhibition in 1851. It survived the fire which melted the Crystal Palace and was then moved to mark the official source of the river at Thames Head in Gloucestershire. In 1947 it was moved to its present resting place to avoid any more vandalism, which it seemed to be attracting.

Our first lock, St John's, with 'Old Father Thames'

After a photograph with the statue and a pleasant chat with the lockkeeper we resumed our journey. Almost immediately we passed beneath the single arched St John's Bridge. The present bridge dates from 1886, it replaced an old stone bridge dating way back to 1229 which in turn had replaced a wooden crossing. The nearby Priory of John, of which no trace remains, had charge of the 'new' stone bridge. The monks built an alms house next to the bridge in around 1220. After the Priory was dissolved by Edward 1V, one monk was left to maintain the bridge and continued to live in the alms house which the enterprising man soon turned into an inn. It was called Ye Sygne of St Baptist's Head but in1704 it was renamed the Trout. (Probably because they had got fed up with being told they had wrongly spelt 'sign')

The garden of The Trout has water on three sides, the fast-flowing weir pool stream on one side, the Thames on another and on the third side the river Leach which joins the Thames at this point. A little further down-stream the River Cole also adds its water to the Thames.

The Trout has long been noted for its good food but unfortunately, as it was just past four in the afternoon, it was closed? We walked across the lawn and peered in through the windows. Ancient fishery rights granted by Royal Charter to the brethren of the Priory are still held by the inn. Appropriately the walls inside are adorned with stuffed fish and fishing prints. We each took a drink from the 'medicinal whisky flask' which we had stowed for such emergencies and took the all-important photograph before returning to the canoe.

Five minutes of paddling took us past the site of an old ferry point known as Bloomers Hole. Named, it is said, after a past local rector the Reverend Bloomer, who was caught bathing here in the nude.

As the Spire of St Lawrence gradually grew smaller the river continued its extravagant meandering course, at times almost doubling back on itself. The scene again became a lonely and rural one.

We passed a small cruiser with a young family as crew who had moored for the evening and were busily lighting their barbecue on the bank. What an idyllic spot. Remote and miles from anywhere with only the sounds of sheep and cattle and the occasional call of a bird to disturb the peace. They gave a friendly wave as we paddled past and quickly disappeared around the next inevitable bend.

We persevered with our tactic of steering diagonally across the river between bends and cutting the corners. Not to be recommended if there are boats about but as we seemed to have the river to ourselves, we decided to persist with this unorthodox and slightly risky method.

We were making good headway and enjoying the late afternoon sun. Progress was so much easier on open water without the hindrance of reeds and fallen trees. Kev suggested we did a hundred strokes in rhythm in the style the Roman galley slaves adopted to get up to 'ramming speed' to see what sort of pace we could maintain. He called out the numbers to keep us in time, one, two, three, four...............It was surprising how quickly our speed picked up. A Roman galley with its one hundred and fifty or so oarsmen must have been very swift.

We were flying along at a fast-jogging speed and all I could hear was the splash of our paddles and Kevin counting up the rhythm, sixty-one, sixty-two, sixty-three. As we rounded a high banked blind left-hand bend on the wrong side of the river we came face to face with a fairly large cruiser, luckily going quite a bit slower than we were. As there was no time to get out the handbook and read up on the appropriate sound signal and as neither of the craft had brakes, I was contemplating abandoning ship.

There was no time for even that. The cruiser swerved out into mid-stream and we took evasive action by steering hard left full tilt into the soft sandy bank. Kevin and I didn't stop quite as abruptly as our canoe. I finished up laying across the bows and Kev came to rest spread-eagled over the blue barrels. Laughter once again came to the rescue and thank goodness even the good people on the cruiser saw the funny side of things. They even turned back to see if we were ok. After an accepted apology from us and a kind donation to UNICEF from them, we extracted the canoe from the bank and proceeded onwards, leaving a ready-made nesting hole for the next pair of lucky kingfishers who passed that way. We decided there and then that from now on we would adhere to the highway code and keep to the right of the river, at least when negotiating blind bends.

Along this stretch of the river between Lechlade and Oxford there are a series of concrete Second World War pill boxes, built along the Thames in 1940 to turn the river into a fortified line of defence. Thankfully never used as they were intended. Now often utilised by cattle and sheep for shelter or by fishermen and ramblers as emergency 'conveniences. Some people are of the opinion that they are an eyesore and should be demolished. Others, and for what it's worth they include me, think they should remain as part of our rich historical heritage, just as castles and other such relics are preserved. As the years have passed their stark concrete appearance has mellowed as moss, lichen and brambles have joined forces to help them blend into the background.

Just before Buscot lock, about a mile from St John's, we passed an island know as Brandy Island. It gets its name from a distillery, now demolished, which stood on the island and distilled spirit from beetroot.

In 1879 an Australian, Robert Campbell, owned the Buscot estate. Somewhat of an eccentric he ruined himself by his financial obsession for introducing the latest farming technology and money-making schemes which included using steam ploughs at night and distilling beetroot. By all accounts the beetroot idea had been fairly successful to begin with as a steady flow of alcohol was exported downriver and then across to France for brandy production. Sadly, beetroot brandy didn't compare favourably with Courvoisier or Remy Martin and the scheme failed.

"Would you like a Remy Martin with your cigar sir, or a Buscot Beetroot Brandy?"

A former owner of the estate, Edward Loveden, was president of a parliamentary committee which was set up in 1793 to improve the navigation on the Thames. The committee was responsible for the construction of straight canal like cuts to bypass some of the long curves in the river. This was at the beginning of the period when the Thames was becoming a very busy freight highway and it became important to get from A to B as quickly as possible.

The 7,500acre estate, which includes Buscot village, is now owned by the National Trust.

The lock keeper at Buscot lock was waiting for us with the gates open. News travels fast on the river and obviously the St John's lockkeeper had contacted his colleague to tell him to expect the 'Red Canoe' as we became known to all subsequent lockkeepers. It became evident that they kept in close contact with one another and knew all about us long before we arrived. They greeted us like old friends and we were always well looked after. Again, we had the lock to ourselves, so we sat tight and rested in the canoe as we were gently lowered five foot and seven inches this time to the river's next level.

According to 'The Ordinance Survey Guide to The River Thames' it was a long and lonely four and a half miles to the next lock. We were beginning to wonder if we would ever reach our night's lodgings before dark. We passed several more pill boxes and met only one boat just after leaving Buscot lock. It seemed in rather a hurry and set up quite a wash which we bravely met head on whilst treating the local wildlife to a rendering of Hawaii Five 0.

The river continued its lonesome way through a wide-open valley with large expanses of unbroken pastureland. It's a very isolated stretch of the river through the very depths of rural England. During the winter and in inclement weather it must be a very bleak and uninviting part of the Thames but thankfully, with the late afternoon sun still warm on our backs, the very fact of the remoteness was quite absorbing. By now the river had made up its mind in which direction it wanted to go and was meandering a lot less, in fact there were some fairly long straightish sections which were perfect for 'hundred stroke ramming speed' sessions.

About a mile and a half from Buscot and just after passing under an attractive wooden footbridge, the Thames does touch civilization briefly as it passes the village of Kelmscott and the Elizabethan Kelmscott Manor built in 1570. Once the home of William Morris, artist, poet, printer, socialist and protector of ancient buildings, who moved there in 1871 from London where he remained until he died in 1896. He described his home as, 'heaven on earth' and had a great affection for this lonely stretch of the Thames between Lechlade and Oxford. He describes this part of the river in one of his poems.

'By this sweet stream knows not of the sea,
That guesses not the city's misery,
This little stream, whose hamlets scarce had names,
This far off, lonely mother of The Thames'

Morris and his family are buried at Kelmscott church. He was passionate about protecting old buildings from unnecessary restoration and modernisation. The entire village and manor, with its original décor, have been left unchanged since Morris live there. The house is now owned by the Society of Antiquities and is open to the public during the summer when it's possible to step back into time.

About half a mile further on we passed an area which was once the village of Eaton Hastings. All that remains of the village, which was probably deserted after the plague of 1665, is a small Norman church, a few cottages and a farm. Perhaps it was a figment of my imagination but even on this fine summer's afternoon the area had a desolate and forlorn feeling about it. Not a spot I would choose for an over-night mooring.

Another three quarters of an hour of steady progress brought us to the isolated outpost of Grafton lock. It must be the loneliest lock on the river. I can imagine a lock keeper of old up before the head lockkeeper and his jury for some misdemeanour, standing with head bowed as sentence is passed. "For your dastardly crime against humanity you are sentenced to be exiled to Grafton lock for the rest of your working days."

In a time before radios, television and telephones it would have been like being banished to outer Mongolia or Hadrian's Wall. Not so bad these days, in fact on that summer's afternoon quite idyllic. Just the place to take your eight favourite gramophone records. Again, the lock keeper was expecting us and we had the lock to ourselves.

By now the late afternoon was thinking of being early evening and we still had a fairway to go before our first day's paddling was over. I must admit that by now we were feeling on the weary side and we were looking forward to a bath, a few beers and a substantial meal.

At last, the three arched Radcot bridge came into view, built in the 13th century and said to be the oldest surviving bridge on the Thames. It has witnessed considerable bloodshed as it has played centre stage to two battles.

The first in 1387 when Henry Bolingbroke, who eleven years later became Henry 1V, lay in wait to ambush Robert De Vere who was on his way south from Oxford to fight for Richard II against Henry. Bolingbroke had demolished the middle arch of the bridge to trap De Vere. Various knights from both sides were killed in the battle but De Vere managed to elude death or capture. The mists of time have confused the details of his escape. Some historians say he spurred his horse forward and leapt the gap in the bridge and galloped off to safety. Others say he abandoned his armour and sword and under cover of darkness swam to safety. In any case he met an untimely end two years later during a boar hunt.

The other skirmish was in 1645 during The Civil War, when a contingent of Prince Rupert's men fought off the Parliamentarians. There were several such engagements around the area as the rival armies fought for the control of Oxford.

Just by the bridge are the remains of a wharf from which many thousands of tons of stone were floated down the Thames to London on rafts for the rebuilding of St Pauls Cathedral after it was destroyed in the Great Fire of 1666. The stone had been cut from Taynton quarry near Burford and brought by road on carts to the river.

The river divides into two here which creates a small island. If we had taken the main channel to the left, we would have passed beneath the new Radcot bridge built in 1787. It consists of a single very narrow arch and is situated around an extremely tight bend if travelling upstream. An abundance of scratches and traces of paint on the sides of the bridge bear testament to the numerous unwary helmsmen who over the years have suddenly been confronted by the narrow bridge after rounding the blind bend.

We passed beneath the old bridge and a few metres further came at last to our first day's destination, The Swan. The time was 6:30pm, it had taken us eight hours to paddle 18 miles which considering the difficult slow beginning wasn't too bad.

The Swan has its own landing stage and boathouse at the end of its garden. We drew up alongside and stiffly disembarked. Whilst Kevin went inside to enquire if we could leave our canoe in the boathouse for the night, I unloaded our baggage. It was then that I noticed the debris we had collected on the way. Bits of reed, broken twigs and branches, leaves, mud and a multitude of minibeasts. All collected earlier in the day as we battled our way along the upper reaches.

We were kindly given permission to use the boathouse and after emptying the canoe of the flotsam and stowaways we meticulously chained and padlocked her securely for the night. We then wearily made our way up the lawn to the inn carrying our barrels, paddles, bucket and dry sack.

The Swan at Radcot was listed in the Domesday book as a hostelry, situated by one of the very few bridges crossing the Thames in those days. The building today is mostly of 15th century origins. It too of course has witnessed the spilling of much gore which continues to this day although to a much lesser extent. At the beginning of May the locals take part in the annual rook shoot and the tradition of making rook pie. I'm told quite a tasty dish not unlike steak pie. It wasn't on the menu that evening otherwise I might have been tempted to try it.

As is the norm for such old buildings it has attracted a ghost. The landlady and staff believe in an ancient, old gentlemen, fondly known as Fred, who plagues and amuses them will his antics of turning off lights at inconvenient times. He also refuses to allow anyone to play 'shove halfpenny' at his end of the bar. He's quite happy to allow it at the other end.

Arrowroot powder is spread over the slate board so that the half penny slides across the board with the minimum of friction. At one end of the bar, no problem, but if you're at Fred's end he forms the powder into lines across the board thus hindering the half pennies progress. This happens apparently whatever the weather, time of day or time of year.

I have met a few cantankerous old characters like that, in fact there is one, very much alive, who drinks regularly in my local and woe betide anyone who sits in his seat. He would soon rearrange their 'arrowroot'!

I wish now, looking back, that we had put Fred to the test but we were content at the time to just sit back and sup a few beers. The truth is we were too knackered to even play 'shove half penny.'

Another regular game they play at the Swan, against other pub teams, is a game called 'Aunt Sally.' Very popular in Oxfordshire just as darts, dominoes and crib, to name just three others, are popular in other parts of the country. I hope these traditional pub games remain and are not abandoned and forgotten for the pub quiz craze and the karaoke evenings that seems to be creeping in.

Aunt Sally is one of those pub games which is played in a very confined locale, in this case it seems to be restricted to pubs in and around Oxford. Within this relatively small area it is a very popular game indeed and there are a number of leagues in-which to compete. It's taken very seriously by the regulars. It may have been introduced by Royalist soldiers during the civil war when Charles set up court in Oxford.

A single white stubby skittle, about six inches high and two and three-quarter inches in diameter, the 'Dolly', is positioned on top of a hollow rod, the 'Iron', which is about two and a half foot high. A team consists of eight players who take it in turn to throw six, eighteen inches long and round ended projectiles call the 'Sticks', from behind a line, the 'Hockey', which is ten yards from the 'Iron'. A point is scored if the 'Stick' strikes the 'Dolly' before the 'Iron'. It's an out-door game so presumably it's a summer sport?

A theory ascribes 'Aunt Sally' as a humane version of a blood sport called, 'Throwing at Cocks'. In the barbaric past a cock was tied by one leg to a stake in the ground and the participants would then pay for a turn at throwing a small club at the unfortunate bird. Whoever killed the bird got to take it home for the pot. If the sad creature was wounded or rendered unconscious it would be supported on sticks until the bitter end. Only one question remains, how did Aunt Sally become involved?

We were lucky enough to witness a game later on in the evening. Although a copious supply of beer seemed to be an intrinsic part of the proceedings, it was taken very seriously and I might add, it isn't as easy as it sounds.

When we first entered The Swan, we immediately noticed a very odd-looking couple sitting up at the bar perched on two high bar stools. They turned to watch, which to them must have seemed to be an odd-looking pair walking into the pub, carrying a blue barrel and a paddle apiece, a white bucket and a large black sack. Some other patrons of the establishment also paused from their conversations and looked our way.

The landlady introduced herself and bid us welcome and noticing we were intrigued by the appearance of the two sitting up to the bar, who were still eyeing us suspiciously, she divulged to us in hushed tones that they were quite harmless. She went on to explain that every evening they were helped onto their stools and there they remained until closing time, keeping an eye on the customers and always ready to accept a crisp when offered.

She led us reverently over to be introduced to them. Their names where Cambric and Lace, two miniature Schnauzers belonging to the landlady.

Now it's fair to say, and Kevin will be the first to admit it, that he is not the most avid dog lover, and Cambric was obviously a very discerning dog. From the outset he showed that the feeling was mutual by revealing a formidable set of teeth in a silent snarl whenever Kevin approached, although he was completely indifferent to me. Kevin did try to offer the hand of friendship later on in the evening by donating a whole packet of crisps as a peace offering. But to no avail, and Cambric remained hostile towards Kev for the rest of the evening much to everyone's amusement.

In the end Kevin gave up and announced that anyway, given the choice, he would much prefer to sit at the other end of the bar with Fred.

Sandra, our landlady, showed us to our room. A twin room just as I had booked and as all good twin room should have, this one had two separate beds. However, this particular room wasn't overly spacious, and I suspect that it just managed to usually house a double bed instead of our two singles. The reason for this supposition was that the two beds were standing side by side, so close that a newspaper wouldn't have been able to slide between them and hanging provocatively from the ceiling above the bedheads, was a white lace canopy. Was this the bridal suite? We couldn't resist a Morecambe and Wise style photograph as a memento of our first night together.

Our first overnight stop.

After a good soak in the bath (separately) we retreated back to the bar and enjoyed a very pleasant steak with a bottle of red wine and then chatted to the locals over a few beers. We watched a game of Aunt Sally for a while but by 10pm the exertions of the day caught up with us and we adjourned back to our boudoir.

We felt pleased with our first day's performance. We had survived without any serious mishaps, and we were handling the canoe with confidence. Our toughest and longest day of paddling was behind us and although feeling tired our fitness training had paid off.

As I settled down, mulling over the day's events, a question crossed my mind. Why is it that the one who snores is always the first to fall asleep? Incidentally, we had placed a pillow between us just in case one of us awoke in the middle of the night confused and forgot who was beside them.

CHAPTER 7

I Name This Ship.........

Radcot to Bablock Hythe - 13.5 miles

It was around 6.30am when I awoke, Kevin had also regained consciousness and was looking at me in a rather accusing manner. I immediately became aware of a very unpleasant, pungent smell wafting around the room. As only exceptionally good friends can do, we both blamed each other for the offending odour. Both of us emphatically denied being responsible for such an unsociable act. "Then if it wasn't you," said Kevin, "that bloody dog must have sneaked in and is still somewhere in the room."

A quick search of the room did not reveal poor maligned Cambric but it did divulge the source of the smell.

Over the course of yesterday and especially during my Humphrey Bogart impression, my trainers had become sodden with river water. I had placed them on top of the radiator with the intention of drying them out overnight. There seems to be an element in river water that leaves an aroma on articles during and after drying out which I can only describe as a cross between rotten cabbages and pig manure. I hurriedly placed the offending articles outside on the windowsill, which was where both pairs of trainers where ceremoniously placed every night for the rest of the trip.

We both felt rejuvenated and raring to go after a good night's sleep. Inevitably we had a few aches and pains after our previous day's strenuous activities but these soon wore off once we got going again.

After an exceptionally full English breakfast, for which the Swan is renowned, we packed our barrels and wandered down to the boathouse to be reunited with our canoe. We had taken the 'evidence' photograph the previous evening. Kev's mate, Cambric, followed us down the garden to see us safely off the premises. It wasn't the fondest of farewells I had ever witnessed!

We had a thirteen-and-a-half-mile day ahead of us paddling to our next evening's port of call, the Ferryman Inn at Bablock Hythe. We were looking forward to a more straightforward and less hazardous journey than the day before with, we hoped, a few more watering holes along the way.

It was 9:15am when we eventually set off after securely fastening down our luggage. A chore which became easier and quicker over the days once a routine was established. We had agreed that we would aim to be on the water by 9am each morning, so it wasn't too bad a start.

I asked Kev if he was superstitious, because did he realise it was Friday the 13th? He said he wasn't but thanks for reminding him.

The weather was overcast but dry and warm as we smoothly paddled out of the boathouse, Kevin at the front this time as we had decided to swap seats every day. It was my turn as helmsman, somehow it felt safer and less exposed at the back.

Cambric stood at the end of the wooden jetty and as a last defiant gesture cocked his leg against the mooring post as we passed. "Bloody dog," I heard Kevin mutter under his breath.

We hadn't gone far when we noticed a middle-aged woman with an exceptionally large dog walking along the bank coming in our direction. I didn't recognise the breed but one of its parents could well have been a grizzly bear. As we approached, she stopped and scrutinized our progress. Just before we passed, she excitedly waved her arms in the air and shouted, "You're those two teachers, aren't you? I heard you on the radio yesterday. Good luck!"

Fame, I thought, people do listen to local radio after all. I was all for stopping and signing autographs, but Kev pointed out that the dog was taking a more than casual interest in us and its front paws were already in the water testing the temperature. He suggested we should just wave and nod in a nonchalant and modest way. We did as Kev suggested and pressed on.

We soon reached Radcot lock where a couple of boats, one a fair size cabin cruiser, the other a brightly coloured narrowboat, were waiting inside for us. They had overtaken us just before and we had exchanged pleasantries as they passed.

The lock keeper beckoned us in behind the other two craft. It was the first time we had shared a lock with any other boats and being in a confined space and at such close proximity to them, made us feel quite small, frail and vulnerable. We had drawn up close behind the narrowboat which obviously, due to the black smoke coming from its exhaust, was powered by a 'past its prime' diesel engine. Unfortunately for my helmsman sitting up front, the engine was left ticking over, (not usually allowed whilst in a lock,) monotonously belching out its smoke in a regular beat. Another valuable lesson learnt the hard way.

Once clear of the lock the two boats soon left us behind and we were left to enjoy the quiet solitude again, although the smell of diesel fumes remained with us for quite a while due to the impregnation of Kevin's T-shirt.

A few minutes further on we passed under a wooden footbridge known as 'Old Man's Bridge'. The footpath once led to a weir known as 'Old Men's Weir' which ceased to exist in 1868. By the weir, on either side of the river once stood two inns. On the Berkshire side was 'The Spotted Cow', and on the Oxfordshire side, 'The Trout.' As it was such a remote spot, the only way of reaching them was either by boat or walking. They both became convenient places for illicit gambling, cock fighting and other shady goings on. Both premises have now disappeared without a trace of them ever having existed.

After leaving Radcot Lock all signs of civilization are quickly left behind and again the river becomes isolated following its own course through flat and featureless water meadows. It again seems unable to decide which way it wants to go as it twists and turns through exaggerated meanders along a three-mile section to Rushey Lock.

While we made steady progress, I took the opportunity to work on my steering skills which soon improved with practice. Once mastered they soon became second nature.

The water meadows on either side of the river seemed to stretch as far as the eye could see. A dull and uninteresting vista apart from the narrow fringe of the riverside flora growing on both banks, making a colourful corridor through which the river flowed.

The names of these plants are as 'colourful' as the flowers themselves. The pink and red flowers were the Ragged Robin, the Marsh Thistle and the Red Rattle. The Marsh Marigold, Marsh Birds Foot Trefoil and the Common Meadow Rue made up the yellow and gold colours. The white flowerheads were of the Sneezewort and the Marsh Bedstraw, the blues were the Water Forget Me-Nots and, the Devil's Bit Scabious, so named because it has a stout root which ends rather abruptly as if it has been bitten off. The story goes that the devil was so envious of the considerable range of herbal properties of the scabious species he tried to destroy it by biting off its root.

These plants, plus many more, are left alone and are unmolested by the plough and modern agricultural methods, to flourish along these important corridors provided by the banks of rivers and streams. They can survive occasional or seasonal flooding but not constant ploughing, grazing or mowing, not to mention the spraying of weed killers.

Intermingled with the bankside herbage, at the very edge of the water and on into the shallows, grow the wetland plants. Celery Leaved Crowsfoot, Brooklime, Great Yellow Cress, Water Mint, Horseradish and Butterbur to name but a few.

Towards the end of April when the flowers of the Butterbur have withered, its enormous leaves appear. I suspect that the old practice of using them to wrap butter gave it its name.

Horseradish was originally of Middle Eastern origin introduced to Britain in the fifteenth century. It's a very adaptable plant and can not only be found growing in damp conditions but also on most types of waste grounds, in fields and along roadsides. It's often found growing by old coaching inns because although its roots are now used exclusively as a condiment, they used to be made into a hot liquid which was drunk by the coach passengers in an attempt to keep out the cold.

This stretch of the bank has an abundance of Teasel. The dried fruiting heads with their stiff hooked bracts, which look like a type of thistle, were once used in the wool trade as a natural comb to raise the nap of the woollen cloth. Hence the saying, 'to tease something out', to untangle it.

Teasels

I also noticed clumps of Hemlock, a member of the carrot family but definitely not to be eaten. All parts of the plant are highly poisonous especially the young leaves which resemble parsley. If eaten, respiratory problems or death by paralysis can result. It was hemlock, made into a drink, which dispatched to Socrates, the Greek philosopher, sentenced to death in 399 BC.

Hemlock

Hemlock is a tall, upright plant growing to about two metres. In the summer it produces 'umbrella like' clusters of white flowers. It has a purple spotted hollow stem and has a distinctive and unpleasant 'mousey' smell.

Thinking back, as kids we used the hollow stems of Cow Parsley, which very much resembles Hemlock, for peashooters, not knowing then anything about the extremely poisonous Hemlock. Luckily for us we never came across it!

The most common plants found along the river margin are the rushes, sedges and grasses. Being wind pollinated they lack the colours and the scent of insect pollinated flowers. They are easily disregarded as dull look-a-likes but there are many individual species with their own characteristics and subtle shades of green. Some are extremely useful.

Our tallest native grass is the Common Reed. Its stems and leaves have been used for thatching, while its creeping roots prevent soil and bank erosion. It grows and spreads quickly and if not kept in check will soon block a shallow river as we had found to our cost as we had battled our way through the upper reaches.

The stem of the Soft Rush can be split open to reveal a soft pith. This was once used for the wicks in candles and rush lights. The dried leaves and stems are still used for basket making and chair seats.

A little further out from the bank in the slightly deeper water, grow the submerged and floating species of flora. Water Crowfoot, Starworts and Water Lilies are just three examples. The plants living beneath the surface oxygenate the water helping to keep it pure and healthy for the fish and invertebrates.

I have only mentioned a miniscule number of the plant life to be found along the upper reaches of the Thames. The profusion of species and the copious variety of colour and shade is forever changing, as the conditions and habitats converge and as the seasons merge into one another.

It's easy to overlook and take for granted this diverse tapestry which is so important for life in and around the river. For the riverbank and water dwelling animals the success of the plant life is essential to their survival by providing shelter and food.

The many types of mini habitats in and around water attract different animals and determine the variety of life to be found in an area. A reed bed will harbour a totally different community to that of a clump of lilies found only a few feet away. For the ecosystem of the river to be maintained all the components need to thrive and work in harmony.

A steady three-mile paddle brought us to Rushey Lock, another far-flung outpost as locks go, but with a beautifully kept garden with a gigantic topiary frog. The charming keepers-cottage once doubled as a guest house. Its isolated location was perfect for those wishing for a peaceful and secretive retreat. In the past it has played host to such celebrities as Douglas Fairbanks and Errol Flynn.

A few craft of various types and sizes had passed us along the way and as we approached the lock, we could see two cruisers awaiting our arrival. Mindful of the diesel smoke incident back at the previous lock we were careful not to linger at the stern of either boat but instead drew alongside one of them. We would not make the same mistake twice.

Both crews were an amiable bunch and we passed the time chatting to them as the lockkeeper went about his business. Already going through locks was second nature to us and we thought nothing of it.

Kev was in the middle of recounting the day before and the swan family encounter to our new acquaintances, when all of a sudden, a steady stream of water was omitted from a hole in the side of the cruiser next to us, straight into Kevin's lap. There was no escape for him, but in any case, I was laughing too much to give any assistance. I did remark to Kev that after all it was Friday the 13th, but that didn't seem to help. Someone on board had decided to pull the plug in the sink to discharge the washing up water into the river. (I didn't think this was still allowed either!) Another valuable lesson learnt. We now knew, Kev especially, that when at canoe height it is best to keep well clear of exhaust pipes and drain holes.

A mile further on, at about 11:30, we moored just below the single arched, 18th century, stone-built Tadpole Bridge, at the end of the well-manicured lawn of The Trout. Apart from the inn and the bridge there is nothing else around within a mile or two in each direction. Someone once said that 'Tadpole bridge is about as far away from it all as you can get on the Thames'. I felt we had passed through more remote areas already, but I know what they meant.

I Name This Ship.......

So here we were, sitting on an old wooden bench at the end of a pub garden supping a pint of ale watching the river slip by, with our canoe moored at our feet and the warm sun on our backs. Nearby, was the quaint old single arched bridge with the dappled sunlight reflected off the water and transferred to the underside of the arch. The only sounds were the high pitched 'clack' of a moorhen somewhere in the reeds across the river and the gentle call of a wood pigeon sitting high in a tree behind us. All our cares and worries put aside for the next ten days.

The memory of that point in time is always one of the first that comes back to me whenever the trip is mentioned or thought of. It somehow encapsulates the whole mood of the expedition and was what we had imagined our days would be like. Kev has asked me more than once over the past years if I remember that time when we sat on the lawn of The Trout at Tadpole Bridge.

The only 'worry' we had, if you can call it a worry, was getting to the next hostelry we had booked in for each night in good time for the evening meal. So reluctantly, after three-quarters of an hour and another beer, we departed from the old seventeenth century Trout and continued our leisurely way down stream.

We hadn't travelled far when the peace was shattered by the shrill call of the 'lesser spotted Nokia', Kev's mobile phone.

You may be asking yourselves why on earth we had taken a mobile phone with us if we were hoping for a carefree and peaceful few days. Well, as mentioned before, family and friends had expressed their wishes to join us on route for a drink or two and so needed to check on our progress and arrange meetings. We had made them solemnly swear that that would be the sole reason they ever rang us. They all kept to their promise.

Radio Oxford had also expressed a wish to keep tabs on us and so had my local newspaper. It was the newspaper that was now on the phone. We spent the next few minutes gently drifting downstream with the current as I related to the reporter our experiences so far. She was duly impressed but seemed somewhat disappointed that we were not suffering from a hangover.

The phone call prompted me to phone home to check that all was well with Jan. It proved to be a very significant few moments which has affected both Kevin and I ever since. She was pleased that all was well with us but she had some rather sad news to tell me.

Kev, being the good friend that he is, could tell something was wrong and after I had said a sombre goodbye, he let us drift on for another couple of minutes in silence.

"What's up mate?" he enquired in a quite concerned tone. I answered with the now immortal statement in a somewhat matter of fact voice, "My lizard is dead."

After a brief moment Kevin collapsed in convulsions of laughter nearly causing our first capsize. "That's a shame," he spluttered. "It must be your age, mine is still in fine working order."

From that moment the canoe was also affectionately known as 'The Lizard'.

Kev and the Lizard

What had actually happened was that for the summer break I had taken home a Sudanese Plated Lizard which I normally kept at school. Unfortunately, whilst I was away it had reached the time of life when all good lizards' journey to the great desert in the sky. Little did he know that he would be forever remembered as a red canoe.

I too soon saw the funny side of the remark and after we have gained control of ourselves and the canoe, we continued on our way downstream as the river twisted and turned through the remote countryside on its way to Shifford lock. Only one boat passed us going in the opposite direction so we seemed to have the river to ourselves again, apart from the usual feathered covered wildlife. Coots, moorhens, ducks, a kingfisher and another family of swans which, I am pleased to say, took little notice of us as we passed by. By now the river had grown considerably but was still no wider than about twenty to thirty meters, a little less in places.

We passed under another wooden footbridge dating from 1869 known as 'Ten Foot Bridge'. The path used to lead to yet another nearby pre-existent weir which had a ten-foot-wide flash lock.

When the Thames was first utilised for industrial transport the main difficulty to overcome was the irregular flow. In summer due to lack of water the many shallow sections had to be negotiated, in the winter months raging floods presented the opposite problem. In order to try to alleviate these problems and regulate the flow, wooden weirs, damn like structures, were built across the river to hold back flood water and to deepen the shallow sections. But this created a new problem. How would the boats and barges be able to continue down or upstream past the weirs? Flash locks, although very hazardous, were the answer of the day.

A section of the weir would be lifted to allow a vessel to be swept downstream with the sudden rush of released water. To travel upstream a vessel had to be winched through the gap against the rushing torrent. Many cargoes and lives were lost over the years during the use of flash locks until the pound locks of today replaced them.

Before reaching Shifford lock the river is artificially straight as it passes through the tree lined Shifford Cut. A fair number of these cuts were made along the Thames mainly in the 19th century to avoid time wasting loops in the river when the waterway was used as a commercial highway and time meant money. This particular section completed in 1898, was the last to be built on the Thames and it cuts out about a two- mile loop.

All that remains of Shifford, once a very important town way back in antiquity, is a church and a few cottages. The name Shifford originates from the Saxon word for 'sheep ford'. In AD890 Alfred-The- Great is reputed to have held one of the first English parliaments in a nearby field known as 'Court Close'. It's hard to imagine this area was once a bustling royal borough, for now it is just another remote and lonely place along the Thames.

As the lock gates were closed allowing the lock to fill to raise a small cruiser up to our level, we waited quietly under a high bank next to a clump of reeds. I noticed, in the bank opposite, just above the water level, a perfectly circular hole about the size of a tennis ball. A movement caught my eye as the resident of the hole emerged and dropped into the water with its characteristic 'plop'.

To me this scenario seemed very reminiscent of another passage from The Wind in the Willows and I make no apologies for quoting part of it now.

'As he (mole) sat on the grass and looked across the river a dark hole in the bank opposite just above the water's edge caught his eye. As he gazed, something bright and small seemed to twinkle down in the heart of it, vanished, then twinkled once more like a tiny star. But it could hardly be a star in such an unlikely situation, and it was too glittering and small for a glow worm. Then, as he looked, it winked at him, and so declared itself to be an eye, and a small face began to gradually grow around it, like a frame round a picture. A brown little face with whiskers. A grave round face with the same twinkle in its eye that had first attracted its notice. Small, neat ears and thick silky hair. It was the water rat'.

Being known as a 'water rat' is rather an unfortunate handle to have. 'Ratty' was really a water vole, there is no such animal as a water rat.

Water Vole

The water vole is about the same size as the brown rat and that's the only similarity they share. The water vole has a blunt nose whereas the rat has a more pointed muzzle. Rats' tails are naked and much longer than the water vole's furry tails. The rat's ears are pointed and stick out, on the other hand voles' small, rounded ears lay flat to the side of their heads.

Rats are extremely common and will thrive in almost any environment including riverbanks. Whereas the water vole, one of the most endearing riverbank creatures is becoming very rare. This sad state of affairs is mainly due to pollution and the degradation of riverbanks which often scarcely provide more than a ribbon of vegetation, the environment a water vole needs to live and prosper. This gentle, unassuming creature needs plenty of vegetation and sturdy undisturbed riverbanks to thrive. Rats are omnivores, eating anything they come across. Water voles are strictly herbivores eating grasses and waterside plants. They make their homes by tunnelling into the riverbank, also excavating an underwater entrance for a safe escape route.

The water vole has many predators including stoats, herons, owls, rats and large pike. One of their greatest enemies is the mink which originally escaped, or were released, from mink farms and are now quite prevalent, feral carnivores, inhabiting our waterways.

We were lucky enough to spot several water voles along this stretch towards Oxford, but none beyond. They are active during the daytime busily eating and patrolling their particular fifty metres of territory they have claimed for themselves along a stretch of the riverbank. On average a water vole lives for about 6 months to 1 ½ years in the wild. Within that time, they have to mature, find a mate, excavate a burrow and have several litters of about five young. At the same time, they need to be constantly on the alert and keep well clear of their predators. And we complain that we have stressful lives.!!

As we sat waiting for the lock to fill and open whilst idly watching the little fellow purposefully working away at surviving, that particular period of time for us was the exact opposite of stressful.

Shifford lock, completed in 1898, was the last to be built on the Thames. We had the lock to ourselves and after a pleasant chat with the lockkeeper we passed through without incident and continued on our way, looking for a pub and lunch.

The river continued to wander through flat farmland between steep banks which in places were heavily overgrown. To pass the time we began to make up verses to a song to the tune of the original version of 'Messing About on The River', recorded by Josh MacRae.

When the weather is fine then you know it's a sign
For messing about on the river.
If you take my advice there's nothing so nice
As messing about on the river....................

Our version was entitled, 'Messing About with the Lizard'. It would be prudent of me not to record the rendering on paper due to the bawdy nature of our lyrics. However, two fishermen, whom we failed to notice until we had passed them, seemed to enjoy our performance as they gave us a round of applause and even called out for more. By the end of our trip, we had amassed about twenty verses.

It was nearing 2 pm when after about three miles the welcoming sight of New Bridge came into view, with the May Bush on one side and The Rose Revived on the other. Although it's called New Bridge it's actually the second oldest bridge still spanning the Thames. It was built in 1250 just after Old Radcot Bridge under which we had passed upstream, so it became known as the new bridge. The six arched structure was built by Benedictine monks, by the order of King John, to connect the Cotswold 'wool towns' with the south. Like many of the old bridges in the area it too has seen action during the Civil War between the Cavaliers and the Round Heads.

The garden of The Maybush was full of people having lunch and judging by the number of craft moored alongside most of them had arrived by river. We had worked off the substantial breakfast from The Trout several hours earlier, so we were more than ready for a drink and a beef and horseradish sandwich.

The Maybush, once a 16th century farmhouse, was licenced to sell beer in around 1745 and was built on the site of a 15th century hermitage. The hermit, named Thomas Briggs, was employed as the bridge keeper.

We found a space between two boats and expertly drew in. The bank had been built up to receive cruisers and not for the likes of lowly canoes, so getting out of the Lizard safely with some resemblance of expertise was not going to be a foregone conclusion. As all eyes seemed to be gazing in our direction, a brief but quiet plan of action was discussed. Happily, for us, but not I suspect, for some onlookers we managed to disembark safely and with some aplomb as if we had been canoeing for years. However, it did cross my mind that we still had getting back on board to negotiate.

The boating fraternity are a friendly lot and after ordering our beers and sandwiches we soon got chatting to those around us. If we had not declined several kind offers to replenish our glasses there would have been little chance of us getting back into the Lizard safely. We could have easily spent the rest of the afternoon in such good company but after a couple of beers we explained that as Teddington was still a good way off, we had to press on.

As we were donning our 'nookies' and getting ready to depart, one gentleman took it upon himself to go around the tables with a hat asking for a contribution for our charity. We had agreed from the start of our venture that we would not ask for donations but we often found that people were so generous and willing to give to a good cause that nothing was needed to be said anyway.

We managed to get back into our canoe without too much unsteadiness and waved goodbye to our newly found acquaintances as we continued what they thought was to be the continuation of our epic journey down the Thames. It caused a deal of hilarity from them when they observed us just a minute later, pulling into the opposite bank at the Rose Revived.

The Rose Revived is now more of a restaurant than a pub but it still has much character and a long history. It began life as the toll house for the bridge then became an inn in the Stuart period known as The Crown. It was later renamed as The Fair House before becoming The Rose Revived. The story goes that a publican by the name of Rose reopened the pub after a period of neglect, hence the name.

The Maybush is on the Berkshire side of the river, The Rose Revived on the other in Oxfordshire. In the times when counties had different licencing hours there was a difference of half an hour between the closing time of the two hostelries. There was always a scurrying across the bridge when last orders were called to get an extra half an hour drinking in on the other side.

We enjoyed another beer each before departing at about 3-o-clock but not before I had walked back across the bridge to collect a promised donation from a lady who had missed the previous collection due to a trip to the toilet. She had been upset to see us paddling across the river without her contribution and had called after us.

We estimated that we still had an hour or two of paddling ahead of us before reaching our intended evening stopover at the Ferryman at Bablock Hythe.

Just beyond the bridge the River Windrush adds its waters to the Thames collected from the Cotswold Hills. The view from the river now began to change as the flat expanses of farmland gradually diminished as the hills closed in from the east and villages became a little closer. About two miles further on, after passing through Northmoor lock which we shared with five other boats, we passed some very attractive woodland which stretched for about half a mile along the right-hand bank making a welcome change to our previous outlook.

We made good time for it was about 4:15 when The Ferryman hove into view. I must admit that my first impression of the place was one of disappointment. It is known that a ford existed here in Roman times, in fact a Roman stone altar was dredged from the river at this very spot. The service for ferrying vehicles ceased in the 1960s, now only a small passenger ferry operates during the summer months. Matthew Arnold, the 19th century poet, refers to the ferry in his poem, 'A Scholar Gypsy', written in 1853, when he mentions, 'crossing the stripling Thames at Bablock Hythe'.

There has been an inn on the site for almost as long as the ferry, so one would expect The Ferryman to be a quaint, olde worlde inn, built of old stone with a thatched roof, or at least an attempt of a modern replica of such a building as the pub was completely rebuilt in the 1990s. Instead, you have the complete opposite. The Ferryman, once called the Chequers, looked to have been modelled on a 1960s holiday camp restaurant bar and dancehall complex. A Billy Butlin's architectural masterpiece. No doubt designed to cater for the sprawling adjacent holiday caravan site.

We alighted at the obvious site of the ferry, a slipway with a large old rusting winch with the remains of a cable haphazardly coiled nearby. We hauled the Lizard halfway up the slipway and Kevin went to book in while I began to unload our luggage.

I had finished unloading and was sitting on one of our barrels when Kev returned looking somewhat concerned. He said that the building seemed locked and he had hammered on the doors but to no avail. He had also explored around the back to the kitchen area but the whole place seemed deserted. I suggested that we phoned their number using the mobile, perhaps they were asleep and hadn't heard his knocking. We tried, but no answer.

Wandering into the garden it was obvious that people had been around earlier due to the numerous glasses on the tables waiting to be cleared. It seemed somewhat reminiscent of the Marie Celeste.

Suddenly we heard a vehicle drive into the car park at the front of the building. We walked around to see the post van and the postman shoving something through the letterbox. Before we could say anything, he shouted, "They open at about five mate." He then got back into his van and roared off.

Luckily it was a fine afternoon, so we sat in the garden and made up a few more verses of 'Messing About with the Lizard'. It had just passed five when we heard another car arrive. It was the landlord and his wife returning from a shopping spree at the local cash and carry. All at once four more cars pulled up containing the staff who were reporting in for the evening shift.

After introducing ourselves we were shown to our room. Much less cramped than our quarters of the previous night with a bed at either end of the room. The landlady warned us not to leave our canoe where is could be easily seen as they were hosting an 18th birthday party that evening in the function room and she was not sure what type of party it would turn out to be, 'if we knew what she meant!!' We carried the canoe around to the kitchen area and hid her behind three very large waste bins, chaining and padlocking her to one of them.

After a shower and a rest, we sauntered down to the bar at about 7pm. It was quite a pleasant room with large windows facing the lawn overlooking the river, the long bar running the full length. We seemed to have the place to ourselves apart from a young family of four who were sitting very quietly in one corner. Mum and dad, a little girl of about six and a boy of about nine were sitting almost motionless. The children were sipping their drinks through a straw, their parents were unenthusiastically nursing two halves of lager apiece. All four seemed unaware of the others existence. Kev decided they needed stirring up, so we took our beers over to join them.

Twenty minutes later mum was on a dry martini and dad had changed from his half of lager to scotch. The children could not stop telling us all about the things they had seen and everything else they had been up to. The family had hired a small cruiser for the week and had decided to moor by the Ferryman for the night.

Several martinis and scotches later mum decided that as they had not yet eaten, they had better return to the boat for dinner. She very kindly invited us to join them but we graciously declined having seen the size of the boat through the window. No wonder the children were used to sitting still!

As they got up to leave dad knocked over two glasses which was met with squeals of delight from the children and a very loud giggle from mum. As all four spilled out of the door and crossed the lawn laughing and chatting, we felt that perhaps we had helped to add a little to their holiday, or was it the scotch and dry martini?

We now had the bar to ourselves apart from the barman who was uninterestingly flicking through the daily paper. The evening ahead didn't seem very promising.

We adjourned to the restaurant for a meal but as soon as we entered the equally deserted room we were pounced upon by the waiter. He was like a spider seizing its prey as soon as it had been trapped in its web. He must have seen us coming as he already had two menus in his hand as he led us to a table smack in the middle of the room. He was a young friendly chap, good at his job and very polite. He informed us we were the only guests staying that night, which surprised me as there was an eighteenth birthday party on the premises. I assumed from that information that it must be a very local affair. He assured us that the place was very busy at weekends and apologised for it being so quiet. Did we look like a couple of ravers? After asking at what time we required breakfast he seemed surprised when we answered 8 am.

He need not have worried about it being too quiet because as we opened the door to go back to the bar, after a very pleasant meal helped along with a bottle of red, we were hit by a wall of sound. The bar was heaving, could it be the Ferryman's Happy Hour? It was packed with people spanning the ages of about four to ninety-four. The majority however were around eighteen to twenty. It then dawned on us that it was the gathering for the party. We soon got chatting to a couple of lads and ascertained that it was being held in honour of Jenny. Suddenly the bar began to empty as the throng flowed out to the adjoining function room. Word must have got round that the food and disco were ready.

The two extra barmen, who had been helping the original one, also left, presumably to man the bar in the function room. Our barman resumed reading his newspaper. It was as if the last few minutes had all been in our imagination.

We stood at the bar feeling somewhat abandoned. "What shall we do now?" asked Kev.

"How about," I suggested, "that we go and wish Jenny a happy birthday?"

We enjoyed a very entertaining evening at the party which was quite a lively but good-natured affair. Nobody asked who we were so we just joined in. We spent a good deal of time sitting at a table with Jenny's grandmother and her two aunts. After a few drinks they unabashedly started to relate some tales of when they were eighteen. Obviously never shy or retiring wallflowers in their youth!

It must have been about 1am when we left. We never did get to meet Jenny. I hope she did have a very happy birthday; I know for fact that her two aunts and her grandmother certainly enjoyed themselves.

Back in our room we sat mulling through another successful day over one last whiskey which we had taken up with us. We had managed to visit another four pubs bringing the total to eight, so all was going to plan. Apart from a few minor mishaps, mainly to Kevin, we had come through unscathed. Friday the 13th had definitely been kinder to me than to him. And, the canoe now had a name, 'The Lizard'. We drank a toast to her, and to Jenny, and then settled down and rapidly succumbed to a pleasant, somewhat alcoholic induced sleep, but not before the important task of hanging our trainers out of the window.

CHAPTER 8

Spires, Punts and Pudding

Bablock Hythe to Oxford - 11 miles

I was awakened at 7.30 by the sound of the small travel alarm clock which we had brought with us. It obviously wasn't loud enough to penetrate Kev's subconscious as he remained soundly asleep at his end of the room impersonating the sound of an ailing motor mower.

It was a fine bright day and as I drew back the curtains the river at the end of the lawn was revealed looking clean and polished as it caught the morning sunlight. Although I had a slightly 'muzzy' head I felt impatient to be on the move again, the Lizard needed to be released from her chains and returned to her natural environment as soon as possible.

We went down to breakfast and on entering the dining room were again shown to the same central table, but this time by the landlord. I enquired as to the whereabouts of last night's amiable waiter. "Oh, I sacked him last night," he replied in a very nonchalant way. He didn't seem inclined to give us the reason why he had been dismissed, although we did recall seeing our waiter at the party in what one could describe as being in a very merry mood. But why not, so were most of the other guests? It did occur to us that he may not have been invited, he may have gate-crashed the party! We did not pursue the matter further.

The landlord seemed very interested in our trip and wanted to know all about it. He said it was the type of thing he would enjoy doing but he had too many commitments to even get away for a weekend. He sat morosely down at an adjacent table looking exceedingly miserable, as if a ton weight had suddenly dropped on his shoulders. He just sat there staring out of the window in silence.

Kevin and I looked at each other not knowing what to say next. A full minute passed without a word from any of us until Kevin broke the silence and asked him if he had any kippers. This question seemed to pull him back from wherever his thoughts had taken him. He apologized for his absence and asked me what I would like for my breakfast. I ordered the full English. "So," he recapitulated, "that's one full English and a pair of kippers."

"No," Kev replied, "two full English please,"

"I thought you'd asked for kippers," he snapped back in a somewhat irritated way.

"I only asked if you had any," Kev explained meekly.

We thought we had upset him as he strode back to the kitchen mumbling something about schoolteachers with their long holidays. But when he returned, not only did he have our breakfast but also a ten-pound note for the charity fund.

On our way out we stopped at reception with our barrels and the rest of our luggage to settle up for the night's stay. The landlady was there to make up the bill. She was also very interested to hear all about the trip and was as generous as her husband giving us another ten-pound note from the till. She was just handing it over as the landlord appeared, he paused, giving her a rather quizzical look before wishing us luck, and asking if we had room for a stowaway?

As we were unchaining the canoe, which had spent a safe and secure night away from the party revellers, behind the dustbins, we could hear a heated discussion coming through the open kitchen window. It seemed to be regarding the breakdown of communications which lead to being over generous to guests. I do not think for a moment he begrudged giving the money to a good cause, he was just making a point.

It was just after nine when we set off to cover the eleven miles to Oxford. We noticed that the boat belonging to the young family we had befriended before the party, and perhaps had led a little astray, still had its curtains firmly closed, so we kept as quiet as possible. Best not to disturb.

The sun was warm on our backs, I felt fitter than I had for years and canoeing held no fears for us now. A motor launch sped past and as we rode the waves; we simultaneously broke into the now familiar Hawaii Five O tune. Confidence and the feel-good factor were at their height.

About a mile down-stream, after passing the caravan site, the eastern side of the river is dominated by the great grassy bank which surrounds the vast Farmoor Reservoir which supplies Swindon, 25 miles to the South West. A large expanse of water, utilised for fishing, sailing and windsurfing and very popular with bird watchers and walkers.

As the river passes the orderly straight lines of the reservoir it again decides to make extravagant bends to its course. It seemed as if it were purposely rebelling against the man-made scar on the natural landscape and was making its point by contrast.

The bends and the straight, grassy bank continued for about a further mile until we came to the isolated Pink Hill Lock. We had the lock to ourselves again and as was becoming the norm the lock keeper greeted us like old friends; knowing who we were and our plans long before we arrived. The Thames grapevine was still obviously working well. He said he had expected us the day before and chatted on until in the end we had to make our excuses and leave.

We left the neat banking of the reservoir behind and again both sides of the river became wild and unkept. The river straightened out a little having made its point. We had been on the move now for well over an hour and the sun was beginning to make itself felt. We both felt in need of refreshment. Having consulted the Thames Ordinance Survey Guide we estimated that it would be at least a couple of hours before reaching Godstow and perhaps our first watering hole of the day. Desperate measures were called for. We stopped for ten minutes at the Oxford Cruisers boatyard for a can of coke and an ice cream each.

We became aware that the river traffic was becoming greater in volume than we had previously experienced. Boats of various sizes were becoming more numerous. It was by no means overcrowded but up till now it had seemed we had had the river almost to ourselves, apart from the few craft we had chanced upon. It then dawned on us that it was Saturday and the weekenders were out. Also, the hired cruisers were on their way back to their boat yards, like starlings returning to roost. There are several hire-boat yards along this stretch into Oxford and Saturday morning is change over time for the next crew of holiday makers.

We would have to get over our unfair feeling of resentment and get used to sharing the Thames with other craft, as below Oxford the villages and towns begin to close in on the river and its casual use would increase. The probable reason that the early settlements tended to shun the reaches above Oxford may have been due to the fact that the vast flat meadows of the upper reaches flooded extensively during the winter months. Therefore, the early settlements needed to be established well back from the river's course on higher ground. Below Oxford the countryside becomes less flat and consequently less susceptible to flooding.

As the river passes the hamlet of Swinford it begins to change direction as its course swings round in a huge ninety-degree loop to Oxford. As it flows out of Oxford it will flow almost due south for several miles.

The exquisite Swinford Bridge, built in 1777 by the Earl of Abington to replace the original ferry, is one of the two remaining toll bridges still charging vehicles to cross the river. The other at Whitchurch, was built near the end of the last century to establish a link with Pangbourne.

The Swinford bridge was commissioned by George III after he had experienced a particularly bad ferry crossing. Under the terms of the original Act of Parliament the toll charges were; wheeled vehicles paid one penny per wheel, one penny for cattle, calves, swine, sheep and horses. Half a penny for foot passengers and a farthing for lambs. When we passed beneath, it cost five pence to drive your car over the bridge, emergency vehicles and post vans crossed without charge.

The original Act also stated that no taxes were payable in connection with the bridge or to its toll income, which, as far as I know, is still the case today. A few years ago, it was estimated that between thirty-five thousand and forty thousand wheels crossed the bridge weekly. The Earl of Abingdon's family still owned the bridge until the late 1960's when it was sold privately. In 1980 it was again sold for offers in the region of £275,000.

As the name suggests, long before the ferry existed at Swinford, there was a ford. Many of the old villages and town names along the Thames are of Anglo-Saxon origin. Swinford means a ford for swine, Shifford a ford for sheep, Moulsford a ford for mules, Oxford a ford for oxen. I can imagine way back in time, a 'jobsworth' ferryman saying, "Sorry mate, oxen only, your swine can only cross up river at Swinford."

Eynsham lock, just around the bend from Swinford was full of boats when we arrived with several others, unable to fit in, being ordered by the lock-keeper to queue outside to await their turn. However, when he saw us, he beckoned us forward to jump the queue and found us the only space available, between two fairly substantial cruisers. We quickly noted the whereabouts of any drain holes and then sat tight feeling rather small and vulnerable. But we needn't have worried because as always, the keeper of the lock kept everything and everyone under control and when it was time to do so, we all left his care in a calm and orderly manner.

By now the sun was getting higher in the sky and it was getting hot, but for the next half a mile or so we were shaded by trees as the river skirted around Wytham Great Wood which falls steeply down Wytham Hill to the water's edge. The wood covers six hundred acres and is owned by Oxford University. It is deemed a site of scientific interest much used by the university's botanists and ornithologists. A treasure chest of flora and fauna. A little further downstream on the opposite side, the river Evenlode, flowing down from The Cotswolds, joins the Thames.

The craving for a thirst-quenching beer was beginning to be an obsession and mirages of pubs were starting to appear. We still had over two and a half miles to go before reaching Godstow and two more locks to get through.

We tried 'a hundred stroke ramming speed session' but gave up after forty strokes, or rather Kevin did. As I was in the front, I didn't notice that he had stopped paddling at forty, but had continued counting whilst I persisted for another twenty or so strokes on my own, before realising by the attempted suppressed laughter from behind.

Kings lock, which happens to mark the most northerly point of the Thames, was pretty busy, packed with rather large cruisers. We passed the time exchanging pleasantries with the crews who seemed to tower above us from all directions. This lock would be the last manually operated lock we would encounter, from now on they would be electrically operated.

Just before the lock, on our left, we had passed the entrance to Duke's cut which joins the Oxford canal to the Thames. This short link between the canal and the river was built by the Fourth Duke of Marlborough and was opened in 1789. He was a main shareholder in the Oxford Canal which passed through part of his Blenheim estate. The cut enabled him to supply the whole of the Thames Valley with Warwickshire coal brought down the canal and thus passing down the Thames via the cut. A wise investment as this resulted in a greatly increased source of income for him from the canal. This is an important junction in our waterways for it enables the Thames to be linked to almost every navigable waterway in the Midlands and the North of England.

It was found necessary to build a lock in the cut as the level in the canal was usually about thirty centimetres above that of the Thames. But, in times of flood the river could be sixty centimetres above the canal. Therefore unusually, the lock gates had to be designed to open in either direction.

After leaving Kings Lock we became gradually aware of a background noise which at first was so faint that it was hardly noticeable, but as we progressed downstream the volume gradually increased and grew to dominate all other sounds. It was a mixture of a roar and hiss. As a modern concrete bridge came into view it became clear as to what was the source of the noise. Traffic!

The structure, called the Thames Bridge, carries the busy A34 trunk road over the river to bypass Oxford. What a sudden and unwelcome contrast to the peace and tranquillity we had been getting used to. The 20th century was suddenly back in our laps almost before we knew it, although of course it had never ever really been very far away. Thankfully it began to recede almost as quickly, as the river and road parted company.

We now had a spectacular horizontal view of Oxford, still three miles away. The skyline of the city is dominated by a forest of church spires, and I now understand why the poet Matthew Arnold christened Oxford, 'the city of dreaming spires'.

The origin of Oxford goes back to Saxon times when a settlement, named Oxnaforda, grew-up around an ox-drovers ford crossing the Thames. When William the Conqueror took the Crown of England in 1066, Oxford was the sixth largest Saxon town in England and so the Normans subsequently built a substantial castle to control the town and the river. But the city's real rise to prominence began in 1167. Henry II was upset with the French because they took the side of Thomas Becket, the exiled Archbishop of Canterbury, and gave him shelter in France. Henry stamped his foot and ordered all English scholars studying on the continent to return home at once. I know not why, but many of the students decided to settle in Oxford and endeavoured to recreate the life they had known in Paris and other continental seats of learning.

To begin with the townsfolk resented the students who were boisterous and drunk too much. (Being a traditionalist, it's reassuring to know that the modern generation of students still respect some of the old traditions!) It all came to a head in 1209 when a number of students were hung by the townspeople for an alleged murder. Some fled back to Paris while another group found refuge in a small town in East Anglia, Cambridge. In 1214 the good folk of Oxford and the few remaining students reached an agreement which was ratified by an ambassador of the Pope. This marked the formal founding of the University, the first in England. Cambridge University was soon to follow.

From then on, the University of Oxford steadily began to develop, rich men realised that the best way to encourage the students was to found colleges where the students could live and work. Balliol and Merton were founded in the 13th century and others soon followed. By Tudor times most students were members of a college, each college had its own library, gardens, hall, chapel and studies.

Christ Church college, founded by Cardinal Wolsey, the one-time chief minister of Henry the VIII, was commandeered as the headquarters for The Royalists during the 1642 civil war.

Oxford is not only noted for its university. James Sadler became the first English aviator when he drifted out over the city in a hot air balloon in 1784 after making his ascent from Christ Church Meadow. Rising to about 3600 feet he landed safely about six miles away. Sarah Cooper, in 1874, produced Frank Coopers Oxford marmalade and in the 1890's William Morris was repairing bicycles in his Oxford home. By 1913 he was making his highly successful Morris Oxford cars. In 1941 penicillin was first administered to a patient in Oxford and in 1954 Dr Roger Bannister was the first athlete to run a sub-four-minute mile. Running around the university's athletic track on a grey damp evening, competing against Oxford University, he won the race with a time of 3 minutes 59.4 seconds. He retired from athletics later that year to concentrate on his medical career.

From such lowly beginnings as a muddy crossing point across the Thames for oxen, Oxford has grown to become one of Britain's chief cultural heritages and concentrations of fine architecture.

About two hundred or so metres from the excessively noisy, concrete Thames bridge, we passed beneath one of the two brick arches of Godstow Bridge which marks the beginning of the lock cut, two bridge constructions of great contrast. The old stone Godstow Bridge is actually in two parts. The more recent part, under which we passed, was built in 1792 to straddle the then new lock cut. The old part, built in the 15th century, crosses the original course of the river leading to the weir and is a grade 2 listed building.

This seemed to be a particularly atmospheric stretch of the river. In the midday sun on a warm summer's day, a scene worthy to adorn any calendar or chocolate box. But I suspect, on a cold dark November evening a complete opposite feeling would be present.

When we emerged from under the bridge the stark ruins of the Benedictine Nunnery of Godstow dominated the scene before us. Built in 1133, or thereabouts, by Lady Edith Launceline of Winchester, after she was instructed in a vision to construct a holy place, 'where the light of heaven touches the ground'. Godstow means God's place. This was well over a hundred years before the first of the Oxford colleges was built. It must have been looked upon as a place of great importance as King Stephen was present at its consecration and it became a place of pilgrimage.

Godstow Nunnery is predominantly remembered through the legend of The Fair Rosamond, a story of both fact and fiction. The facts are that a fair maiden, by the name of Rosamund de Clifford, was receiving her education at the nunnery when Henry II was smitten by her beauty. He persuaded her to become his mistress and took her to live in his palace at Woodstock which was sited in what is now the grounds of Blenheim Palace. Eventually Queen Eleanor found out about this arrangement and not surprisingly was a little aggrieved.

The story goes on to say that the jealous Queen poisoned the Fair Rosamund, her body was then taken back to the nunnery and buried before the high altar in a tomb erected and lavishly ornamented at the expense of the King. The poisoning by the Queen is undoubtedly the fictional part of the story. Rosamund died in 1176 but the Queen had been imprisoned since 1173 for conspiracy against Henry, where she remained until his death in 1189.

When the affair was discovered, Rosamund ended the relationship and rejoined the Nunnery at Godstow where she remained until her death. She was actually given the luxury of the lavish tomb by Henry. However, in 1191, Hugh Bishop of Lincoln whilst visiting Godstow was appalled by the example set to the nuns by the 'illicit and adulterous intercourse' and ordered the body to be removed and the tomb demolished. The sisters secretly collected Rosamund's bones and placed them in a lavender perfumed leather pouch, enclosing it in lead. They then reburied her in the church beneath a stone slab.

During the Dissolution of the Monasteries in 1536, Henry VIII gave Godstow Nunnery to his physician, William Butts.

During the civil war the old nunnery was used as a Royalists barracks, but it was partly destroyed by a disastrous fire and was then dismantled later by the victorious Parliamentary forces. All that remains today are the forlorn looking outer walls and the ruined ivy clad chapter house. On the opposite bank however, a building, once the hospice of the nunnery, still survives giving sustenance to weary travellers.

A hospice in the Middle Ages offered shelter and rest to pilgrims and travellers as well as tending to any illnesses or injuries they may have had. From the word hospice the words hospitality and hospital were derived. The earliest scholars who rode to 'Oxenford' may well have rested in Godstow's hospice when monasteries and abbeys offered the hospitality that inns and pubs provide today - and now two very thirsty and weary travellers in a red canoe were impatient for a visit. Now called The Trout, it's an authentic picture book inn which over many years has been enlarged using the tumbled stone of the old nunnery. It was the favourite haunt of undergraduates in the days when they were forbidden to frequent bars and taverns. The enforcers of the Academic Law, the Proctors, would always find student lawbreakers when they raided The Trout.

To get to The Trout we needed to paddle down the lock cut past the ruins, and on through the lock then turn back on ourselves into the weir stream to paddle the length of the cut again. The lock was busy but as before we were waved through to the front of the queue. When we turned left into the weir stream, we found progress a little harder than we were used to as we were now paddling against the flow towards the weir. Lunch and beer were going to taste all the better for our labours.

On the way up the weir stream we passed two fishermen sitting mid-stream in a punt obviously spinning, using large artificial lures, for predatory pike. As we passed them and before I could stop him Kev asked his stock question. "Caught any roach yet?"

"Not yet mate," came the sarcastic reply, "but they're bloody huge around here."

It was well worth the extra effort. The Trout is a picturesque stone building with a shady terrace overlooking the weir pool. The pool is full of large chub and carp swimming near the surface, grown fat on the food thrown to them from the terrace by the customers. The sound of the water tumbling over the weir is ever present, punctuated every so often by the haunting call of peacocks roaming the garden.

The Fair Rosamund is said to haunt The Trout appearing as a white lady. The apparition is identified as being Rosamund because as mentioned before, the nuns had wrapped her bones in a lavender scented pouch, when the phantom appears it's always reported to being accompanied by the fragrance of lavender.

It was 12.25 when we arrived. We took a leisurely hour enjoying our lunch of beer and 'door stop' beef and horseradish sandwiches in the idyllic surroundings. After the mandatory photograph with drinks in hand, we set off back down the weir stream feeling refreshed and contented.

We passed the two fishermen in the punt who informed us, without any prompting, that they still hadn't managed to land any monster roach. I was just beginning to explain to Kevin the art of pike fishing, explaining to him that as pike grew to be our largest native freshwater fish the methods used were somewhat different to catching roach, when we fortuitously came across a recently deceased pike of about 10 pounds floating belly up.

With their unmistakable torpedo shape, olive-green colour and large powerful jaws displaying a full set of needle-sharp teeth, the pike is

Pike

an impressive looking fish. Built for speed with a powerful seizing lunge, it's a deadly hunter, attacking fish almost its own size. Large pike, and there is no doubt that in British waters they have been known to weigh in excess of fifty pounds, extend their diet beyond fish. Ducklings are readily taken and occasionally fully grown mallard ducks have been their victims. Other swimming water birds have been found in their stomachs as have water voles and brown rats.

A pike relies on stealth to catch its prey. Lying up in vegetation, where its dappled colouring keeps it well camouflaged, it waits for fish to pass close by, then, propelled by its large tail, it makes a lighting dash at its victim. Once grasped in its jaws there is little chance of the victim escaping as all of the pike's teeth point backwards. A captured pike needs to be handled with respect when being unhooked. Many an angler has suffered from bites from this voracious predator. Having on many occasions fished for pike, the largest I have managed to land was of about fifteen pounds, I have to say that in my opinion they are one of the most exciting freshwater fish to catch.

The French eat pike as a delicacy so I decided to take a healthy looking ten pound specimen home once to give it a try. Having dispatched it with a sharp blow between the eyes, with what is known in fishing terms as a priest, (a small club), I drove home with it wrapped in a bin liner. Once home I unwrapped it and laid it on the draining board ready for preparation. By now it had been out of the water for a good three quarters of an hour. As I reached forward to turn it over, it suddenly twisted around trying to take a bite out of my hand. After peeling myself down from the ceiling I sat down for a few minutes to allow my pulse rate to return to normal. I returned once again to the vicinity of the draining board with greater caution. The pike watched my approach daring me to come within striking distance again. I'm sure I saw its eyes narrow and its mouth open slightly as it prepared to extract retribution on the mugger and kidnapper who had so unmercifully extracted it from its home. I stayed well out of reach and apologised to this brave specimen of a freshwater predator.

I began to feel rather ashamed of the way I had treated the noble creature and rather wished that I had released it back into the river. I decided there was only one course of action I could now take!

It tasted a little on the 'muddy' side but cooked in white wine and onions and wrapped in foil to steam, it was nevertheless quite a palatable dish. The flesh when cooked is not unlike the texture of chicken breast but tastes rather like a very meaty trout. Its only drawback is that it's packed with large 'y' shaped bones which I'm sure if swallowed would cause more than a little discomfort. Even on a dinner plate a pike still demands to be handled with respect.

This stretch of the Thames between Godstow and Oxford was often frequented by The Reverend Charles, Lutwidge Dodson, alias Lewis Carroll, who was a maths tutor at Christchurch College. In 1862 he regularly rowed up from Oxford with the three young daughters of Dr Liddel, the Dean of Christchurch, and while picnicking on the bank near Godstow began to make up the story of Alice in Wonderland to entertain them. The ten-year-old Alice persuaded him to write the story down for her. In 1865 the book was published. It's a story I never really got to grips with and often wondered whether any 'extra' ingredients had been added to the sandwiches and cakes? The Beatles song, Lucy in the Sky with Diamonds, always puts me in mind of Alice in Wonderland!

Almost as soon as we rejoined the main stream we began to pass on our left the huge expanse of Port Meadow. It's sandwiched between the Thames and the Oxford Canal, covering four hundred and forty acres and stretching for two miles from Godstow down to Oxford. It's a vast flat green area of ancient common land, dating well back to Saxon times. The word 'port', meaning a trading place, is a clear indication of its Saxon use. The meadow may well have been given to the people of Oxford by King Alfred as a thank you for their help in his fight against the Danes. Its historic interest goes even further back than Alfred as it contains burial mounds dating back to 1500BC. During the English Civil War, the Royalist army was encamped for a time on the meadow and in 1940 the men of the Oxon and Bucks Light Infantry rested here after their evacuation from Dunkirk. There is a story of an overseas visitor to Oxford asking to see the oldest part of the city. He was directed to the green space of Port Meadow.

Port Meadow is now protected forever by public rights of access and extensive common rights to graze cattle, horses and geese. The ground has never been ploughed and rare plants flourish amongst the grass. It's now a site of Special Scientific Interest. Over the years the city fathers have tried several times to snatch the land to build on but, on each occasion, they have been repulsed by the time hallowed status of the commoners' rights of grazing.

In the winter the Meadow's southern end often floods becoming a giant mirror for Oxford's 'dreaming spires'. On the occasions when it's frozen over it is utilised as a huge outdoor skating rink.

About fifteen minutes after leaving The Trout we came upon another pub named after a fish, The Perch, at Binsey. Kev said he was looking forward to finding one named The Roach; alas we never did. We would now come across pubs and inns more often and our progress would be frequently interrupted. A nuisance we were just going to have to put up with!!

Until early in the last century there was a ford at Binsey which connected the village to Port Meadow on the opposite bank. It's thought that this may well have been the site of the original ox-ford. It's an unspoilt village with the church of St Frideswide and St Margaret dating back to AD 750. Nicholas Breakspear, the first recorded incumbent of the church, was the first Englishman to become Pope,(Adrian 1V) in 1159.

It was here, in the eighth century, that St Frideswide built her chapel and the Holywell of St Margaret which was reputed to cure 'the lame, the epileptic and otherwise afflicted'. St Frideswide's blindness is also said to have been cured at the well. It soon became a famous place of pilgrimage and people flocked to Binsey seeking the cure. Henry VIII and Catherine of Aragon are said to have made a pilgrimage to the well. By all accounts, by this time he was afflicted with all sorts of ailments and whether or not the waters of the Holywell did him any good was not recorded. Lewis Carroll's inspiration for the treacle well in Alice's Adventures in Wonderland is reputed to have been St Margaret's Well.

We drew into the jetty belonging to The Perch and were just about to walk the fifty or so yards up the path to the pub for our drinks and the photograph when a female voice calling Kevin's name stopped us in our tracks. Looking up the towpath in the direction from which the call came, we saw a robust looking lady heading our way in a rather a precarious manner, riding the most dilapidated 'sit up and beg' style of bicycle I have ever seen.

She approached weaving back and forth from one side of the path to another in a style which suggested she was cycling up a very steep incline. As she got nearer, we could hear the machine squeaking and squealing like a distressed piglet. It wasn't possible to tell the original colour of the bike as it was now a subtle shade of rust from its handlebars to every spoke. The only part of the contraption which looked remotely worth keeping was the basket strapped between handlebars, although even this was hanging at a lobsided angle.

Twice I had to avert my eyes from which I thought was going to be a disaster, when it looked as if the poor distressed velocipede was going to tip its tormenter into the river. But, on both occasions, she gained control and urged it on towards us. A young couple walking arm in arm only just averted being mown down by flattening themselves into the hedge as she wobbled by.

Her momentum had slightly increased as we stepped to either side of the path to allow her to pass between us, with both brakes full on and one leg outstretched, endeavouring to act as an extra brake. She eventually stopped a good twenty metres further on down the path. She half alighted and half fell from her tormented steed and then after a laboured three-point turn, pushed the complaining bicycle back to us.

The lady in question was Anne, a friend and colleague of Kev's who knowing of our itinerary had ventured out along the towpath from Oxford, on this bright sunny Saturday afternoon, with the hope of meeting us. She informed us that she often cycled along the towpath for a bit of exercise. I was tempted to suggest that she ought to consider wearing a buoyancy aid and a crash helmet on her outings, but I refrained because as I had only just met her, I wasn't yet sure of her sense of humour. In retrospect I needn't have worried because it soon became apparent that she had a very humorous side to her nature. During the week she lived and worked in Coventry as a Senior Adviser for the Education Authority but at the weekends she retreated to her Victorian terraced house in Oxford.

We invited Anne to join us for a drink at the Perch which she readily accepted. She lent her bicycle up against the fence and produced from the basket a large padlock and chain with which she used elaborately to secure the bike to the railings. She remarked that one couldn't be too careful as some people would pinch anything these days!

The Perch lies about fifty yards back from the river at the end of a path crossing its sizeable lawn. The present building is a large, attractive, thatched 17th century pub but there has been a hostelry on this site for over eight hundred years. The ghost of a heartbroken sailor is said to appear in the low-ceilinged bar. Nobody seems to know who he is or why his heart was broken, but it's thought that he drowned himself in the Thames a short distance away in an area known as Black Jack's Hole, an extremely deep part of the river, his ghost then returned to The Perch to forever drown its sorrows. There is an old myth, which used to be told to children to dissuade them from bathing at this dangerous spot, about an evil goblin living in Black Jacks Hole who would catch them and keep them in his underwater cave.

We sat for about an hour beneath a large weeping willow tree in the garden enjoying Anne's company and a couple of pints of Guinness each, her favourite tipple since she had become a regular visitor to Ireland. She kindly invited us back to her house for dinner that evening and arranged to pick us up in her car from The Head of the River, our overnight stopover, at about 6:30. As we watched her unsteadily riding off back towards Oxford on her bike, I couldn't help wondering what type of car she would be turning up in and in what condition it would be?

We soon passed under the iron, rainbow shaped Medley Footbridge which allows people access across to Fiddler's Island. The navigation channel below Binsey becomes comparatively narrow and tree lined. It was cut by the monks of Osney Abbey in around 1227 to direct the flow of the river to drive their mill.

At the end of the half mile cut we came to a 'crossroads'. The unnavigable Bulstake Stream ran off to our right whilst to our left a short, narrow cut leads to the Oxford Canal beneath a low railway bridge.

Slowly, urbanisation began to creep in around us providing a surprisingly welcome contrast to the seeming endless tranquil water meadows we had been travelling through. Victorian terraced houses backed on to the towpath and several well-maintained allotments with their assorted sheds shared the scene. The towpath was being well used by cyclists, joggers and walkers who had to manoeuvre around the numerous sedentary fishermen and women who had staked their claims along the bank.

We soon came to the notoriously low Osney Bridge which is looked upon as the beginning of Oxford if you're travelling downstream. Built in 1888 after the previous eighteenth century structure collapsed, it has a headroom of only seven foot, six inches, the lowest on the river. It's an obstacle which prevents the large 'gin palace' type cruisers from penetrating upstream. From now on we would be sharing the locks with some much larger craft than we had become used to.

Nothing remains of the great Augustinian Abbey of Osney, once looked upon as one of the most magnificent monastic houses in Europe, the abbey church was Oxford's first cathedral. After it was destroyed during The Dissolution of the Monasteries, Osney's wealth and stones were taken by Cardinal Wolsey to build Christchurch in Oxford, which then became the city's cathedral.

The bells of the monastery were taken and hung at Christchurch including, 'Great Tom', which has been run every night since 1682 at 9pm as the curfew bell. It informs all students that they should be 'within bounds', a rule that I expect has seldom been kept by past or present students.

Osney Abbey was founded in 1129 by Robert d' Oilli who was procured to do so by his wife Edith, a favourite of Henry I. Legend tells that as she was walking one day along the riverbank close to the castle, she came across a tree in which were several magpies chattering ceaselessly at her. Edith asked a passing monk the meaning of this, to which he replied, 'they are not magpies at all, they are souls in purgatory imploring you to do some good deed'.

Edith decided that her good deed would be to persuade her husband into coughing up the readies to build a magnificent abbey because a 'parliament' of magpies in a tree had told her to. It makes one wonder if she and the monk had enjoyed a similar picnic to Lewis Carroll?

Just before Osney lock we came upon the Watermans Arms. By now it was 3pm so we decided to just have a quick 'short' each for the photograph. It's a fine riverside local built in the 1850s, once used by the railway workers and the bargees making their way to and from the nearby canal.

The lock was built by prisoners from Oxford Castle in 1790. The castle dates from 1071 and for most of its existence was partly used, right up until 1996, as a prison. Adjacent to the lock is a stone barn, the only surviving building from the Abbey.

We negotiated the lock without incident, sharing it with several other craft, and proceeded on downstream towards Osney railway bridge. Before the bridge is a touching memorial to an Edgar Wilson who, according to the inscription on a large stone obelisk, lost his life on the 15th of June 1889 at the age of twenty-one, whilst saving the lives of two little boys who have fallen into the river.

This section of urban waterway, winding its way through the Victorian backstreets of the city, is not particularly picturesque but it provides plenty of interest. Terraced houses, once the homes of the poorer folk, are now much sought-after dwellings, made all the more desirable because of their close proximity to the Thames, or should I say The Isis, as this is the name the river is known as while it flows through Oxford.

Where the Thames becomes the Isis and vice versa has never really been clearly defined. The origin of its alias is uncertain, some historians suggest the name Isis is from the word Tamesis, the Latin name for the Thames. Julius Caesar named the river Tamesis, before the Romans it was called 'Tems'. In Anglo Saxon times it was spelt Tamyse . Only since about 1600 has it been called The Thames.

Rounding a bend, we discovered that we had almost reached Folly Bridge with our night's lodging, The Head of The River, alongside. But first, much to my consternation as I was in the front, we had to run the gauntlet of about fifty swans. They always gather around popular areas of the river where they're likely to be fed by tourists. They took little notice of us and we remained unmolested as we quickly paddled by trying to look as nonchalant as possible.

Just before reaching the bridge, we passed a floating jetty with numerous punts tied alongside. Punts were originally built as cargo vessels or used as platforms for fishing or shooting wildfowl. Punting is a traditional Oxford pastime and you can hire one and entertain the other tourists as you try to master the technique of propelling and controlling the punt using the long pole. Or you can hire a 'chauffeur driven' one for half an hour with a free glass of wine. The main centre of the activity is actually on the River Cherwell, one of the Thames major tributaries which flows in at Oxford. At peak times during the summer months, The Cherwell becomes jammed with students and tourists in punts. A number of backwaters of the Cherwell flow through Oxford and it's this reason, plus the rivers gravelly bed, which makes it an ideal place for pleasure boating, especially punting.

The present, elegant, four arched, stone Folly Bridge was built in 1827 to replace a previous structure dating from 1085 which was very narrow and had eighteen arches and a tower. In this tower, there lived for a time in the 13th century, a Roger Bacon once described as England's Leonardo da Vinci. Amongst other things he was an astronomer using the tower as his observatory. In the 18th century a man by the name of Welcome restored the then ruins of the tower which subsequently became known as Welcomes Folly, which is the origin of the present name of the bridge. The tower was demolished in 1779.

We passed beneath the low middle arch at around 3:45 and at once came upon The Head of the River situated on the left bank. The pub is a large three-story building originally built as a warehouse for grain in around the 1820's. In 1858 it became Salter Brothers boat yard, one of their cranes still survives amongst the many tables situated along its waterfrontage. It was converted into a pub in 1977. The tables were packed with customers, eating and drinking and enjoying the late afternoon sun, obviously one of the 'in' places to be.

As we paddled towards our stopover, dodging several out of control punts which were keeping the pub's customers amused, our daily problem was demanding attention. We needed to find a safe anchorage for 'the lizard' to spend the night.

A few metres past The Head of the River was another floating pier with yet more punts for hire. An idea landed on my shoulder, perhaps the owner of the said punts would allow us to chain the lizard amongst them for the night. Permission was kindly granted and we were assured that our canoe would be perfectly safe as the wooden plank used as the walkway from bank to the pier was removed in the evening, thus leaving the punts marooned well out of harm's way.

I left Kev unloading and went to report our arrival. The interior of The Head of the River was as crowded as the exterior but I eventually found the manager and booked in. The building has been very cleverly and tastefully transformed. The walls of the large ground floor bar are covered in old Thames photographs and the original beams and upright wooden supports have been kept in situ. A large imposing staircase leads up to the first-floor restaurant and above that are the guest rooms.

Our room was spacious and comfortable, overlooking the river, with a large bathroom equipped with an extremely deep, old fashioned styled bath. I lost the toss so I passed the time waiting for my turn in the bath sitting by the open window enjoying a beer. We had each taken a pint up to the room with us to help us unwind.

My attention was drawn to the antics, of I presumed a first-time punter, showing his girlfriend how it should be done. How he managed to remain dry I will never know. He performed balancing tricks any circus performer would be proud of, while all he was endeavouring to do was propel the punt in a straight line. At one point he was leaning out over the water at a precarious angle of about 45 degrees, clinging with all his worth to the pole which was at a similar angle. Through superhuman effort only possible when total fear has taken hold, he managed to close the gap by somehow pulling the punt back to the pole until he and the pole were back in a vertical position. I now feel slightly ashamed to say that I felt disappointed when he escaped his ducking, and so I expect did the many other onlookers from the pub's terrace and the bridge. A spontaneous round of applause followed but both he and his girlfriend were so engrossed in their 'relaxing' pastime, they didn't appear to notice. I think she may have been aware but did not dare look around, having not moved a muscle since I had been watching. She sat bolt upright in her seat staring straight ahead with both arms outstretched, hands gripping each side of the punt.

By the time it was my turn for the bath, a good 20 minutes later, they had managed to travel about 30 metres, but as it had been in a circle, they were back where I had first become aware of them, almost in mid-stream. Watching them brought back memories of our first outing at Longridge!

Kev took over and gave me a running commentary as I enjoyed the bath. The couple were eventually rescued by a rowing boat which took pity on them and towed them back to terra firma and safety.

We were lucky enough to find a vacant table out on the patio and were enjoying another pint when a man I vaguely recognised and his family approached us and introduced himself. It was David Moorcroft MBE, once world record holder of the 5000 meters and now the head of British Athletics. They had taken the time to seek us out to buy us a drink and wish us luck with the fund raising. Kevin used to work with his wife and she knew of our planned trip. They were on their way home from a holiday and knowing we were spending the night at The Head of the River, had made a detour to find us. We spent a very pleasant hour with David and his wife, his two young daughters and the dog, recounting our adventure so far. They were very patient and listen attentively to our miscellaneous ramblings.

Anne picked us up as promised and drove the few minutes from Folly Bridge to her delightful Victorian house where she had prepared the most delicious meal. The pub food we had been eating up till now was all very well but nothing compares to good home cooking after a hard day's paddling. I can highly recommend her homemade chocolate pudding with chocolate sauce topped with cream and brandy. Her love of Ireland was made evident as Guinness and Irish whiskey where much to the fore during the evening!

Incidentally, Anne's car was in immaculate condition and of a much later vintage than her bicycle.

We thought it would be prudent and wiser to relieve our very generous hostess of the task of driving so we persuaded her to let us walk back. The pub was still fairly busy when we returned at about 11pm, mostly by the young and trendy, so we naturally decided to join them for a 'night cap' before retiring, but we soon fell into chatting with a slightly older dishevelled looking character who was propping up the bar.

I suppose he must have been in his late thirties although his weather-beaten features made him appear rather older. He told us he was the owner of the first collection of punts for hire that we had passed just before Folly Bridge. During the punting season, April to September, he slept in an old punt he had adapted into a bed, in a small shed situated on his floating jetty, cooking over an old Primus stove. Just as his father and his father before him had done. We didn't enquire about his washing and toilet arrangements, but I suspect he used the facilities of the pub. He went on to say that most evenings were spent in The Head Of The River and he had almost become part of the furniture.

During the 'closed season' in the winter months, he moved back into his cottage in a small village several miles out of Oxford. When Kev asked why he put up with such a frugal, solitary existence during the summer months, he replied that as it was a seven day a week job and couldn't afford to pay anyone else to work for him and as he didn't drive, he failed to see any alternative. A look of horror came onto his face when I suggested that he could sell up and do something else. The cottage and business had been in the family for generations and he wasn't going to be the one to break the mould. I wondered what chance there was of him producing a son and heir to continue the business while he continued to abide in his present dwelling. Although thinking about it, his father and grandfather must have managed to persuade females to share their quarters with them at some time or other.

Eventually, after several more nightcaps than we had intended, we took our leave and unsteadily found the way back to our room. I don't recall actually getting into bed, but with our damp trainers safely dangling out of the window we must have very quickly settled down for the night. Another successful day completed.

Can you spot the two pairs of trainers dangling from the bedroom window?

CHAPTER 9

What Shall We Do with the Drunken Sailors

Oxford to Abingdon – 7.5 miles

As Sunday the 15th of August was scheduled to be our shortest day's paddling, a mere seven and a half miles and three locks, we were in no hurry to get up. Which was just as well because we were both suffering somewhat from the night before. We both blamed our condition, unfairly I have to add, on Anne's chocolate pudding and brandy sauce. Not, on the near full bottle of Famous Grouse whisky, or 'her indoors', as my dear late father fondly dubbed it, which we had finished off with the help of our shed dwelling friend.

However, as Kevin's blue, curry smelling barrel seemed even more pungent that morning, we were persuaded not to linger in our beds for too long. We agreed on a gentle stroll into Oxford to clear the head and settle the stomach before partaking of breakfast.

We decided to cross Folly Bridge for a view of the river and to check on the 'lizard'. From our vantage point halfway across we could see her still safely birthed where we had left her amongst the maroon punts. Looking back at the hotel we were amused to see two pairs of trainers dangling from an upstairs window swinging gently in the breeze.

The bridge is in two parts separated by a small island. Several houses via for space on the island, one, a red brick castellated structure with iron balconies has niches filled with statues. It was once a brothel and it's thought that the sculptures represent the women who worked there.

Sunday morning isn't complete without a newspaper, so we entered a somewhat crowded newsagents to purchase one. Not necessarily to read, it just seems to be a ritual one has to honour on a Sunday. How often do newspapers remain unread in hotel rooms after they've been ordered for the Sunday morning?

An hour's stroll around Oxford in the fresh air helped to restore our equilibrium and we returned to The Head of the River for a late breakfast. It was around 11am when we eventually went to reclaim the 'lizard', but it wasn't going to be as straightforward as we had supposed.

As we approached, it immediately became apparent that we had a problem. The wooden walkway which had joined the floating pier to the bank had, as promised, been removed the night before, it was now lying against an iron fence to which it was firmly chained and padlocked. Between us and our canoe was a five-meter expanse of river of unknown depth.

A nearby notice informed all interested parties that punts were for hire between the hours of 12:30pm and 6pm. We couldn't hang around for another hour and a half, so there was only one course of action open to us.

After a brief discussion and the toss of a coin, Kev began to wade out to the 'lizard'. The look on his face and several expletives made it clear to me and passers-by, that the water had instantly been transported from Antarctica. For the first few steps the water reached just below knee level, but as faltering progress was made it gradually crept higher and higher. As it reached middle thigh, I just couldn't resist lobbing in half a brick just behind our hero. More expletives! Just before the critical stage of 'crotch level', he disappointingly reached the canoe. After unlocking her, Kevin towed her back to the bank.

We were just about to set off when a female voice from the bridge called down to us to wait. Looking up we were surprised to see the mother and daughter of the family we had befriended at The Ferry at Bablock Hythe. They rapidly joined us at the water's edge and explained they had moored at Oxford for the day and were out shopping for provisions whilst father and son were fishing. Mum wished us luck and insisted on giving a generous contribution to the funds of our charity.

It was overcast but dry and warm as we paddled past Christ Church Meadow on our left bank. Just as Port Meadow, Christ Church Meadow is one of the oldest uncultivated meadows in Britain having never been built upon or touched by the machines of agriculture. It's held in trust by Christ Church College and during the summer it's thronged with tourists and sunbathers enjoying a slice of green countryside in the heart of the city. In 1965 a successful campaign was fought against the proposal to build a road through it. At the time it was described as, 'the bloodiest battle ever fought over an environmental issue'.

Christ Church Meadow is flanked on one side by the Thames/Isis, and on the other by the River Cherwell which flows into the Thames/Isis at this point. The Cherwell actually has two tributaries into the Thames because as it skirts around Christ Church Meadow it divides into two channels, one joins at the bottom right of the meadow and the other about a quarter of a mile further downstream.

The Thames now becomes broader and more imposing as it leaves Oxford. It's almost as if it has suddenly matured and grown up after the experience of passing through the University City. We had accompanied it through its infancy and childhood stage, through its teenage years, and now we were maintaining our presence as it passed into its early middle age.

Between the two tributaries of the Cherwell, we passed the numerous university boat clubs. Similar in design they're purposefully built for the serious all year-round sport of modern competitive rowing. Originally, each college used as its club headquarters its own unique, ornately decorated barge, permanently moored on the river, but these have sadly gradually been replaced. The Oxford squad, for the annual University Boat Race, rowed between Putney and

Mortlake is drawn from these clubs. Competitive rowing has long been a part of Oxford University life.

In May the traditional festival called Eights Week takes place. The races are rowed along the river in front of Christ Church Meadow between Iffley Lock and Folly Bridge, a distance of about a mile. Entry is limited to 420 oarsmen in crews of 8, that's 3780 competitors. If you're thinking my maths is incorrect, you're forgetting that each boat also has a cox! On the Saturday the place to be is on the banks of the river and the wearing of a boater and blazer is the order of the day and the drinking of Pimm's is compulsory.

Torpids is the other major university rowing event, held in February. Drinking hot chocolate and wearing a woolly hat and thermals is probably best for spectators at this event.

The City of Oxford Rowing Club run the 'bumping races' in September. This competition is not restricted to Oxford University clubs, any rowing club may enter. Participating crews are grouped into divisions racing four times in one day. A number of boats chase each other in single file with the object of 'bumping' (catch up or overtake) and by doing so exchange places in the starting order. A crew which is consistently successful will rise up the starting order until it reaches the top, earning the title of, 'The Head of the River'.

The Thames quickly becomes rural again as it leaves Oxford, urbanisation keeping well back leaving a green corridor for the river to flow through. In took us barely twenty minutes to paddle the mile to the picturesque Iffley Lock but before passing through we were duty bound to call at the nearby Isis pub.

The Isis began life as a farmhouse but became an ale house in 1842. Up until 1979 its beer supply was delivered by river as there was no direct road access. The interior is full of memorabilia of the university's boat clubs. We found it to be a very pleasant pub with a large garden and as we expected an easy day ahead of us were in no hurry to leave. It's obviously a very popular watering hole in the summer for Sunday lunchtime drinkers who were arriving by bike or had walked along the towpath from both directions.

A couple of pints each later and after making several new acquaintances we resumed our journey. It was now about 1pm and the pub garden was full to bursting. Iffley Lock, a mere two minutes away, was also obviously a very popular place to be on a fine Sunday afternoon as there was quite a large gathering of onlookers watching the comings and goings of the boats. The lock was almost full of various types and sizes of craft but as usual the lockkeeper called us forward. We partook in plenty of banter and chat with all in our vicinity and the total of the donations substantially increased.

Iffley Lock dates from about 1632 and was one of the first pound locks to be built on the Thames. Two more of the earliest pound locks are at Sandford and Abingdon. As mentioned before, up until then the only way for boats or barges to negotiate the many weirs that had been constructed along the Thames to control the flow and alleviate shallow areas was by way of a flash lock. Weirs were also built by the hundreds of mill owners along the river. The weir would hold back the flow to establish a head of water to drive the machinery for paper mills, fulling cloth or grinding corn. The control of the weir would normally be by the miller. When a flash lock was opened, which literally was just lifting one or two paddles in the weir to create a gap, a great amount of water would be lost downstream. Therefore, the miller was loath to remove the paddles and he might hold up the bargemen wanting to pass for a day or two until a number of them had assembled, so he could let them through for just one opening of the paddles. Tolls could also be collected which would in part compensate him for the loss of waterpower. One can imagine the ill feeling from both parties and the arguments and fights which must inevitably have occurred on many occasions.

Pound locks, which only use the volume of water contained in the lock itself and are so much less hazardous to negotiate, gradually replaced the flash locks during the 18th and 19th centuries. They were introduced to make the river more competitive with the then newly developing canal system and led to a huge increase in commercial traffic on the river.

Iffley Lock has a delightful setting overlooked by a fine Norman church where, in the 13th century, a recluse by the name of Annora once lived for nineteen years confined in a cell beside the church. Born in 1179, her father was William de Braose, a powerful Baron in the reigns of Richard I and King John. William quarrelled with King John and he was outlawed. His wife and eldest son were imprisoned in Windsor Castle and left to starve to death. Annora was incarcerated in Bristol Castle but was released in 1214 but continued to worry that she would meet the same painful fate of her mother and brother. In 1239 she decided to become a recluse and retired to the cell at Iffley. Not such a strange decision to take then as it would be now. She was still feeling very unsafe and to live in a cell by a church was to be in the safest of places. In the 13th century there were ninety-two women living this solitary life in England, they were known as anchoresses, men were known as anchorites, of which there were only twenty. Anchoresses and anchorites were under the protection of the bishop who had to satisfy himself that they intended to remain in their cells until they died.

Adjoining Annora's cell was another room where her maid would have lived, cooking for her, attending the fire and collecting water. Gifts of food and firewood would have been sent to her by the people of Iffley. The maid would visit the locals and bring back news of importance. Annora would have passed the time in contemplation, prayer, reading psalms, and writing. In her cell would have been an altar and a stone coffin lid as a constant reminder of mortality. After her death she was buried beneath the floor of her cell. An ancient blocked-in door, visible in the north wall of the chancel, may have led to her tiny chamber.

We paddled happily on. It was the kind of happy type of feeling you get after a leisurely two or three pints of strong ale. I don't think shooting through an open flash lock would have held any fears for us right then. We soon once again passed under a modern road bridge carrying the busy Oxford ring road, another unpleasant noisy few seconds but an impromptu loud rendering of Hawaii Five-O helped us through. A young amorous couple who had taken refuge under the arches from prying eyes and hadn't seen us approaching were taken completely by surprise.

Some of the boats we were now sharing the river with were large enough to be capable of crossing the channel without any difficulty. Surprisingly, they caused little wash as their powerful engines were having to do little more than just tick over to propel them along at a reasonable speed. They patrolled the river gliding effortlessly along in a haughty contemptuous manner, rather like gigantic swans. Oxford is as far upstream as they can go as the notoriously low Osney Bridge, as previously mentioned, prevents them venturing further.

Some of the owners of these magnificent craft, but not all it has to be said, seemed to look down upon the smaller craft, especially the hire boats, in every sense of the word. The captain's lady is always readily recognised as she will be wearing dark sunglasses, sunny or not, clutching a gin and tonic, with nose in the air as if looking out to sea at an imaginary horizon. But I must be fair and shouldn't tar them all with the same brush for we did meet some very genuine and down to earth owners of the 'larger vessels' during our trip.

For instance, just after passing under the Kennington railway bridge, a little further down-stream, a stunning 'sixty footer' going in our direction, began to silently slide past. Just as it came alongside the lady of the boat, a round sturdy looking woman of about sixty-five with bright red lipstick, chemically enhanced auburn hair and wearing the regulation sunglasses, stood up, pushed her sunglasses to the top of her head and waving her gin and tonic in the air shouted at the top of her voice, "Ere aren't you the two blokes we erd on the wireless? Ow many pubs you bin to?"

"Thirteen," Kev replied without even having to think about it. And he was spot on.

The captain of the ship, a man about the same age and the same rounded physique as his good lady, wearing a peaked cap and sucking on a large cigar called back, "Is that today's total or since you started?" And with that remark he stopped his boat midstream, "Come and have a couple of beers with us, you look as if you need it," he bellowed.

It would have been rude to have declined his offer so we manoeuvred the 'lizard' alongside. "Get the boys a drink Marj," he commanded. "Beer or lager?" We opted for lager.

We drifted downstream in the middle of the river with boats passing us on both sides. The captain seemed oblivious to what was going on around him as his boat now began to drift sideways on.

Marj meanwhile had opened two cans of larger and was endeavouring to hand them down to us. She was extremely well-endowed in the chest area and as she precariously lent over the side to hand us the cans her 'assets', which up until then had barely been covered by her bright red singlet, decided to introduce themselves. With a can of lager in each hand there was nothing she could do to prevent it happening. Without a hint of embarrassment, she handed over the lagers, sat back upright again and proceeded to wrestle the escapees backed to where they belonged.

By now the considerably sized boat was drifting backwards, still in mid-stream. "Enjoy your drinks boys," he said. "See you at the Kings Arms." And with Marj waving both arms high in the air, he turned his boat around and headed off downstream.

The incident reminded me of a story my father used to tell of a business acquaintance of his, a self-made man who bought himself a large ostentatious cruiser. Being quite a 'rough diamond' and not having had any previous experience of boating he quickly earned an infamous reputation amongst the boating fraternity by committing misdemeanours regarding the etiquette of the river.

When you owned such a boat it used to be the 'done thing' to belong to a prestigious yacht club, but you needed to convince a committee that you were worthy to be a member of their club. If you were accepted you were allowed to proudly fly a pennant from the bow of your boat depicting the initials of your club. For instance,

M.A.H.Y.C. Marlow and Henley Yacht Club or, U.T.Y.C. Upper Thames Yacht Club.

For several months my father's acquaintance tried in vain to be accepted into the folds of such a club. Then at last he was seen to be exhibiting a pennant on his boat which fluttered proudly in the breeze. From then on whenever he was asked which yacht club he belonged to with the initials M.O.B.Y.C. his reply was, "My own bloody yacht club!"

We proceeded on at a gentle pace enjoying the early afternoon sun but it wasn't long before the nagging feeling for a 'comfort stop' began creeping into our minds, and elsewhere. The beers and lagers were making themselves felt. This hadn't been a problem in the upper reaches above Oxford, but now there were many more boats and walkers around. When there is nowhere to answer the call, it is surprising how quickly the nagging becomes an order not to be disobeyed and a sense of panic sets in. All likely looking spots with trees or bushes either had a boat moored nearby or had people in close proximity. Paddling became more frenzied which unfortunately made the sound of splashing water more audible and provocative.

The situation was becoming desperate, when rounding a bend, a perfect spot presented itself. On the bank was a deserted clump of thickly growing hawthorn bushes. The feeling of relief must have been similar to a thirsty man finding an oasis in the desert, although for the completely opposite reason. However, we were about to experience the same emotions the thirsty desert traveller would have felt if he had found the well dry. The bank was too high and too steep for us to climb out!

There was no time to even try. Having our hopes raised and then snatched away so quickly did nothing to relieve the situation, in fact it made it many times worse. Up until then our predicament had been controlled with the well proven ploy of humour. Neither of us were laughing or joking now. We paddled on in silence.

A small sandy beach came into view on the opposite side and without a word from either of us we changed direction and headed straight across the river at ramming speed. We ran aground, the momentum of our headlong dash taking a good deal of the canoe beyond the waterline. I half jumped and was half catapulted out of the canoe onto the beach. Kev followed but managed to fall over in the process, but I didn't have time to stop and help him as I scrambled up the bank and sprinted behind a clump of nearby bushes. Two seconds later Kevin joined me complete with grazed elbow and a bloodied knee. We didn't hesitate to check if anyone was around, if they had been it wouldn't have made any difference anyway. If there was, I do apologise.

We soon passed on our right; the treacherous fast flowing weir known as The Sandford Lasher. It empties into the notorious Sandford Pool which has claimed the lives of several bathers over the years. A stone memorial beside the weir records the names of these unfortunate souls. One such individual was a Michael Llewelyn, an undergraduate of Christ Church College, who drowned in 1921. He is thought to be the inspiration for Peter Pan because he was the ward of J. M. Barrie who wrote the story for Michael and his brother in 1904.

It was getting on for 2pm when we reached the quiet village of Sandford-on-Thames. It's only about 3 miles from Folly Bridge but it had taken us very nearly three hours to cover the distance, but why worry, we hadn't far to go and it was Sunday. As the name suggests there was once a river crossing here, a sandy ford, and there are references throughout history to the Sandford Ferry. In May 1644, during the English Civil War, the Earl of Essex took his troops across the river at Sandford to join the battle of Cropredy.

If ever you find yourself in Sandford on a Christmas Eve beware of meeting George Napier. In the early reign of Queen Elizabeth I, George Napier lived near the village at Temple Farm. He was a Jesuit priest who paid the ultimate price for his religious beliefs. In 1568 he was tried and executed in Oxford. Each of his limbs were placed over the four gates of the city and his head was placed in front of Christ Church. A few nights after his execution his relatives secretly collected his remains for burial back in Sandford, but unfortunately forgot to collect his head.

The good people of Sandford will tell you of the headless George Napier who every Christmas Eve drives a ghostly coach and horses to Temple Farm in search of his missing head. Few people will admit to seeing the spectre as it is believed that whoever has the misfortune to meet the coach will die within the year.

Try to imagine the scene. It's Christmas Eve on a cold moonlit night and the skeletal trees cast their moving shadows over a carpet of snow while a keen breeze whispers through their branches and the leafless hedges. The only other sounds come from the occasional distant call of a lonely owl and the church clock which has just struck midnight.

As a cloud slides silently across the moon, dimming its light, a new sound is heard. The muffled drumming of hooves. As the sound gets closer and louder the breeze subsides and the atmosphere becomes still. An extra chill is felt in the air.

The noise swells to roar as a coach pulled by four fiery eyed black horses, their manes flying wildly about their heads, careers seemingly out of control along the narrow country lane. The frenzied steeds are being urged on by the headless driver, George Napier.

Napier and his coach and horses thunder on around a blind bend and only just avoid, coming in the opposite direction, an old gentleman dressed in red, with a flowing white beard, driving a sleigh pulled by six reindeer!

The Kings Arms at Sandford- On-Thames is a fine old lock side pub. As we approached, we couldn't fail to notice the impressive sixty foot cruiser we had drifted down stream with earlier, moored nearby. The garden was noisy and crowded with more than the usual number of children present. Above the din however, we plainly heard the familiar voice of Marj. "Ere they come Henry. Over ere boys." Maj was standing up by a table in the garden waving both arms in the air as was her custom.

After shedding our buoyancy aids, we joined Marj and Henry at their table on which were two pints of lager awaiting us. They were good company, chatting as if they had known us from years back and we had just re-met after a long absence. It didn't take long for Marj to relate their history including Henry's hernia operation and her own irritable bowel and ingrowing toenail which, I'm pleased to report, was nearly better.

Henry had made his money in the scrap metal business, now retired, they were enjoying the fruits of his labour. They spent the summer cruising the Thames in their splendid vessel, meeting old friends and making new ones. The winter was spent at their villa in Spain. They were the most genuine and down to earth couple you would wish to meet, wanting nothing more than to share their enjoyment of life with friends and acquaintances. They had worked hard for their retirement and deserved the lifestyle they were now enjoying. Good luck to them.

It was now nearing 3 o'clock and we hadn't eaten since breakfast. We invited Marj and Henry to join us for lunch and another round of drinks but they declined as they had arranged to meet some old friends further downstream. They wished us well and went back to their boat but not before giving a generous donation to the fund.

We vacated our table and picked our way through the crowded garden to go inside to order ourselves some sandwiches and another pint. The noisy chatter, shouts and screams reminded me of the school playground. Inside, the pub was deceptively large with a wealth of beams and comfortable furniture. Every chair and table were taken by an adult but the sounds of children were still very audible. The reason was glaringly obvious. In an adjacent room, running the full length of the pub, with a plate glass wall dividing the two was, 'The Funky Forest', a Childrens in-door playground. Every so often children would emerge from the 'forest' and scuttle across the room to their parents table, take a bite from a sandwich and a swig of Coke and then scuttle back. Kevin remarked that they reminded him of wood ants foraging back and forth.

Call us old fashioned, but we both agreed that when it comes to pubs, children should be seen and not heard. Definitely not encouraged. We didn't dally long over our lunch.

Sandford lock is the deepest on the river above Teddington with a fall of eight feet, nine inches. It was around 3:30 when we began to descend into its depths. As the water drains away and you slowly descend the dripping walls seem to close in around you. Quite an intimidating experience when you're sitting practically at water level in a canoe.

Below the lock the river passes through open country and for the first time it was now flowing along a recognisable valley. About two miles downstream where the hills begin to creep closer from the east, we passed on our right, the Radley College boathouse. The college, famous as a rowing school, was founded in 1847 and old boys include cricketer Ted Dexter and comedian Peter Cook.

Half a mile further, on the opposite bank, standing on a hill overlooking a great sweeping bend in the river is the impressive Nuneham house. It was built in the early 18th century by the Harcourt family before moving from their old manor at Stanton Harcourt. The magnificently landscaped grounds were laid out by 'Capability' Brown. It was here that Queen Victoria spent her honeymoon.

Lord Harcourt felt that the nearby medieval village of Nuneham was too near to the house and obstructed his view - so he had it removed! This provoked the poet Oliver Goldsmith to write his lengthy poem in 1770 entitled 'The Deserted Village'. Here is a very short extract.

> 'The man of wealth and pride
> Takes up a space that many poor supplied
> Space for his lake, his parks extended bounds,
> Space for his horses, equipage, and hounds,
> The robe that wraps his limbs in silken sloth,
> Has robbed the neighbouring fields of half their growth;
> His seat, where solitary sports are seen,
> Indignant spurns the cottage from the green'.

To be fair to the Earl, he did build a new model village for the displaced villagers nearby, along the Oxford to Henley road, called Nuneham Courtenay. He also built himself a church close to the house. Built in the style of a temple with a copper domed roof which is visible amongst the trees. The house and extensive grounds are now owned by the Oxford University.

A little further on down-stream but still in the grounds of Nuneham House, we passed what looks like a large, ornately carved stone. It's known as the Carfax Conduit. It is in fact a stone cistern built in 1615 that once stood in the middle of Oxford drawing fresh drinking water from a spring outside of the city. When in use it was a very elaborate public drinking fountain. When the high street was widened in 1797 it was removed and given to the Nuneham estate as a garden ornament.

In Victorian times this area of the river was a popular summer destination for people from Oxford who would travel down by boat for picnics and parties in the grounds of Nuneham . Lewis Carroll was one such person and it's said that he may well have had the idea for 'the pool of tears' in Alice's Adventures in Wonderland after a visit on a rainy June day in 1862. I would really love to know what was in his picnic basket!

The steep wooded slopes of Lock Wood, just below Nuneham, forces the river to flow westwards for a couple of miles; the only time it flows in that direction. When it reaches Abingdon, it curls completely around into an easterly direction.

While passing Lock Wood we became aware of a noise sounding not unlike a swarm of excessively angry wasps. As we paddled on down-stream they seemed to be getting even angrier and judging by the velocity of the noise, larger by the minute. It occurred to me that the insect repellent spray we had thoughtfully brought with us was going to be rather inadequate as judging by the noise an anti-aircraft gun was going to be more appropriate.

Rounding a slight bend, we had a brief glimpse of one of the 'wasps' as it appeared fleetingly above the tops of some trees before diving back to earth again. It was closely pursued by a second and a third 'wasp' before a multitude of others followed the same trajectory. They were in fact riders on motorbikes taking part in a motocross meeting. As they came over a brow of a hill beyond the trees at full throttle they took off and flew through the air giving the impression that they were flying over the trees. The river took us past the racetrack so we stopped for a while to watch. But we soon tired of the noise and zealous activity and it wasn't long before the tranquil peace of the river enticed us back to resume our journey.

As we approached Abingdon lock, we passed on our left, the entrance to a now very overgrown, non-navigable half mile backwater known as Swift Ditch, 'swift' meaning shortcut. It was once the original course of the Thames, but the river was rerouted as early as AD973 by the monks of Abingdon Abbey to avail them with running water. The main channel now skirts Abingdon around a long sweeping bend.

The Swift Ditch however remained in use as a shortcut until 1550 and then again between 1630 to 1790. The very first pound lock on the Thames was built in 1630 at the entrance to the 'Ditch', the remains of which can still be seen.

For eight and a half centuries Abingdon, 'abbey town', grew around the Saxon Abbey, not around a fording point, as some other towns along the Thames began as their names suggest; for example, Oxford, Wallingford, Shillingford. The Benedictine Abbey, founded in AD675, steadily became extremely rich and powerful until its abolition in 1538. Little now remains of the abbey apart from its impressive gateway and the ruins of the guest house and the prior's house.

In 1084 William the Conqueror came to spend Easter at the abbey leaving his son to be taught by the monks. The Domesday Book records that, apart from the king, the abbey was the largest landowner in Berkshire at the time.

Abingdon is one of the oldest continuously inhabited towns in Britain and during its long history it has been a wealthy wool town and a thriving market town reflected in its magnificent County Hall built in around 1678. Mondays has been market day since 1086 and up until 1867 it was Berkshire's County town.

The town's Michaelmas Fair, originally a medieval hiring fair for rural farm workers to find work in the local area, is held every October. It's said to be Europe's longest street fair.

MG cars were built here from 1829 until 1980. One of their prototype saloon cars was painted a stippled black on a gold-coloured background. The locals nicknamed the car 'the old speckled one'. In 1979, Morlands the local brewery, was asked to brew a special beer to celebrate MGs Golden Jubilee. It was decided to call the brew 'Old Speckled Hen' after the prototype car. It's still a very popular bitter.

Naturally enough for a town with such a long and varied history it has some strange customs and traditions. Non so strange as a decree dating back to the Coronation of George III in 1760 that states that; 'buns should be thrown from the County Hall on all similar occasions.' As coronations are few and far between there is a designated bun throwing day in June, when the mayor throws buns down to the waiting crowd from the top of the old County Hall.

On the nearest Saturday to June the 19th the whole town is given up for a weekend of Morris dancing, which, I'm told is eagerly looked forward to by the good folk of Abingdon. This event originates from about 1700 when the men of Och Street and the men of Vineyard competed in a Morris dancing 'battle' for the horns of a black ox. One wonders how this 'battle' was conducted? I imagine two teams of strangely dressed men with bells strapped to their legs, trying to knock the hell out of each other with inflated pigs' bladders tied to sticks, whilst at the same time waving their handkerchiefs in the air in time to music. All this while they are being hampered by the onlookers who are pelting them with stale buns!

Abingdon lock was very busy with a queue of boats at both ends, but again we were waved to the front by the lock keeper who managed to squeeze us in. Below the lock the town soon presents itself along the right-hand bank, but strangely the opposite side is only occupied by open meadows and a sports ground. It's as if the town is afraid to cross the river in fear of trespassing on the other side.

We paddled slowly along looking out for The Old Anchor Inn, our accommodation for the night, enjoying the pleasant river frontage of Abingdon consisting of ancient and modern properties. As we passed under the old multi arched stone bridge, originally built in 1416 by the wool merchants of the town, we made note of two river-side hostelries that we needed to return to later, The Mill House and The Broad Face.

A ghostly apparition of an unidentified woman's head and arm is said to appear beneath the water under the bridge. We had a good look, but alas, we didn't spot her.

Immediately, on the other side of the bridge, the river is overlooked by the imposing Victorian Abingdon gaol. The first inmates were incarcerated in 1811 but it was closed down in 1868 because it was deemed unfit for purpose. During the 1970s it was partially rebuilt as a leisure centre and there are plans to convert it further into flats and apartments.

During its heyday as a prison, it was the main gaol for the area and many a lawbreaker was dispatched on the prison gallows. It's probable that the youngest recorded person ever to be hanged in England, met his end in Abingdon gaol. He was an eight-year-old boy accused of setting light to two barns.

It's not surprising that there are stories of ghostly encounters in the sports centre backed up the chilling experiences of the staff. Doors banging, strange noises and voices and figures seen lurking in corners. Staff have reported hearing the sound of a child laughing and speaking just as they're locking up for the night.

A few hundred yards further on we came upon The Old Anchor. A welcoming looking building built alongside the confluence of the River Ock, once famous for its salmon. The inn, however, is situated across the road and is protected from invasion from the Thames by Saint Helens Wharf, along the top of which runs stout iron railings which seem to defy any craft to moor alongside the wall and make a landing. It may well have been The North Face of the Eiger as far as we were concerned as there was no way we would be able to disembark and haul the canoe and our luggage up and over the imposing wall.

We sat for a while midstream pondering on the problem. It seemed the only option was to paddle back up stream to find a suitable landing place and then walk back several 100 yards along the road carrying 'the lizard' and accompanying baggage. A prospect neither of us relished.

It was then I spied, tucked under an elder bush growing out of the wall, a flight of narrow stone steps ascending to the top of the wharf. We paddled over to investigate further. They had obviously been unused for some time, except for the bottom three steps which were plainly used frequently by the local duck population as their public convenience.

Duck guano is a treacherous substance creating little friction between itself and the soles of trainers which I instantly found to my cost. As I stepped from the canoe onto the bottom step my feet slid from under me and I found myself kneeling as in prayer, my hands clutching the third step up with duck dung oozing through my fingers and my knees embedded in the sludge. Three young fishermen between the ages of about eight and twelve, fishing a little way along the wharf who had witnessed the event, fell about laughing, as did my friend who almost managed to upset our canoe.

It took a good ten minutes with much grunting and cursing to unload the canoe and manhandle her and our luggage to the top of the steps. Some of the duck manure had inevitably transferred itself to various items, so while Kev stayed to clean up as best he could, I crossed the road to report our arrival. I had endeavoured to scrape my knees clean to the best of my ability, but they were still obviously soiled, and although I had rinsed my hands in the river, I found that duck deposits leave stubborn stains and a putrid lingering odour.

With fetid hands and knees, I entered The Old Anchor, which for 5pm on a Sunday afternoon had quite a gathering of customers around the bar. They didn't seem to notice my presence at first, but as I wafted past them on my way up to the bar, they abruptly stopped talking and gave each other rather accusing looks.

I explained to the barman who I was and he went to fetch the landlady. As she approached, I went to shake her hand but just as we were about to, I suddenly remembered the state my hand was in so I hastily withdrew it. Thinking I was trying to be funny she politely gave a false laugh. As we spoke, I noticed the gap between us steadily increasing as my 'essence of duck aftershave' took effect. By now the customers had realised the source of the odour which had invaded their conversation and had moved well away from the bar and were talking in hushed tones looking in my direction. While our hostess went to check that our room was ready, I took the opportunity to go to the gents in search of soap and water. Unfortunately, the customers had gathered in the vicinity of the toilets and as I approached, thinking I was about to join them in conversation, hurriedly downed their drinks and left.

Our garret for the night was way up in the attic and I couldn't help wondering if the original location of our room had been hurriedly changed after our initial introduction. It meant negotiating, with our barrels, paddles and our other bits and pieces, a flight of steep and narrow stairs which for some unknown reason caused us much hilarity. At one point in the proceedings one of the blue barrels went crashing from top to bottom of the stairs. Thinking one of us had fallen, the landlady and the barman rushed to administer first aid only to find us in fits of laughter. They must have wondered who on earth they had staying under their roof that night! In spite of the first impressions we had presented, our hostess was very amenable and allowed us to stow the canoe in the courtyard come beer garden. As an extra precaution we chained and padlock her to one of the wrought iron tables. (I do mean 'the lizard'!)

After a shower and a change of clothes we went back down to the bar to introduce ourselves properly and hopefully prove that we were actually fairly sane and didn't always leave a noxious smell in our wake.

The Old Anchor Inn, where Jerome K. Jerome had his 'Three Men in a Boat' stopping for lunch, was first licenced as a pub in 1884. It was originally three attached houses which were converted into one building to create the pub. The game of Aunt Sally is taken very seriously and the Anchor competes in the Abingdon and District Aunt Sally League, one of their great rivals being The Swan at Radcot.

We fancied a change from pub food so after a couple of pints each we set out to explore the town in search of a Chinese restaurant, remembering to take the camera with us as we needed to visit the two pubs we had passed earlier which fronted the river. It didn't take long to find a restaurant. After the meal, accompanied by a very decent bottle of house red, we set off again to find the two yet unvisited pubs.

Abingdon has many fine taverns, some so fine that we found them impossible to pass without sampling their hospitality. And so, by the time we had found our way to the two 'official' pubs we were in quite a jovial and carefree mood.

The Broad Face was erected in 1840 but there are records of a tavern of that name in the same vicinity back in 1734. The origin of the unusual name is a mystery but one macabre theory is that it refers to the bloated face of a man who was hanged at the old gaol which is situated opposite the pub. After a pint and a photograph, we moved on.

The Mill House sits on its own island in the middle of the river halfway across Abingdon Bridge. Once called the Nags Head, it's a Grade 2 listed building of 18th century origin. Its large garden was heaving with customers and as it took us some time to get served, we only had the one before deciding to head back, nearly forgetting the all-important photo. With these two pubs, plus The Old Anchor, our 'official' tally at the end of day four was seventeen.

Although now quite late The Old Anchor was still full with some customers spilling out across the road and leaning on the railings overlooking the river, enjoying the balmy summer evening. We purchased a couple of beers and joined those on the railings. As the river slipped silently past below us, we soon got into conversation with our fellow drinkers.

When Kev's had a few and is well lubricated he can, it is fair to say, talk the words off a page. Generally, a load of nonsense, often prone to exaggerate but always very entertaining. I tend to listen and smile a lot, chipping in now and then with what I consider to be witty and intelligent comments.

Kevin soon captured an audience of Dutch holiday makers, three middle aged couples, all of whom could speak fluent English. They were on a tour of England and were eager to know all about the River Thames. As we had known the river intimately for four whole days now, there wasn't very much Kevin didn't know on the subject, and what he didn't know he made up.

During one particularly bad case of verbal diarrhoea he was instructing them on the best method he had found for roach fishing which, he said, he had always found fool proof. In fact, he went on to say, it was so successful that he had won several prestigious angling competitions and was, at this very moment, in training for the All-England Left-Handed Fisherman's Golden Maggot Award.

It was well past 11:30 when our Dutch friends managed to say goodnight during a brief lull in the dialogue. They wished us good luck with the rest of the trip and, giving me a knowing look, also wished us success for Kev's quest for 'the golden maggot award'.

We stopped for a brief nightcap with the landlord and landlady on our way through the bar. As we hadn't met him before we thought it only polite to do so. He was very taken by our River Thames campaign.

Somehow the stairs up to our attic room seemed steeper than before and we found them best negotiated on 'all fours'. Sleep very quickly took over but I do recall dreaming of a forest full of golden maggots riding motorbikes.

CHAPTER 10

Things That Go Bump in the Night

Abingdon to Dorchester – 12 miles

The morning of the 16th August began, I'm sorry to say, much as the previous three days for us both. Headaches and a general feeling of 'muzzyness'. But this morning's hangover, and yes, I shamefully admit that is what we were both suffering from, had the added ingredient of the feeling of wanting to be left alone in a sound proofed darkened room. We both made a pact that this sorry state of affairs was not going to become a habit.

We gingerly and very quietly ascended the stairs with the intention of having nothing more than a coffee and a piece of dry toast for breakfast. Our landlord had other ideas.

"This is on the house lads," he announced in an unnecessarily loud voice, as he emerged from the kitchen. "This is my contribution to a good cause."

He was carrying two large plates almost the size of dustbin lids. Each plate was crammed full with fried eggs, bacon, tomatoes, fried bread, mushrooms, beans, sausages and black pudding.

I felt a sense of panic grip me and the desire to vacate the room as quickly as possible. I looked at Kev for some support only to find he was staring at me for I expect the same reason. "Thank you," I heard myself whisper.

"Yes, very kind of you," Kevin murmured, not daring to look again in the direction of the gastronomic ordeal which was being laid before us without mercy.

How we managed to consume our host's generous gesture without disgracing ourselves I'll never know. Any other day we would have enjoyed every mouthful, but on that particular morning we were in danger of 'enjoying' every mouthful more than once.

There was no escape as our benefactor remained with us throughout the whole ordeal recounting some of the unusual schemes he had come up with over the years to raise money for charity. Apparently, he was well known for his annual madcap ideas for a worthy cause. Once, he recalled, he had been sponsored to wear nothing on his feet for a year except a pair of green wellingtons!

It was getting on for 9am when we finally said farewell. We had done our best with the breakfasts. One of the fried eggs and a sausage had beaten me and I noticed that Kevin's black pudding was untouched.

With difficulty we negotiated the narrow stone steps down to the water and re-floated 'the lizard' without too much duck excrement attaching itself to us or our belongings. It was rather overcast and the clouds were threatening to rain on us whenever they felt the urge, but we were glad to be on the move again and in the fresh air, little was said as we paddled out of Abingdon.

As we passed the other end of Swift Ditch, we could see it was crossed by three bridges. A wooden footbridge stands beside the old road bridge which was built in 1416 and was still in use carrying the A415 road up until 1928. Beside that sits its modern replacement.

Grey Heron

We soon left the town behind us and headed into open country along a wide, straight, placid half mile stretch of the river lined with alder trees and willows, known as Culham Reach. Ahead of us, in the distance, we could see the rather imposing view of the cooling towers of Didcot Power Station.

It seemed that we had this quiet stretch of the river to ourselves apart from a solitary Grey Heron. It was standing motionless, knee deep in the shallows waiting patiently for its prey to pass. They are magnificent birds with their long legs, grey-white plumage, with black markings on the front of the neck and on the edge of each wing. On the back of their head is a distinctive black drooping crest. Their long, yellow dagger shaped beak is used like a pair of forceps to you seize their prey, which consists of fish, eels, frogs, water voles and large insects. They are the top bird predator of the freshwater food chain.

Being in a canoe we were able to approach quite close to the bird before it became wary of us. When it did, it rose effortlessly into the air and flew lazily, with its long neck tucked against its body and its legs trailing behind, a further hundred metres downstream, whereupon it landed and resumed fishing. With a large wingspan of about a hundred and ninety-five centimetres and their legs trailing behind they are easily recognised in flight. This pattern continued the whole length of the reach, the heron allowing us to approach to within ten metres before taking flight and moving on.

Although solitary hunters, herons' nest in large colonies in trees. They begin to lay their clutches of three to five eggs as early as February, they are about the size of a hen's egg. The colonies are generally on traditional sites, the oldest recorded in 1293 is in Chilham in Kent. The collective noun for a group of herons is a 'siege' of herons.

Herons have a long lifespan for a bird, about eighteen years. They have no natural predators, but they have been known to choke on large fish and severe winters can be devastating. They will fly long distances to find new sources of food. Goldfish in garden ponds are easy prey, once found a heron will keep returning until all are consumed. Herons are a protected species, much to the annoyance of many a Koi Carp breeder, but in the past Herons were the highlight of a medieval banquet and so, on land deeds, a heronry was always noted. In the Middle Ages when falconry was an aristocratic sport, herons were very much a sought-after prey.

Our heron left us at the end of Culham Reach and continued on to fish along the original course of the river which flows through the village of Sutton Courtenay. Eric Blair, better known as George Orwell, who wrote his political satire Animal Farm, is buried in the village churchyard. However, we turned sharply to our left at almost a right angle to continue our way along the main canal like navigation route known as The Culham Cut. The cut was dug in 1809 when time saved meant more money for the Thames hauliers. Another example of river corner cutting.

I always felt cheated in a way when passing along these cuts. It seemed to me as if certain parts of the Thames were being kept aside and secret from us. We could have followed the true course of the river, but it may have meant negotiating weirs and we would quite possibly miss important 'watering holes'. We did briefly discuss the idea but decided that sticking to the recognised navigation route was the best option.

After passing beneath a fine old wooden footbridge, we entered Culham Lock at the end of the cut which we shared with a traditional, beautifully painted narrowboat. The middle-aged couple aboard lived on their boat all year round, travelling the canals and rivers of England making a living by selling their remarkable art work and hand-made crafts along the way.

Immediately after leaving the lock, we passed under Culham Bridge before rejoining the 'proper' river again. We had now somewhat recovered and the usual banter and carefree feeling had returned although the sun was still reluctant to share the day with us.

The river again becomes wide and lazy as it flows unhurriedly through lush open meadows to its next destination, Clifton Hampden. A couple of boats passed us traveling in our direction but the only other sign of human presence occurred as we passed under the steel girded Appleford Railway Bridge, at the same time as the Oxford to Paddington train thundered overhead.

In the distance, ahead of us, we could see the dual hillocks of the Sinodun Hills which overlook Dorchester, our evenings stopover. They look like two islands rising above a vast sea of flat meadowland, four miles away as the crow flies, nine by river.

We continued our leisurely progress selfishly enjoying not having to share the river with other humans for a while. We disturbed another heron from its fishing who no doubt felt they were two too many humans around.

About a mile further on we were again diverted into yet another cut, this time to be denied the secret delights of the village of Long Wittenham. The Clifton Cut was opened in 1822 following the success of the Culham Cut opened a decade before.

At the far end of the half mile or so cut, Clifton Lock was in the process of being filled to bring two very large cruisers up to our level. We waited for them to vacate the lock against the bank by our tried and tested method of holding on to tufts of long grass to prevent us from drifting away. As the sun was well over the yard arm, or it would have been if it had shown itself, we decided it was time for the 'medicinal' flask to see the light of day from the white bucket. We also took the opportunity to consult the O.S map and to our dismay, there only seemed to be one inn marked along our day's route. It was at Clifton Hampden half a mile further downstream, but on closer inspection it became apparent that it wasn't strictly speaking a waterside pub.

A planning meeting was immediately held to discuss this grave situation. After the 'medicinal' flask has been passed around several times it was decided that as the inn in question was the famous old Barley Mow, which Jerome K Jerome describes in 'Three Men in a Boat' as, 'the quaintest and most old-world inn on the river', we could not pass it by. An exception would have to be made and it was unanimously passed that the Barley Mow would count as one of our 'official' pubs visited.

We had the lock to ourselves, but the congenial lock keeper was not in any hurry to let us out, wanting to know all about our river experiences so far. It wasn't until a smallish cruiser arrived going upstream, that he opened the gates to release us. The lock marks the end of the cut and we rejoined the original course of the Thames almost immediately.

Ten minutes or so later the six red brick arches of the elegant, narrow, Clifton Hampden Bridge came into view. It was built in 1867 from a design by Sir George Gilbert Scott who, amongst other things, also designed the Albert Memorial. The story goes that he was dining one evening with Lord Aldenham who had inherited the village in 1842. Lord Aldenham was complaining that his servants were constantly late through frequently missing the ferry that was then in existence and was the only way of crossing the river at this point. Whilst sitting at the dining table Sir George promptly drew a design for the bridge on his starched shirt cuff.

In the 1950s the bridge was recorded as having the largest colony of house martins in the UK with over four hundred nests beneath its arches and it was declared a site of scientific interest. We checked, but sadly there is now no evidence of the colony having ever existed.

We left 'the lizard' to go in search of the Barley Mow in the safe keeping of three children who were sitting on the bank. They were between the ages of about eight and ten and seemed thrilled to be trusted with such an important task. We told them we would be no longer than half an hour, it was now ten-thirty. We didn't have far to walk as the inn was situated just about a two minutes' walk across the bridge and along the road out of Clifton Hampden.

According to the date on the outside wall the Barley Mow was built in 1352 and in spite of a devastating fire in 1975, anyone looking for an almost perfect 'olde world' vision would not be disappointed. Its thatched roof, low pitched gables, half- timbered walls and great curving timbers on the end wall seemed to confirm its genuine antiquity. It's an example of a cruck framed construction, the oldest type of domestic building in England.

The interior lives up to the exteriors promise. On entering through the low door, you're met with flag stoned floors, a wealth of beams and steps up and down to several anti-rooms. It's very tastefully furnished and old engravings and artefacts adorn the walls. One wall is dedicated to photographs of the near devastating fire.

All that's missing is a jovial landlord and landlady. The Barley Mow is now owned by a well-known chain of pub-restaurants and therefore lacks the atmosphere and welcome which comes from the personal touch of proud and dedicated hosts. The bar was manned by young men and women dressed in the company's uniform and although very efficient at their job, to them it was only work. They didn't have time or the inclination to chat and pass the time of day.

The old inn must have a wealth of stories to tell but alas we could find nobody with the knowledge to relate any of them. However, I did find some information printed on the quite extensive menu and I quote. 'Oliver Cromwell is said to have passed this way on several occasions. Jerome K Jerome is supposed to have written several chapters of his book whilst staying at the inn. The toll bridge keeper and the ferry man before the bridge was built used to sit in the inglenook fireplace watching for customers through the window which gives an excellent view to the river. The existing mantlepiece is worn where they used to pull themselves to their feet. During the Second World War the rafters rang to the chatter and laughter of Canadian airmen stationed in the area, enticed to the Barley Mow by the excellent reputation the ales and beer had at the inn'. It goes on to say that the Barley Mow is 'open all day every day eight days a week'!

They say walls have ears. What a shame they couldn't speak and tell more of the characters and incidents which they must have witnessed during the inn's six hundred years existence.

We spent a pleasant enough half an hour over a pint and after the photograph wandered back down the road to the bridge. We took with us three cans of Coke and some crisps as a payment for our canoe guardians. They eagerly accepted their wages and solemnly reported that they had saved the canoe from a dog that came along and began sniffing around. After thanking them again we resumed our journey leaving them sitting in a circle on the riverbank enjoying their picnic of Coke and crisps.

The river now turns completely back on itself in one enormous three-mile bend as it gently curves to the right. The inner bank consists of lush water meadows. The outer bank is dotted with some very desirable riverside residences with their lawns sweeping down to the water's edge complete with their obligatory boathouses. They prompted a discussion on what we would spend the money on if we were lucky enough to win the lottery.

Cars, houses, boats and travel were all mulled over. Eventually Kev came up with an idea which I readily accepted and I hereby put in writing lest he forgets. 'Whichever one of us wins the lottery will pay for the other to accompany him, in style and luxury, to every major sporting event in the world'. Dream on!

As we passed the village of Burcot at the apex of the bend, the first drops of rain began to fall. To begin with it wasn't worth worrying about and it was quite pleasant to see the occasional drop of rain disturbing the river's surface, but as it became more persistent it grew evident that the waterproofs would need to be utilised.

Our wet weather gear was packed in the plastic watertight sack which was stowed in the bottom of the canoe between the two blue barrels. We were near mid-stream at the time along a particularly wide part of the river and so decided to save time by donning our waterproof there and then instead of pulling over to the bank. Big mistake!

To begin with Kev had trouble undoing the cord around the neck of the sack. After talking nicely to the knot, he lost his temper with it and in doing so he somehow managed to lose his paddle overboard which had been resting across his knees. It was eventually retrieved but by then had floated some distance away from us. The reason for the delay was because I was in the front and didn't find it easy to steer from the bow seat. We pirouetted a few times and even headed off in the wrong direction before Kevin was reunited with his paddle. It didn't occur to us at the time for me to hand my paddle over to Kev who from his position in the back of the canoe would have steered more easily. Meanwhile the rain was becoming more persistent and the heavy drops were bouncing off the surface of the river. We were still in mid-stream.

After threatening the knot with his Swiss Army Penknife, it gave in and Kevin was able to distribute our waterproof leggings and jackets. It was now raining seriously. I wonder if you've ever tried putting on waterproof trousers whilst in a canoe drifting backwards in mid-stream during a heavy rainstorm. It was my turn to lose my temper when my foot, still in its trainer - left on to save time, became stuck down one trouser leg.

Meanwhile, Kevin was attempting the very risky manoeuvre of standing up in a Canadian canoe in order to pull up his trousers. He didn't quite make it but remained in the squat position, trousers round ankles, as we rocked dangerously from side to side. Somehow, we managed to stay upright and thus escaped a ducking. Mind you, we wouldn't have got any wetter than we were already for by now it was raining so hard we could hardly see either bank.

A good ten minutes had elapsed by the time we were completely waterproofed. Two minutes later it stopped raining and the sun appeared, so we paddled over to the bank and took them off to dry.

Burcot is easily missed as it lays a little way back from the river but up until 1636 this was a most significant spot on the Thames. It was the point where commercial navigation could not continue further upstream due to shallow water from here on. Passengers and goods en route to Oxford had to be transferred to the road to continue their journey. This led eventually to the Oxford-Burcot Commission, appointed by an Act of Parliament of 1605 by James I to improve navigation on the Thames between Oxford and Burcot. It was the first Commission to be concerned with the navigation of the river.

As we continued around the huge bend and headed due south, we both began to steam in the warm sun. Didcot Power Station was becoming much less imposing and had been deposed by the two mysterious Sinodun Hills as the prominent landmark. In the distance we could also see the line of the Chiltern Hills capped in beech trees. Somewhere there I have left all the petty worries and tribulations of everyday life behind.

The surprisingly regular shaped, smoothly rounded Sinodun Hills are commonly known as Wittenham Clumps because of the copse of beech trees which crown the two hills, possibly the oldest recorded planted tree clumps in Britain. The old local nickname for the hills is, 'Mother Dunch's Buttocks', named after the mother of the seventeenth century owner of the nearby manor house.

On the top of one of the hills is the remains of a ten-acre Iron Age Hill Fort consisting of a single ditch and ramparts. This place was of great strategic importance in Celtic times and only from the fort can it be appreciated how much territory they surveyed. The dominant vantage point overlooks the rivers Thame and Thames and not far away are the ancient byways, The Ridgeway and The Icknield Way.

The remains of a Roman Villa with mosaic floors and painted wall plaster, has been discovered on the southern slope of the other hill.

The 'clumps' are owned by the Northmoor Trust and managed as a nature reserve with public access to the land. Once a year Oxfordshire County Council presents the trust with a single red rose as a token payment for the public use of the land.

In 1844, Joseph Tubb carved a poem in the bark of a large beech tree growing in the fort. It's now difficult to make out the words but a nearby plaque recounts the poem for us. The beginning goes:

> As up the Hill with the labouring steps we tread,
> Where the twin clumps their sheltering branches spread,
> The summit gained, at ease reclining lay
> And all around the widespread scene survey.

Paul Nash, who is served as an official war artist in both wars and was also one of the finest English landscape painters of his generation had a special affinity for the Wittenham Clumps. They were a great source of inspiration for him and he returned many times during his life to paint them. He wrote, 'ever since I remember them the clumps have meant something to me. I felt their importance long before I knew their history. They were the pyramids of my small world.'

It had just begun to rain again as we approached Day's Lock at the base of the Sinodun Hills. As we are quick learners, we went ashore to re-clothe ourselves in our wet weather gear. This time only taking a minute or so over the task.

Day's Lock, named after the lock keeper in the eighteen twenties, is an indication that the locks were once privately owned, the lock keeper charging a toll to all who passed through. Most locks are now named after their location but some, as in this case, have retained their past owner's name.

Day's Lock has a major role to play as it is the main gauging station for measuring the flow of water in the Upper Thames.

The lock gates were open and inside were two boats, which had passed us a minute or two earlier, kindly awaiting our arrival. The two crews and the lockkeeper were eager to hear of our exploits and on leaving kindly donated to the now swelling charity fund.

Close by, just downstream from the lock, we passed under Little Wittenham footbridge which is the venue for the annual Poohsticks World Championships. The event is held at noon on the first Sunday in January and has been held every year since 1984, apart from 1997 when the river froze over.

The game of Poohsticks was invented by AA Milne in his book House at Pooh Corner published in 1928. It was played by Rabbit, Piglet, Roo, and Winnie the Pooh. It's a simple game, each player drops a stick on the upstream side of a bridge and the one whose stick first appears on the downstream side is declared the winner. Kev and I are still unsure as to whether this event will be included in our major sporting events schedule when we win the lottery.

Because the twin hills bar the way, the Thames is forced to take a sharp easterly turn after leaving the lock. It was now raining quite steadily but we didn't have far to go now until our final destination for the day. But it did involve a short detour up the River Thame to Dorchester and we didn't know what this much smaller river had in store for us.

There was a good reason for this brief deviation from the Thames. As I mentioned earlier, when planning the trip, I experienced difficulty in splitting the days into manageable chunks whilst at the same time finding available accommodation. Without venturing up the Thame to Dorchester it would have meant a further thirteen miles paddling to Goring. We had already decided that The George Inn, our overnight accommodation, would qualify for the final tally of pubs visited, after all, we would have arrived by canoe.

We had been looking forward to sampling this ancient inn's hospitality, said to be one of the oldest in the country, ever since I had booked our night stay all those weeks before. A friend of mine had eaten there on several occasions and praised the menu and the food with unbridled enthusiasm and a colleague of Kevin's had stayed overnight and reported that the atmosphere and comfort of The George was unsurpassed. So, we had decided this was to be a stopover of extravagance and we would go the whole way and have the luxury of a room each. This was to be our birthday treat, our Golden Jubilee celebration.

It was midday and raining quite heavily when just below Day's Lock, we turned left at the confluence of the two rivers and headed up the River Thame. For the first few hundred metres it was quite wide but then it became very reminiscent of our first day's paddling as the river become narrower and overgrown. It was hard work, with the wind and rain now lashing into our faces and a fast-flowing current working against us. The river twisted and turned below overhanging willows and in places the reeds becoming quite intrusive.

Nevertheless, we found it a welcome change from having it relatively easy. We were much fitter from when we first set out four and a half days ago, in spite of the alcohol intake and the full English breakfasts, and it was quite exhilarating to be battling against nature. How long this feeling of exhilaration and bravado would have lasted if this particular part of the journey had been longer is another question, but we knew it was only a short diversion, so we set about enjoying the challenge.

Half an hour's hard work brought us to the bridge which takes the A407 across the Thame to Dorchester. The rain had by now eased off. The question now was, "where do we go from here?" Climb out and walk the short distance along the road into Dorchester or press on further upriver. We decided on the latter.

The river took us along the backs of gardens obviously owned by some opulent dwellers of Dorchester. The only option which seemed available to us now, if we were to gain access to Dorchester from the river, would be via one of the gardens. Now there were new uncertainties to ponder. How would we be received when we suddenly appeared from the river from the bottom of the garden? Did they own a dog? How big was it? Did they own more than one dog?

The next garden, with overhanging willows, looked as good a place as any to try so we stopped beneath a tree to think through the situation. The garden was blessed with several mature trees and stretched a good hundred metres or so up to the house. Kev suggested that as I had a dog at home and therefore would know what to do if attacked by a pack of Rottweilers, it should be me who went forth to establish contact with the owners. As I couldn't think of a reason why he should go, I prepared for martyrdom. I couldn't decide what was best. To keep my waterproofs on for added padding or shed them for extra speed. I left them on and clambered from the canoe leaving Kev hanging on to a branch to avoid being swept back down stream. I gave several dog type owner whistles and called out; "Here boy, come on good dog," and such like, followed by more whistling. I wanted them to know I was friendly.

"Can I help you?" came a voice as its owner, a large man with rake in hand appeared from behind a nearby tree. "Have you lost your dog?"

I was about to explain when I noticed he was staring with a rather quizzical look on his face at something going on behind me. I turned to see Kevin hanging from a branch in a 'gibbon like' manner, desperately trying to prevent the canoe from being swept away with the strong current by gripping his seat with his feet. He was at full stretch, arms and legs extended to their full length.

We both watched mesmerized as Kev slowly drew the canoe back to directly beneath him, only to have it pulled away again to full stretch by the river before he could sit down. We continued to observe his highly entertaining gymnastic labours through several repetitions until, in less than a polite manner, he enquired whether or not we would be assisting him.

Having retrieved Kev and 'the lizard' and got them both safely on dry land, we were able to introduce ourselves to the gardener, for that's who he turned out to be. After explaining our overall mission and our immediate goal of The George, he proved to be a most helpful new acquaintance. He informed us that The George was almost opposite the house and that his employer, Mr. Morrison, was at home and he would introduce us to him, and he assured us, there were no dogs.

Mr. Morrison and his wife were extremely obliging people and they readily agreed to grant us access to Dorchester via their garden. They also said that our canoe would be perfectly safe left on the lawn but if we wished we could move her to the garage.

We left 'the lizard' on the lawn chained to a tree in case of a flood, and laden down with our luggage crossed Dorchester's high street to The George. We were looking forward to a night of unashamed indulgent delectation.

The present building dates from around 1449, almost a century before Henry VIII closed the nearby monastery. It's built around the abbey's brewhouse which dates way back as far as 1140.

During the great coaching era of the 18th century, it became an important coaching inn on the route between Oxford and London. An abandoned coach at the front of the inn doesn't seem out of place as it waits patiently for the ostler to come and hitch up its team of horses.

With the passing of the coaching era The George fell on hard times. Part of it became a private residence and the beautiful courtyard became a wheelwright's shop and coal merchants. Thankfully it has now been expertly and carefully restored back to its original career of providing hospitality to weary travellers. The arch and courtyard and the galleried travellers' lodgings are reported to be an example of the earliest of their kind in England.

Inside, The George has lost none of its original character with a wealth of beams, open log fireplace and furniture to match the period. The dining room, with its high ceiling and half-timbered walls, was originally the monks brewhouse and is a fine example of medieval domestic architecture.

I don't think we quite matched the ambience of the place when we entered dressed head to toe in waterproofs, wearing buoyancy aids and fetid trainers and carrying a blue barrel apiece plus the rest of our paraphernalia. Despite our appearance we were made extremely welcome and shown up to our rooms.

When I was shown into my room, I was relieved to see that my bed was not of the four-poster variety. A white lady is supposed to haunt one of the rooms and appear at the foot of the four-poster bed. I followed Kev further down the corridor to his room to see if he had a four poster. He hadn't, but as I knew, Kev was always reluctant to lock his door at night in case of fire, so I was still fairly sure he would be having a visit from the white lady sometime during the night.

By now it was getting on for two o'clock so we decided that after a quick shower and a change of clothes we would meet down in the bar for a gin and tonic and a spot of lunch. After perusing the superb evening menu, we refrained from having very much for lunch, just a sandwich to help the gin and tonic down and to keep our appetites keen for our 'official' birthday celebration dinner.

After lunch, as the sun had again decided to make an appearance, a gentle stroll around Dorchester was suggested. Some people refer to it as the town of Dorchester but in fact it's no bigger than a village. Once upon a time however it was a city. If it were not for the random fate of history it could now well be the nation's capital.

The area was once densely populated by people of the Iron Age who left a massive one hundred and fourteen acres of earthworks known as Dyke Hills situated between the Thames and Dorchester. Later, the Romans built a military settlement calling their town Dorcina Castra. After the Romans withdrew back to Rome in the 5th century the Anglo Saxons built themselves a settlement from its ruins.

In AD635 the missionary St Birinius came to Dorchester to baptise the heathen King Cynegils of Wessex in the river Thame, which resulted in a Saxon cathedral being built on the site. This baptism had the momentous effect of converting much of southern Britain to Christianity.

By the 10th century Dorchester had become the Cathedral City of Wessex and was the centre of a huge diocese that included Worcester, Bath, Salisbury, Lichfield and Winchester. It was one of the most important places in Saxon England.

A great abbey was later built and the Abbey Church of St Peter and St Paul, founded in the 12th century, replaced the Saxon cathedral. At one point in time Dorchester had a cathedral, an abbey, a monastery and seven other churches.

St Birinus died in AD650 at Dorchester and was buried in the church. Tradition says that he died from a snake bite. The oldest of the abbey's eight bells, cast in about 1380, bears the inscription in Latin, 'Protect Birinus, those who I call forever'. From that day, so the story goes, no snakes could stay within the sound of the bell and crawled away and hid.

A shrine was erected for St Birinus in the abbey which brought fame and riches to Dorchester in Medieval times. Many pilgrims thronged around it leaving rich offerings to obtain the indulgence, ('a way to reduce the amount of punishment one has to undergo for sins'), granted to all those who visited the shrine.

The cloisters, chapter house and other monastic buildings have long disappeared and all that is left of the great Abbey of Dorchester is the guest house and the abbey church.

We wandered around the beautiful and peaceful abbey church which along with the guest house, used in the 17th century as a grammar school and now a museum, is well worth a visit. Both have been expertly restored thanks to The American Friends of Dorchester Abbey.

A visiting wealthy American woman by the name of Miss Stedman, who passed away in 1978, was greatly impressed with the lovely old ruins of the abbey but was saddened to find there were no plans or finance to stop further decay. On returning to America, she formed The American Friends of Dorchester Abbey who, with various fundraising activities, raised enough money to renovate the remaining buildings and ensure their upkeep.

It made a welcome change to be stretching our legs and we spent a very pleasant couple of hours wandering around the remains of the abbey and its grounds and exploring Dorchester. It was late afternoon when we returned to the George and retired to our respective rooms to relax on our own for a while.

I lay on my bed reflecting on how much a success our trip had so far turned out to be. The previous days seemed to merge into one another as I recalled our exploits and incidents of the journey. I suddenly felt a sense of panic as I realised we were almost halfway through our adventure. Time was passing too quickly and I wanted it to slow down.

I must have dozed off because I suddenly became aware it was almost 7pm, the time we had arranged to meet back down in the bar. Kev hadn't arrived but I bought us both of whiskey and settled down in an easy chair to await his appearance, but by the time he had surfaced I had finished both. Kevin had also fallen asleep. It's not until you relax in comfortable surroundings that fatigue eventually catches up but we both now felt refreshed and totally at ease and ready for an indulgent evening.

In the unique surroundings of the old dining room, we lingered over a splendid three course meal accompanied by an expensive bottle of exquisite red wine and reminisced over our long friendship. We have been the best of friends since the first time we met on our first day of secondary school when were both eleven years old. A great deal had happened to us over the years, both good and bad, and here we were, almost 39 years on, still the greatest of friends, a little wiser and experienced but at times, according to some sources, still behaving as if we were eleven years old.

Eventually we adjourned to the bar to round off the evening with a few brandies. The recollections continued around the log fire until about midnight when sleep and our comfortable rooms began to beckon. Before retiring I reminded Kev of the story about the white lady, for I felt she might be paying one of us a visit later.

It was as much as I could do to stay awake but after giving Kevin a good half an hour to settle down and fall asleep, I quietly crept along the dark corridor to his room with the white sheet from my bed draped around my shoulders. It was very quiet and eerie as I made my way through the old travellers' lodgings and I found myself wondering what I would do if the white lady or another apparition were to really suddenly appear. I was beginning to wish I had stayed in the comfort and safety of my own room.

Luckily, Kev had left his door unlocked. I pushed it quietly open and stepped inside pulling the sheet over my head so just my face was showing. I could just make out the bed in the darkness and judging by the snoring he was already sound asleep. I carefully made my way across the room, but before I reached the foot of his bed I inadvertently stepped on the corner of my trailing sheet and stepped sideways into his blue barrel sending it crashing into his paddle which was leaning against the wall, which in turn slid sideways into the bedside table knocking the lamp onto the floor.

A 'snore' stopped for a second in mid-flow and then to my amazement continued. I rearranged.

my sheet and stood at the foot of the bed and gave a ghost like moan. The snoring didn't falter. I tried again, much louder this time. Still no reaction.

In desperation I pulled the bed clothes off him and stood with arms outstretched. He sat bolt upright, looked at the ghostly spectre before him and yelled at the top of his voice, words which would have turned any ghostly white lady a deep shade of crimson. What he meant to say was, "who are you and would you kindly leave my room?" The wide-eyed look on his face was worth a photograph and I only wish I had thought to have taken the camera. After several seconds he realized who it was, probably the laughter gave me away. I gathered up my sheet and made a hasty exit helped by a pillow followed by a shoe.

As I made my way back to my room, still laughing to myself, I noticed that some of the adjacent rooms had lights shining from under their doors. The visit of the white lady had obviously not gone unnoticed. I just hoped that nobody would venture out of their room to investigate because I would have had quite some explaining to do wandering around the corridors at night with a sheet under my arm dressed only in my 'boxers'.

I gained the sanctuary of my room without being discovered and soon fell asleep, but not before I had double checked that my door was well and truly locked.

CHAPTER 11

Stormy Waters

Dorchester to Goring - 13 miles

Kev took his visit from the 'white lady' during the night very well and we had a good chuckle over it during breakfast. Overall, we agreed, it had been a very enjoyable and gratifying evening, a fitting way to have celebrated our half centuries.

It had obviously rained extremely hard during the night but it had abated and only the occasional spots of rain made their presence felt as we left the George under a grey overcast sky. We thanked Mr. and Mrs. Morrison for minding the canoe and squelched down their rain sodden garden to be reunited with her.

The river Thame was very high, threatening to burst its banks and running extremely fast. We needed to secure 'the lizard' front and aft very securely to prevent her from being swept away as we stowed our gear on board. It was around 9:30 when we were eventually ready to head off back down the Thame to re-join the Thames.

As it was his turn to sit in the front Kev took his place and I settled down behind. The river was doing its utmost to tear us free from our moorings and sweep us downstream, so it was agreed that the best course of action would be to release front and aft moorings simultaneously to ensure a smooth and straight departure. Unfortunately, Kev encountered some difficulty with his mooring rope and was several seconds behind the release of mine. The current instantly swept the back of the canoe out into midstream in an arc. By the time Kev managed to release his mooring rope we were pointing upstream.

We shot off downstream backwards at a rate of knots at the mercy of the current. It was not unlike a theme park ride devised by some sadist who delighted in the passengers being lashed and flogged by overhanging branches and brambles. We eventually gained control and enjoyed an exhilarating journey downstream, all we had to do was steer. We were spat out back onto the Thames as one would eject an annoying grape pip.

The Thames was much calmer and sedate than the excitable Thame and we were able to continue along at our usual pace. Open farmland flanks the river on both sides for about a mile as it approaches the village of Shillingford. Just before Shillingford bridge, with its adjacent hotel imaginatively named, The Shillingford Bridge Hotel, the river takes an almost ninety-degree, right-hand bend. As we approached the bend, an Elizabethan style house seemed to be blocking the way as it sits on the bank with its extra-large boathouse resembling a gaping mouth facing us, giving the impression from a distance that it's swallowing the river.

The Shillingford Bridge Hotel is a large white modern box like building with a generous expanse of lawn sweeping down to the river. The lawn was dominated by a deserted, sizeable outdoor swimming pool. A smaller hostelry, called the Swan Inn, once stood on the site now occupied by the present building.

It was only 10:15 and there was a distinct chill in the air, so we felt instead of beer a couple of Irish whiskeys each were needed to restore our bodies back to their optimum working temperature. We stayed for about 40 minutes before resuming our campaign but not before reclothing ourselves with our, still very damp, wet weather gear, as the rain was now beginning to pit the surface of the river in a rather meaningful way. If you listened carefully, you could hear a constant high pitched ringing sound as the raindrops dived headlong into the, now looking, murky depths of the river.

Almost immediately we passed beneath the fine three arched Shillingford Bridge which was built in 1827 to replace a much earlier wooden bridge. Before that, it was obviously yet another fordable part of the river. Kev wondered if the name bore reference to the charge made for using the old ferry!!

The rain was now quite steady and our waterproofs were being tested to the full. The river takes on a completely different persona on a wet murky day. From being welcoming, cheerful and friendly the now grey, dirty looking river seemed threatening and much deeper. It made it impossible to converse with our hoods up and the noise of the rain bouncing off our waterproofs, so we paddled on in silence.

Half a mile or so on we passed the village of Benson, marked by a caravan park and a host of moored boats clustered around a marina. Benson was once a coaching stop but is now better known for its RAF base. Three miles inland is the village of Ewelme, the last resting place of Jerome K Jerome. The 'K' stands for Klapka.

We passed through Benson lock, which we had to ourselves, with only a cursory nod from the lockkeeper who was dressed in a similar fashion to ourselves. The first pound lock here was built by the previously mentioned Thames Navigation Commission in 1788 and was replaced by the present lock in 1870. It would be a further six and a half miles before we reached the next lock, the longest stretch on the non-tidal Thames between locks.

The river was deserted, even by the wildlife. Every river dweller and user, it seemed, had taken shelter but being the fearless, intrepid canoeists, we had become, we carried on. Our next brush with civilization would be the ancient town of Wallingford and hopefully there would be one or two stops to make.

For at least a mile the river takes an uncharacteristic natural straight course on its way to Wallingford passing through flat uninspiring farmland. Just before the town it passes Howbery Park Institute of Hydrology. Once the home of Jethro Tull, a wealthy landowner and inventor. Not to be confused with the early 70s band of that name. He was a pioneer of mechanised farming who, amongst other things, invented in 1701, the seed drill for planting beans and wheat thus eliminating the haphazard and uneven method of scattering the seeds by hand.

Before someone had the bright idea of building bridges across the Thames, Wallingford was the most convenient and important place to ford the river above London. The Romans were the first to utilise the spot and it remained a ford until its first bridge was built in 1141. The present stone bridge, parts of it dating from 1250, is an impressive affair with no less than seventeen arches of various widths. The river only flows through five of them now but the necessity to build such a huge span says much about the width of the river and the danger of flooding at the time it was built.

Wallingford has a long and interesting history. During Saxon times it was a tribal capital, and it was here that a great battle was fought when Offer, the king of Mercia, repelled the West Saxons.

William the Conqueror made his first crossing of the Thames at Wallingford six days after the Battle of Hastings. His conquering army was prevented from crossing London Bridge, so he followed the south bank until a suitable shallow fording point was found at Wallingford. The Normans recognised the importance of the then very shallow area of the Thames which allowed an easy crossing and fortified the town with an impressive castle which became one of the most important in England and was visited by many English kings and queens.

During King Stephen's troubled reign, it was the refuge for his cousin Matilda, who had laid claim to the throne which had led to a bloody civil war. She had escaped from the besieged Oxford Castle in 1142 by fleeing across the frozen Thames dressed in a white robe as camouflage against the snow-covered landscape. Wallingford castle then became her stronghold against Steven. Later, in 1153, the castle was witness to her signing The Treaty of Wallingford that surrendered her claims to the throne. It allowed Steven to keep the throne until his death but insured that he would be succeeded by Matilda's son, who became Henry II. He granted the town its Royal

Charter in 1155 and ever since then, on every Friday, a market has been held in the old marketplace.

The castle's final act was during another civil war, the one between James I and Parliament. It was the last Oxfordshire stronghold of the Crown and it held off the Cromwellian general Fairfax for quite some time. It was finally captured in 1646 after a sixteen-week siege and was demolished soon after on the orders of Fairfax.

All that remains now of the once imposing Wallingford Castle is the castle mound and a few remnants of some of its walls.

The name, Wallingford, is thought to mean 'Welsh peoples ford' as it was situated along the ancient main London to Wales road. Like Abingdon, it's 'lopsided', being built largely on only one side of the river seeming to use the Thames as a natural barrier between itself and London. In 1641 the Royalist troops used this fact as part of the town's defences. They blew up the four central arches of the bridge and installed a drawbridge thus using the Thames as a moat.

The George, in the high street, another old coaching inn, dates from 1517. During the Civil War it was frequented by the royalist soldiers one of which, a sergeant by the name of John Hobson, became engaged to the landlord's daughter. One night he became involved in a drunken brawl which resulted in him being stabbed to death in front of his fiancé. Being distraught she locked herself in her room for days and with soot from the fireplace mixed with her tears, she painted large teardrops on the wall which can still be seen. As The George is back from the river, we didn't investigate but I intend to at a later date. Dick Turpin, the infamous highwayman, is reported to have been a regular visitor to The George.

There are two pubs with a frontage to the Thames in Wallingford. The Mill House dating from 1890 and The Town Inn another former 16th century coaching inn. The former we arrived at 11:40 and the latter we left at 12:30 having shared our time equally between them. Whiskey Macs were the favoured drinks in an attempt to compete against the cold and damp awaiting us out on the river. The bowls of hot homemade chicken soup, purchased at the Town Inn, would, we hoped, also be a help.

As we left Wallingford we passed, on the left bank, the tiny Norman church of St Leonards. There has been a church here since at least the Saxon period, way before the Norman Conquest. The church was badly damaged during the siege of Wallingford in 1646 when parliamentary troops used the church as a barracks.

A little further downstream on the opposite bank, just before Winterbrook Bridge, is Winterbrook House, once the home of Agatha Christie where she lived for a good number of years until her death in 1976. She wrote several of her mysteries whilst living there including the stage play The Mousetrap which opened in 1952 and is still playing in London, making it the longest continuous running play in the world. Her second marriage was to an architect. She is reported to have said that an architect was the best husband a woman could have because the older she gets the more interested he is in her.

The wind was against us driving the now heavy rain straight into our faces making it very hard going. It felt as if we were paddling through treacle, each pull on the paddles only took us forward about half the length of the canoe. Without doubt the next hour was the toughest we were to experience during the whole trip.

This stretch of the river is broad and straight with little on either side to act as a windbreak. Large open arable fields stretched away into the distance towards the beech wooded Chiltern escarpment, which was barely visible through the driving rain. Only second to Henley, this is the longest straight stretch of water on the Thames. It's often used as a practice course for Olympic rowers, the Oxford boat race crews as well as the crews for the Oxford Eights Week. Nobody was out practising today!

The strong headwind was creating fairly substantial waves topped with 'white horses', often breaking over the front of the canoe. This, together with the heavy rain meant that 'the lizard' was gradually filling up with water. It was now ankle deep. I was in the front and as I turned around to make myself heard, in order to point this fact out to Kevin, as if he didn't know already, I noticed the sky behind us. The next time you pour a Guinness take note of its appearance as it swirls around the glass before settling. This is the impression the jaundiced coloured sky gave me as it approached, strangely against the direction of the prevailing wind.

At the time we were about six feet out from the right-hand bank, at a particularly wide part of the river, trying in vain to gain a little shelter from the wind. On the opposite bank a large empty boathouse was offering us shelter. After drawing Kev's attention to what was approaching from above, I shouted to him that perhaps it might be a good idea to accept the boathouse's hospitality.

After carefully considering the proposal for at least two seconds, Kev shouted back that there was no way he was going to head out across the river, which would mean the waves hitting us broadside on and then getting caught midway across by whatever was threatening us from above. I accepted his decision without comment and returned to my labours.

A minute later the 'Guinness sky' emptied over us in a sudden deluge.

The heavens opened!

I've never experienced rain like it. It was as if huge buckets of water were being poured over us. While I paddled gamely on, Kevin found it necessary to swap his paddle for a plastic pint mug, which happened to be floating around inside the canoe, in order to attempt to keep us afloat by frantically bailing out the water which was increasing in volume at an alarming rate.

The torrent lasted for perhaps a couple of minutes and then abated into a steady 'every day' pour which was just as well as Kevin was losing his battle with the rising tide inside the canoe. We pressed on regardless, saying little.

On a more clement day, undoubtably this broad, majestic stretch of the river would be pleasant enough. However, on a day such as this it was boring and tedious without even a lock to break the monotony.

At last, after about a two-and-a-half-mile slog, the strikingly visual, four red brick arches of Isambard Kingdom Brunel's Moulsford railway bridge came into view. The magnificent looking bridge was built in 1839 to carry the Great Western Railway across the Thames. From the river, the perspective view of the bridge is very different to most other bridges, because owing to the direction the railway approaches, it straddles the Thames at a skewed angle of sixty-degree, whereas most bridges tend to go straight across a river.

About half a mile further on the river passes the village of Moulsford. Way back, the river was fordable here and as the towpath switched banks at this point it allowed the mules, pulling the barges, to be transferred across the river. Later, after the river became deeper, a ferry was introduced to take the towing mules and horses across, the bargees having to pay a 'penny-ha'penny for the service.

By now it was around 1:30. It had been a long and exhausting morning and we were more than ready for another stop so the landing stage of The Beetle and Wedge at Moulsford was a welcome sight. The rain had eased to a steady drizzle and the hostelry looked dry and inviting but before sampling its hospitality we finished the job Kev had started and emptied the bilges.

The Beetle and Wedge dates back to before 1860 and is situated next to the site of the old ferry which ceased to be operational in 1967. Its built where a former timber wharf used to exist from which planks of timber where floated downstream to London. The planks were obtained by using a large mallet, called a beetle, to drive a wedge into felled tree trunks in order to split them.

Having been submerged up to our knees in rainwater our trainers were somewhat sodden. As we squelched our way into the main bar, dressed head to toe in our wet weather gear, the clientele, of which there were a fair number, paused over their gin and tonics and eyed us with astonishment and whimsical uncertainty. If I mention the makes of the cars parked in the car park were made up of such models as, Porsches, Jags, Rolls-Royces, Bentleys and the like, it will give you an idea of the type of patron The Beetle and Wedge attracts. It has a reputation of having a restaurant of high standards. Apart from the main building and restaurant it has another facility called the boathouse, in which one can eat from a huge indoor barbecue - and I'm not talking over-cooked hamburgers and charcoal sausages.

H.G Wells stayed here in 1910 and wrote The History of Mr. Polly in which The Beetle and Wedge was immortalised as The Potwell Inn. Bernard Shaw is also reported to have stayed and the fictional 'three men in a boat', also paid a visit.

We peeled off our wet weather gear in the gents and then returned to the welcome warmth of the bar. We must have stood out like a couple of sumo wrestlers at a slimmer of the year award ceremony, dressed in our t-shirts, shorts and Thames sodden trainers. The other suited and groomed customers chose to ignore the strange apparitions in their midst. We drank another couple of Whiskey Macs each, but then decided that it might be prudent to leave as the warmth of the bar was having the usual effect on our footwear. The pungent aroma of Thames water was beginning to overpower the expensive aftershave and perfume of the other customers.

We retired to the gents once again to don our wet weather regalia and then bid a cherry farewell to everyone as we left to return to the friendly grey drizzle outside. I have to say that subsequently I have returned to The Beetle and Wedge and enjoyed a very pleasant evening in their boathouse restaurant, this time wearing more conventional attire for the establishment.

Feeling somewhat refreshed, it was about 2pm when we resumed our journey. We estimated that we had about an hour's work ahead of us before reaching Goring and the end of our day's toil.

The Thames had now become a wider and more mature river, now at last seeming to have made up its mind in which direction it wanted to go. The many twists and turns were replaced by long graceful sweeping curves.

We soon passed The Leatherne Bottle on the left bank, unfortunately for us no longer a pub. In the 16th and 17th centuries it was popular not only for its beer, but also for its medicinal water taken from a spring in its garden which had also been known to the Romans. At the time of our trip, it was purely a restaurant often frequented by celebrities.

A little further on is Cleeve Lock. It had been six and a half miles since our last locking manoeuvre at Benson, the longest stretch between locks on the non-tidal Thames. Strangely, the next stretch to Goring lock is the shortest, a mere five-eighths of a mile.

A small island, next to the lock and weir, is owned by Pete Townsend of the rock band, The Who.

Cleeve Lock has the smallest fall on the river at just two feet three inches. We had seen a few other craft during the morning but we had the lock to ourselves. As there were no other boats waiting to enter the lock, the lock keeper kept us pleasantly chatting, wanting to know all about our exploits on the river so far.

As the river approaches Goring the river valley becomes narrower with steep, tree lined sides. The Chiltern Hills on the north side and the Berkshire Downs to the south gradually become nearer until they almost touch at the narrowest part of the Thames Valley known as the Goring Gap. In my opinion one of the most dramatic and beautiful parts of the Thames. It was gouged out during the last ice age making a diversion for the river through the chalk hills which had previously formed a barrier across its path.

The Chiltern Hills and the Berkshire Downs have both been deservedly given the accolade of 'An Area of Outstanding Natural Beauty' and as you pass through the Goring gap it's easy to see why. But that pleasure was awaiting us until the next morning.

We arrived at Goring Lock at exactly three-o-clock, it was still drizzling slightly. The lockkeeper, a very jovial character, greeted us with a smile and a wave as we approached the lock gates. Yet again we had his attention to ourselves. When we enquired if he knew of a suitable berth for our canoe, he immediately offered the use of his garden. We gratefully accepted his offer and with his help, which he insisted on giving, unpacked 'the lizard' and put her to bed.

I had booked us in to stay at The Miller of Mansfield which was situated a little way up Goring high street. Laden with the barrels and our other bits and pieces we bade our new friend farewell and set off in search of our night's accommodation. By 3:45 we were enjoying a pint in the bar before being shown to our room.

On the wall in the public bar, I noticed a rather compelling inscription which reads:

> 'This bar is dedicated to those splendid fellows who
> make drinking a pleasure,
> Who reach contentment prior to capacity,
> And who,
> Whatever they drink,
> Can,
> Take it,
> Hold it,
> Enjoy it,
> And remain, gentlemen'.
> *Stolen from The Lairds Arms, Matjiesfontain.*

'Food for thought' for those engaged in the present craze of binge drinking!

We arrived up in our room just in time to take a phone call on Kev's mobile from BBC radio Oxford. It was to inform us that Jeremy would be calling us in the morning at 8:30 for a live on the air progress report.

After a shower and a change of clothes we went down and booked a table for dinner before having a wander around Goring. After sitting in a canoe for most of the day, a necessary but pleasant exercise.

It had stopped raining but the sky still threatened more as we strolled down the high street. Goring sits on the side of the Thames directly opposite Streatley, both connected by a bridge built in 1923. It's the only point on the Thames where two settlements of similar size face each other.

Strangely, there was not a bridge at all until 1837. Before that a ferry was the only means of visiting either settlement. In 1647 a major tragedy occurred when the ferry was swept across the weir costing the lives of 15 men, women and children. Before the ferry it was a pre- Roman and Roman fording point for it's here that the prehistoric track the Ridgeway and the Roman road the Icknield Way join to cross the river at the Thames Valley's narrowest point. In ancient times it was the most important crossing point of the Thames.

Goring church has perhaps the oldest Bell in England. A Latin inscription on it reads, 'Pray for Peter, Bishop of Exeter. Richard de Wymbis made me'. It can be dated to some accuracy because Peter, Bishop of Exeter, was Peter de Quivel who was Bishop from 1280 to 1291. If the inscription had been made after his lifetime it would read, Pray for the soul of Peter. Richard de Wymbis, who made the bell, was a member of a well-known family of bell founders who worked in London at the end of the 13th century.

It's a mystery how the bell found its way to Goring from Exeter. It may have something to do with the Augustinian nunnery which was founded here in 1150. At the time when the bell was cast the prioress was Sarah of Exeter. Perhaps the bell was a present to her from Bishop Peter? The nunnery was destroyed during The Dissolution of the Monasteries.

We strolled on across the bridge to Streatley for a couple of pints and a photograph at The Swan Hotel, which dates from about 1650. I had originally tried to book our overnight's accommodation at The Swan but there was 'no room at the inn'. It was once owned by the entertainer Danny La Rue who bought it in 1970 as a forty-third birthday present to himself. The Swan is situated just below the weir with picturesque views from its bar back across the river to Goring.

It's thought that Streatley's name evolved because one of our most ancient trackways or 'streets', The Ridgeway, descends from the Berkshire Downs and crosses the Thames at this point and then continues eastwards along the ridges of the Chiltern Hills.

Situated on Streatley's high street is The Bull public house. A monk and a nun are reputed to be buried in the garden under two yew trees. In around 1440 they were discovered at The Bull, which they used for their intimate secret meetings. They were put to death as punishment and buried in unconsecrated ground in the pub garden.

We lingered in The Swan for some time enjoying our drinks and the ambience before returning for our dinner. We paused whilst crossing the bridge to view the steep hill which climbs out of Streatley, from the top of which, I have read, is the most stunning vista of the river and the Chiltern Hills beyond. It's a climb not for the faint hearted but, I am told, well worth the effort. For a brief moment we were tempted but decided it could wait for another day. Not that we couldn't have managed it you understand, but the time for our pre-booked meal was drawing near. Evidently, we were not the first to decline the challenge of the hill as an extract from the Punch magazine entitled 'A Streatley Sonata' explains.

'Ah! Here I am! I've drifted down.
The sun is hot, my face is brown
Before the wind from Moulsford town,
So pleasantly and fleetly!

I am not certain what's o'clock,
And so I won't go through the lock,
But wisely steer, the 'Shuttlecock'
Beside the Swan at Streatley!

But from the Hill I understand
You gaze across rich pasture land;
And fancy you see Oxford and
Perhaps Wallingford and Wheatley:

Upon the winding Thames you gaze,
And though the view, beyond all praise,
I'd rather much sit here and laze
Than scale the Hill at Streatley!

And when you're here, I'm told that you
Should mount the Hill and see the view;
And gaze and wonder, if you do
Its merits most completely:

The air is clear, the day is fine,
The prospect is, I know, divine,
But most distinctly I decline
To climb the Hill at Streatley.

We returned to The Miller of Mansfield and enjoyed a pleasant meal in the pub's restaurant and then joined a very convivial assembly in the public bar. They were saying goodbye to a colleague who was returning to Australia. More than a fair amount of alcohol was consumed!

During the course of the evening, I discovered why the pub had such an unusual name. A legend tells the story of Henry III who was out hunting near Mansfield. He stopped at a mill for refreshment and being incognito was unrecognised by the hospitable miller. The king was offered wine and venison which, the miller confessed, had been poached from the king's forest. Henry enjoyed his meal and then made himself known to the miller who proceeded to beg for mercy as poaching was a capital offence. However, Henry was so impressed by his generous host that he knighted him and granted him a plot of land at Goring, well away from his hunting forest, on the proviso that he built a tavern and continued providing hospitality to hungry travellers.

It was around 11:30 when we decided it would be better for us to retire before reaching 'hangover territory'. We bade bon-voyage to our new Australian acquaintance and retreated back to our room. After last night's luxury it was back to sharing a room and the first asleep snoring the loudest.

CHAPTER 12

Relics and Rain

Goring to Sonning – 13.5 miles

Kevin's phone rang at exactly 8:30am. It was BBC Radio Oxford wanting their live, on-air report of our progress. We had made notes and drawn lots to select who was to be the 'lucky' interviewee, we had also sworn an oath not to make noises, pull faces, or strike poses in an attempt to disrupt the flow of the other's verbal intercourse. I was selected and immediately made Kev repeat the oath of conduct.

I was able to report to Jeremy and his listeners that after six days we had paddled seventy-two miles and visited twenty-five pubs and had the photographs to prove it. We had managed to remain in the canoe whilst afloat and had met many helpful, generous and kind people on the way. He went on to ask several other questions regarding our plans for the next half of the trip.

I felt the interview went very well, in spite of the fact that throughout, Kevin was standing in the middle of the room wearing nothing but his socks and his boxers, impersonating a drunken chimpanzee.

After another 'Full English', we set off down Goring high street to resume our journey. We were a little later than usual and it was 9:45 before the relief lockkeeper eventually saw us off. Even lockkeepers have an occasional day of rest. As he stood in the doorway of the lockkeeper's office with his peaked cap slightly askew and pulled well down over his forehead, a cheerful grin spreading across his face and saluting us on our way, he reminded me of the Benny Hill character, Fred Scuttle. Kev had also seen the likeness, which prompted a rendering, once we were out of ear shot, of 'Ernie, The Fastest Milkman in the West'.

As rain was threatening yet again, we already had our full wet weather gear on as we headed on through the Goring Gap. In every book you read relating to the Thames they always describe the Goring Gap as one of the most beautiful stretches on the river. Even on that grey damp morning it was easy to endorse their opinion.

The river had broken through the chalk escarpment, now known as the Chilterns, during the last ice age forming a deep valley. Steep sided woods tumble down to the riverbank on both sides forming, in summertime, a green backdrop to the river, and in the autumn, when the beech trees give their ostentatious display of colour, the spectacle is stunning. The only place to be able to really appreciate the unadorned natural beauty of the gap is from a boat or walking along the towpath.

At this point the Thames separates the two counties of Berkshire and Buckinghamshire and both banks share the honour of being awarded Areas of Outstanding Natural Beauty. There are only thirty-three AONB in the whole of England, all protected by law to maintain their exceptional natural character and splendour.

The Goring gap is a haven for wildlife, especially it seemed to Great Crested Grebes. We had already seen several during our

journey but they seemed more prevalent along this stretch. They are quite a striking looking bird to look at with a dagger like bill, black crest and prominent chestnut and black frills on either side of the head. They have a slender body that sits rather low in the water when swimming and a long thin neck which is generally held upright. Although quite capable of flying they spend most of their time swimming, in fact, I don't ever recall seeing a Grebe in flight. If approached they dive to re-surface at a safe distance several meters away. Their diet is almost entirely of fish which they catch by diving and chasing their prey beneath the surface. They nest on floating platforms made up of waterweed at the water's edge amongst vegetation. The striped young are taken on to the water as soon as they have hatched and can swim and dive almost immediately. The brood, of two or three, often rides on the back of one of the parents whilst the other dives for food. The male and female are very similar except the male is a little larger with a heavier bill and larger crest. In early spring the pairs exhibit a very elaborate courtship display on the water which consists of an elegant dance routine.

Great Crested Grebes are fairly common now but it was a very different story about a hundred or so years ago when they were brought to the brink of extinction in this country. It became highly fashionable for ladies to wear the skins of Crested Grebes, with their thick layers of soft silky feathers as a decorative accessory. It is thought that as a result of being hunted there may have been as little as thirty-two pairs left in this country. Laws were passed in the late 1800's to stop this exploitation and happily the numbers of pairs slowly increased. At the time of the last census in 1975, there were some six-and-a-half thousand pairs nesting in Britain.

We tried to get as close as possible to any Grebes we came across, but they never allowed us very close. They would submerge gracefully with hardly a ripple, we would then try to guess where they would re-surface, sometimes they would reappear behind us. They swim entirely with their feet, keeping their wings tightly folded to their sides.

We were glad we had bothered to put on our wet weather attire before starting out because by the time we had reached the end of the Goring Gap it had started to drizzle again. Here, at the southern end, the Great Western Railway yet again crosses the Thames via another of Brunel's impressive brick built, arched bridges.

The valley briefly narrows quite considerably again as it passes Hartslock Wood on the left bank. The trees seem to be scrambling out of the water and on up to the top of a lofty hill which forms the southern end of the Chilterns.

As the valley begins to broaden out again, we passed Basildon Park on our right bank. This area of the river has a profusion of fine, 'mansion type' houses and Basildon House on the slope of a hill overlooking the Thames is one of the best. It's said to be the finest Georgian mansion in Berkshire. It was bought by Lord and Lady Iliffe in 1952 when it was virtually derelict, who then restored it into the splendid house it is today. The National Trust now looks after it.

Almost adjoining Basildon Park is the Child Beale Wildlife Park. By all accounts it's a curious mixture of exotic animals and birds, statues, modern and antique model boats, gardens and play areas, in a water and woodland setting. It was formed in 1956 by Gilbert Beale on a three-hundred-and-fifty-acre site of his farmland. He wanted to 'give to the people' through a non-profit making charitable trust. He died in 1967 but his great nephew, Richard Howard, continued to make additions to the park. Evidently well worth a visit but not on a grey drizzling day. We passed by on the other side.

The reach above Whitchurch Lock is very wide and often busy with sailing and rowing boats from Pangbourne college, but all sane folks who had a choice in the matter were keeping well away from 'Old Father Thames' on such a dreary day and so we mostly had the river to ourselves. There were, still of course, those who did not have the choice of staying away. I refer to the holiday makers who had saved and spent a great deal of money to hire a cruiser for a week or two. Life afloat on warm sunny days and barmy evenings is ideal. When it's wet and cold it's a whole different world.

Several 'holiday boats' had passed us and those on board all seemed to have the same expression on their faces which conveyed the same message. We are bored and wish we had gone to Spain for our holiday. However, some seemed to brighten up momentarily when they saw the two rain sodden, hooded canoeists at the mercy of the elements gamely paddling along.

As we approached Pangbourne and Whitchurch Lock we passed on the Berkshire side, seven distinctive Edwardian houses known as 'The Seven Deadly Sins'. They were built by D.H Evans, the shop owner who, it was alleged, kept a mistress in each of them.

The relentless drizzle had been replaced by a steady heavy downpour, when at eleven, we reached the sanctuary of The Swan, just above Whitchurch Lock and weir. Ironically, The Swan plays a prominent part in Jerome K. Jerome's Three Men in a Boat, for it's here, on their way back, that the three of them, and a 'shame faced dog,' decide to 'run away from the rain' and abandon their trip by returning to London by train from Pangbourne station. The two of us where in complete sympathy with their feelings and fleetingly considered following suit but a very brief discussion dismissed any ideas of abandonment by a unanimous vote. Incidentally, the book was published in 1889 on the 3rd of September, which happens to be the day and month of my birthday.

We hastily adjourned to the warmth of The Swan, both feeling I think, a little embarrassed for even fleetingly contemplating a premature end to our trip. Having abandoned our waterproofs in the gents we settled down at a window seat overlooking the river with a pint each, a whiskey chaser and some dry roasted.

The Swan is a beautifully situated 17th century listed building with a wealth of traditional oak beams. A fanciful story goes that once upon a time the county boundary between Oxfordshire and Berkshire ran down the middle of the bar. The two counties had differing licensing hours, and it is alleged that when the landlord called time at one end of the bar the customers simply picked up their drinks and continued drinking at the other end!

We had the bar to ourselves which was just as well because the 'wet trainer aroma' didn't take long to kick in. The barman didn't comment but his regular glances in our direction made it clear that he was noticing the atmospheric change in his bar since we had walked in. When I went up to the bar for a couple of refills, I somehow felt he expected an explanation of who and what we were. After I had introduced ourselves and outlined our mission, he became an intent inquisitor wanting to know every detail of the past six days and of our future plans. His curiosity seemed insatiable and he seemed genuinely intrigued in all the whys and wherefores of our trip.

Kev soon joined us and we sat at the bar with our new found friend. Several whiskies later the usual verbal diarrhoea set in and we were swapping life stories and future plans as if the three of us had been comrades for years. He was twenty-six, came from New Zealand and was on a tour of Europe. He had been working at The Swan for two weeks and was planning to head off up to Scotland in a few weeks' time to meet up with an Australian girl he had met in London. So far, he had been away for five months and had been to France, Switzerland, Holland and Germany. He had three brothers and a sister; his mother's name was Francis and his dog was called Jake.

Kevin soon got into his stride and with a certain amount of embellishment, retold some of our experiences from the past forty or so years, some of which I didn't actually recall! A glass or three of scotch always seems to jog Kev's memory and imagination.

Our story swopping came to an abrupt end when a party of six entered the bar and needed serving. Just as well as the whiskey was beginning to flow all too easily. A glimpse through the window confirmed that it was still raining hard so we retired to the gents to be reunited with our waterproofs. For some reason this caused a certain amount of hilarity between the two of us. When we re-emerged back into the bar, we received some very inquiring looks from the party of six who must have heard our raucous laughter emanating from the toilet.

It was by now nearly twelve-thirty and we had lingered for longer than intended but before setting off we found it necessary to again bail out several inches of rain water which had accumulated in the canoe. We found this chore also unaccountably funny, which was witnessed by the seven incredulous faces peering through the window from the sanctuary of The Swan. This being one of our longer days, thirteen and a half miles, we still had about nine and a half to go before reaching the evening stop over at Sonning. But not even the pouring rain could dampen our enthusiasm as we set off in high spirits. Spirits, I'm afraid, being the significant word.

Within a few minutes we reached Whitchurch Lock and not surprisingly had it to ourselves. It's situated on an island and is the only lock solely accessible by boat. In spite of the weather the lock keeper was very cheerful and as usual, was expecting us.

Beside the weir is a splendid boathouse in which Jimmy Page once lived. It was here in 1968 that he and Robert Plant met and formed what was to become the legendary English rock band, 'Led Zeppelin'.

As soon as we left the lock, we passed under the distinctive white painted, Victorian, iron lattice work road bridge which links Whitchurch to Pangbourne. It's one of the only two Thames bridges still charging a toll to cross, Swinford being the other. Pedestrians, pigs and sheep used to be charged one half penny each, carriages were charged two pennies for each wheel. Today motor vehicles are charged sixty new pence, regardless of how many wheels they have; pedestrians cross free of charge.

Between the lock and the toll bridge, the river Pang joins the Thames. The large village of Pangbourne, bourne meaning stream, derives its name from this tiny river. Kenneth Graham, the author of the classic book, The Wind in The Willows, published in 1908, lived opposite the church in Pangbourne until his death in 1932 and he's buried in the churchyard. He wrote his book from stories he made up for his four-year-old son as together they explored the rivers Pang and Thames. For his funeral, the church was decorated with willow branches collected that morning from the riverside.

Willows, more than any other tree, are associated with rivers and there are many species of the tree. The White Willow, the Crack Willow, the Cricket Bat Willow and the Chinese Golden Weeping

Willow, are some of the commonest to be found growing along the streams and riverbanks of Britain.

The White and Crack Willow are the largest native species and are often planted along banks to help prevent water erosion of the soil. The White Willow is rich in salicin, a chemical used in the tanning of leather and formerly for making aspirin.

The Crack Willow has extremely fragile twigs which snap easily, hence its name. The seeds are dispersed by being carried downstream on the broken twigs. Willow seeds need to find very moist conditions within a few days if they are to germinate. All Willows grow very easily from cuttings and often Willow fence posts will sprout new growth.

The Crack and the White Willow hybridize freely and the commonest hybrid between the two is the Cricket Bat Willow. It's fast growing, the wood is tough, pliable and light, making it ideal for constructing cricket bats. It's said you can get a dozen bats from one fully grown tree. The trees are often pollarded to produce straight branches, used for hurdle making, fence posts and such like.

Weeping Willow

The Chinese, Golden Weeping Willow, which droop their branches into the water like curtains, were only introduced into this country about two-hundred-and-fifty years ago. They cannot propagate on their own, they need the intervention of man to spread. Which explains why you only tend to see them at the water's edge at the ends of gardens and not along wild, uncultivated stretches of rivers and streams. Many of Whitchurch's houses and gardens run down to the river and many fine species of the Weeping Willow are present along this stretch of the Thames.

Below Pangbourne and Whitchurch the river flows through exposed open farmland for a couple of miles. On the Oxfordshire bank we passed a large expanse of meadowland which was occupied by a substantial herd of Peruvian Alpacas looking pretty miserable in the rain. They were part of Europe's leading Alpaca stud.

It was now raining with a vengeance, but our refuelling stop at The Swan and taking it in turns to make up and sing, at the tops of our voices, new verses of 'Messing About With the Lizard', kept us going. A couple of boats passed us going in our direction and judging by the gloomy looks on the crews faces they had passed The Swan without stopping.

There is little sign of human habitation along this two-and-a-half-mile stretch to Mapledurham, apart from the very impressive Hardwick House, one of the oldest houses along the Thames. The house nestles amongst some trees whilst its lawn sweeps down majestically to the river. Queen Elizabeth I stayed on one her 'Grande Progresses' around England. Whenever Elizabeth became tired of living in London, she would let it be known that she would be staying uninvited in one of her wealthy subject's grand houses for several weeks. She would take her entire entourage with her who needed to be accommodated and fed at the expense of the host. This was known as her 'Grande Progresses'. Another royal connection to the house was that Charles I is known to have played bowls on the lawn towards the end of his reign.

It was damaged during the Civil War but was restored soon after. There are rumours that a considerable stash of money was secreted somewhere in the grounds at the beginning of hostilities. It has never been found in spite of subsequent owners making numerous searches. The house boasts of having two 'real tennis' courts.

Hardwick House is now privately owned by Sir Julian Rose whose great grandfather is said by some to be the model for 'Toad' and the house, Kenneth Grahame's inspiration for 'Toad Hall'. But there are two more houses which also lay claim to stimulating Grahame's imagination, one nearby which we would soon pass and the other a couple of days further downstream at Cookham Dean where he spent his childhood.

The wide-open meadows on our right seemed to be used extensively for cattle grazing and there were many obvious places where the bank had been worn down by the cows enabling them to wade into the river to drink. At one such spot we passed a group of eight standing in the water up to their udders.

As we approached Mapledurham lock in torrential rain, Kev's mobile rang. He answered then immediately handed it to me as I was in the front and he needed to steer from the back. It was Star FM Radio, Slough, wanting to make a tape for airing later of our progress and plans. The female researcher asked if we were enjoying the trip. I tried to sound as cheerful as I could and answered in the affirmative just as a deafening clap of thunder erupted directly overhead triggering the rain to fall in an even greater volume. Kev felt the need to stop paddling and commence his bailing out routine with the plastic pint mug which we had saved for such emergencies. As there was now no steerage 'the lizard' decided to turn herself around. As we gently drifted backwards downstream in the middle of the river while Kevin gamely battled against the rain to keep the water level in the canoe below shin level, I answered her questions while endeavouring to remain positive and calm amongst the lightning and trying to make myself heard above the booming thunderclaps. We've often wondered how the interview sounded over the radio. I wish we could have heard it!

In retrospect we had been in a very dangerous and vulnerable situation. We should have pulled over to the side and stopped, tucking ourselves as close into the bank as possible. Our attitude had been far too macho and blasé, which reinforces the message, 'don't drink and drive'!

The thunder soon abated and moved on, unfortunately leaving the rain behind. It was a pity that the weather was so appalling because Mapledurham Lock and its adjacent mill are particularly picturesque. Over the years the lock has won a number of awards for the best kept lock and best garden. It was the first to be mechanised, in 1956.

The 15th century brick and timber mill is the only flour mill still working on the Thames albeit now driven by electricity. It was fully restored to working order in 1977 after lying dormant for thirty years. It can, I'm informed, now produce one ton of flour in six hours. Fringed by trees, on a fine day it's an artist dream. It's featured on the cover of an album, released in 1970, by the heavy metal band, Black Sabbath.

We shared the lock with a medium sized cruiser. All of its crew remained ensconced in the cabin apart from one dejected looking youngster who had been assigned for the rope duty, I don't think he had volunteered! We tried to engage him in conversation but to no avail.

About a quarter of a mile from the lock the extensive lawn of Mapledurham House runs down to the river. It's privately owned, still occupied by the descendants of the Blount family who bought the original Manor in 1390. The present building is of Elizabethan origin. It's one of a very few English houses that have never been sold on to other families. Mapledurham House is the other house in the area said to be the inspiration for 'Toad Hall'.

A beautifully maintained timber built Edwardian boathouse with its characteristic living quarters above for the boatman and a balcony over the water, is situated at the end of the lawn. At one time, no self-respecting, well to do householder with a frontage on the river would have been without one. They are now becoming rare but a few still remain between Oxford and Windsor.

The rain had decreased to a drizzle as we passed the outskirts of the village of Purley which marks the beginning of the Reading conurbation. The river soon began to run alongside the railway separating us from Tilehurst, with open farmland to our left. Now a suburb or Reading, Tilehurst was once a centre for brick and tile making.

Relics and Rain

We parted company with the railway after about a mile when the river curved to the left across a wide flood plain, the site of the annual Reading rock festival, held during the August bank holiday weekend and preparations were well under way. The Thames is quite wide here as it passes Caversham, sprawling away to our left, another suburb of Reading.

We approached Reading with a somewhat apprehensive attitude. Remembering that Jerome K. Jerome had written, perhaps unkindly, 'one does not linger in the neighbourhood of Reading'. Having watched the film Deliverance, a week or two before setting out, we were on the lookout for any locals sitting on bridges playing banjos! In fact, the run into Reading was not at all unpleasant with small, well-kept gardens of chalets and bungalows lining the north bank. The Thames actually bisects Reading and Caversham and flows well away from the centre of the town itself thus little of Reading is actually sampled.

Just above Caversham Bridge is a landscaped public garden called Caversham Court which is listed as Grade 2 in the National Register of Historic Parks and Gardens. The area was once the centre of the medieval community of Caversham. In the 12th century the Earl of Buckingham donated the land, now occupied by the gardens, to an Augustinian Abbey then situated near Long Crendon in Buckinghamshire, who established a small monastic cell on the site. Later, a shrine was also built for Our Lady of Caversham, which became the 'home' to such relics as, the head of the spear that pierced the side of Christ on the cross. During the Middle Ages it became one the most important shrines to the Virgin Mary. It was demolished during the years of the Dissolution but in 1663 a brick and flint gazebo was erected on the site of the shrine, which is still there to this day.

After the Dissolution of the Monasteries between 1536 and 1541 the land was given over to Christchurch, Oxford who built a rectory on the site which became known as Caversham Court, in the

1840s it was redesigned as a gothic mansion. In 1933 the house was demolished but the gardens remain as a public park.

The Three Men In A Boat pub is situated just before Caversham bridge. It was 2pm, pouring with rain again and we were wet and hungry. The area was obviously the meeting place for all the local swans for at least sixty of them were cruising around, most of them by the pubs landing stage, the place where they were usually supplied with plenty of food. Today, they were disappointed as nobody had ventured out in such inclement weather, except for the two who were approaching in the red canoe. We were soon surrounded and we seemed in danger of being boarded but the pub with its promise of food and warmth awakened the bravery within us and we battled unflinching through the mob to the sanctuary of the inn. It's a very modern building and an unlikely looking Thames pub but it has a fine view of the bridge and Caversham church amongst the trees on the far bank.

The present concrete Caversham bridge was built in 1926 but the original was erected in the 13th century and at one time had St Ann's chapel upon it which supposedly housed two more notable relics. A piece of the rope with which Judas hung himself and the 'blessed knife' that killed St Edward. These relics were delivered to the chapel by an angel with only one wing. No mean feat as surely an angel with such a disability would have tended to fly around in circles! How the angel obtained the relics and why St Ann's chapel was selected as their resting place remains a mystery. The chapel became a popular place of pilgrimage in the Middle Ages, as did the nearby St Anne's Well for people with eye diseases.

Before entering The Three Men In A Boat, we noticed a large poster pinned to the door informing all who entered that the selling or taking of drugs would not be tolerated on the premises. There was no mention of the playing of banjos.

The interior was spacious with oars and old photographs of the Thames adorning the walls and large windows overlooked the river. Again, we removed our top layer of clothes in the gents and utilised the hand blow-dryers to attempt to dry ourselves off a little but we still looked like competitors for a wet T-shirt competition when we re- entered the bar. Soup, sandwiches and beer were taken which soon had the desired effect of reviving our damp souls.

We spent a pleasant hour recuperating in the pub before resuming our journey which was immediately interrupted, as almost opposite there was another quite modern 'pavilion looking' hostelry called, Pipers Island. The building takes up most of a tiny island and the only access is by a footbridge that connects the island to the centre of Caversham Bridge, or via the river and its landing stage. A quick whiskey each was downed and photograph taken before we continued on our way. It was our twenty-eighth 'stop' since leaving Cricklade six and a half days ago.

Half a mile down from Caversham bridge we passed Fry's Island on which is the only bowls club in Britain reached by ferry. It's also known as De Montford Island, so named after a duel fought there in 1163 between Henry Earl of Essex, the King's constable and standard-bearer, and Robert De Montford.

De Montford had accused Essex of cowardice by dropping the Royal Standard and fleeing during the Battle of Coleshill in 1157. Essex strongly denied the charge saying that he had thought the King had been slain and the battle lost. So, the King, Henry II, decreed that the dispute was to be resolved by a trial by combat. 'Let God judge between them'. It was watched by thousands including the King. Essex fell, believed dead, and was taken to Reading Abbey to be buried but he was found to be still alive and was tended night and day by the monks until he recovered. As he had lost the combat, he was adjudged of being a traitor to the King. His lands were confiscated and he was stripped of his honours but he was permitted to become a monk. He remained at the Abbey for the rest of his life.

Soon after passing Fry's Island, we passed under the graceful looking Reading Bridge which links the centre of Reading to Caversham. Built in 1923 it was the first bridge to be built on this site.

We shared Caversham lock, just below the bridge, with a small cruiser manned by a young, bedraggled family on their first holiday afloat. They were very chatty and were trying very hard to put on a brave face. We pointed out to them that things weren't so bad because at least they had a warm cabin into which they could retreat and when the sun came out the mood and ambience of the river would completely change. The burgers and sausages would be on the barbecue, mum and dad would be on their second glass of wine and the two boys would be happily fishing in the warm, early evening sun. Hopefully, they left us with this vision in their heads and waved as they headed off into the rest of the dreary day.

A half a mile below the lock the river Kennet joins the Thames. It's one the rivers major tributaries, flowing through the centre of Reading. The Kennet is the start of one of England's major inland waterways, The Kennett and Avon canal. It was opened in 1810 to link London to Bristol taking a route through Reading, Devizes and Bath. It closed in the 1950s and fell into decay. Since then, it has been painstakingly restored and is now completely navigable once more.

Perhaps Jerome K. Jerome and I have given an unfair impression of Reading because Kevin and I had quite a pleasant paddle along this particular stretch of the river, apart from the rain. Reading has a long and interesting history attached to it.

Evidence of an Iron Age settlement has been found and Romano-British artifacts have been unearthed all over the town. Alfred the Great lost a battle in AD870 against the invading Danes on the water meadow between the Thames and Kennett, known today as Kings Meadow. He defeated them in the following battle on the Downs above Wantage. In the Norman Doomsday Book 'Radynges' is recorded as a small village with thirty houses.

An Abbey was founded in 1121 by Henry I and no expense was spared. It eventually became one of the greatest in the Kingdom. It became the focus of enormous reverence as it boasted of having yet more, exceptional holy relics. A piece of the Lord's shoe, a tooth belonging to St Luke and a small piece from Mose's rod. The area around Reading seems to have attracted relics! In 1135 Henry was buried before the high altar before his church was completed. He had died in Normandy supposedly of food poisoning from eating too many eels. It took forty years for the vast church of the abbey to be finalised and was eventually consecrated by Thomas Becket in the presence of Henry II.

In 1539, Henry VIII closed the Abbey during the Dissolution and had the Abbot, Hugh Farrington, together with two of his priests, publicly hung, drawn and quartered for denying the King's supremacy. The tomb of Henry I was destroyed and the King's bones thrown out with other debris to make room for a stable. Soon after, the Abbey became a royal residence. Parliament frequently sat at Reading when driven out of London by plague.

Early prosperity came to the town through its cloth trade which had Royal backing. A story relates that a rich Reading clothier by the name of Thomas Cole, obtained from Edward I, the first standard measure for cloth, the yard, the precise length of his majesty's arm. A Mulberry tree, on which silkworms feed on the leaves, was sent to Reading by Queen Elizabeth I to encourage its silk industry.

Reading also became well known for its beer. In 1700 you could have visited one-hundred and four pubs which were supplied by twenty-one breweries within the town. I wonder how many of the pubs had a frontage onto the river?

Oscar Wilde was imprisoned in Reading gaol in 1897 for 'homosexual practices'. While there he wrote, De Profundis. He actually wrote, The Ballad of Reading Gael, a year later whilst in Paris.

> 'I never saw a man who looked with such a wistful eye,
> Upon that little tent of blue which prisoners call the sky.'

Later Reading became synonymous with two well-known businesses, Huntley and Palmers Biscuits and Suttons Seeds, neither remain. Fragmented ruins of the abbey can still be seen, and the 13th century gatehouse is still standing.

Reading is the County town of Berkshire. Chris Tarrant, Arthur Negus, Ricky Gervais, Kate Winslet and Mike Oldfield, amongst many others, were born in the town.

After Caversham lock the river veers around King's Meadow and then heads off through some uninspiring scenery of pylons, gasometers and factories. On the left bank we passed extensive gravel workings, from what was originally meadowland, in various stages of production.

After about half an hour we had left the ugliness behind and rounded a right-hand bend to approach Sonning Lock. It had almost stopped raining and the sun was making a valiant effort to break through the clouds. Several more boats had now passed us going in either direction, had they been privy to the forthcoming weather forecast?

We reached the picturesque Sonning Lock at 4:25 and sought permission from the lockkeeper to leave the canoe in his garden. Permission was kindly granted so we left her safety padlocked to his fence and set off the few hundred metres along the towpath with our baggage to Sonning village in search of The Bull. It always felt good to get one's legs working again after a few hours paddling and the walk along the path was particularly pleasant. It had stopped raining at last and the hazy sun was making its presence felt as it pushed its way through the clouds making the various shades of the prominent colour green seem fresh and new.

James Sadler, a former poet and lockkeeper of Sonning Lock, wrote:

'Is there a spot more lovely than the rest;

By art improved, by Nature really blest?

A noble river at its base is running,

It is a little village known as Sonning'.

A few metres down from the lock we passed an ornate metal gate with two crossed oars. An inscription read, 'The Denys Amos

Gate, a master of Reading Blue Coat School who drowned on January the 26th 1953'.

Centuries ago, the bishops of Salisbury had a palace here, the site of which can be seen just above Sonning Lock as a mound in the grounds of a Victorian Gothic mansion known as Holme Park, now the home of Reading Blue Coat School. It was here at the palace in 1399 that Henry IV locked away Isabella of France, the young queen of the deposed Richard II. She was a child bride of only eight years old when she married Richard. He was forbidden to ever see her again. It is said that her 'fair and youthful ghost' can often be seen walking by the river sobbing and sighing.

At the height the English Civil War in 1646, a wealthy London merchant left a sum of money to the corporation of Reading which was 'to be devoted to the education and upbringing of twenty-four male children'. That was the inception of the Reading Blue Coat School.

The school is now ranked as one of the best ten private schools in the country. It caters for boys from the age of eleven to eighteen and for girls in the sixth form, totalling over seven-hundred pupils. It's renowned for its sporting prowess, rowing being especially strong, annually competing at the Royal Henley Regatta.

We rounded a bend and the eleven, soft red brick arches of Sonning Bridge immediately caught our eyes set against a backdrop of Weeping Willows, a popular subject for numerous artists throughout the years. The present bridge was built in 1775 to replace an earlier wooden one and is a Grade 2 listed building. To the right of the bridge the tower of the village church peered over the treetops and to the left, situated on its own island and surrounded by giant Plane trees, was Sonning Mill.

A mill was in existence here from Saxon times right up until 1969 when the then 18th century flour mill, which supplied flour for the Huntley and Palmer biscuits, was converted into a theatre where many well-known actors have performed. For the price of your ticket, you are served with dinner before watching the performance, and from past experience I can say it's well worth a visit!

Legend has it that it was along this stretch between the lock and the bridge that Dick Turpin would often swim across the river to the Oxford side to escape his pursuers after a successful hold up on the nearby Bath Road. The Berkshire authorities having no jurisdiction in Oxfordshire and the river being the boundary between the two counties. The legend goes on to say that his horse, Black Bess, would meanwhile find her way back to a stable at his aunt's house in Sonning village to await his return. The original cottage was the middle one of a group of three, but they have now been knocked into two, one named Rich's Cottage and the other Turpin's Cottage.

We found The Bull in the centre of the village. Built in the 16th century and originally known as Church House, it was used as the guest house for pilgrims visiting the medieval chapel in St Andrew's church which stands opposite. The chapel became a popular place of pilgrimage in the Middle Ages for the mentally ill.

The Bull is aptly described by Jerome K. Jerome in Three Men in a Boat as: 'a veritable picture of a country inn, with green, square courtyard in front, where, on seats beneath the trees, the old men group of an evening to drink their ale and gossip over village politics; with low, quaint windows and latticed windows, and awkward stairs and winding passages.' Little has changed.

We were shown to our large, low ceilinged room whose uneven floor sloped very obviously towards the window at quite an incline. A very substantial wooden double bed dominated the room. Next to it was a small metal camp bed. I lost the toss!

After showering and a change of dry clothes we went for a wander around the village. Charles Dickens had a liking for Sonning, referring to the village he wrote: 'a few minutes' walk inland will disclose as pretty a little place as could be desired, containing many excellent houses with good old-fashioned gardens.'

We found Dick Turpin's aunt's cottage and then headed back towards the river as we needed to have a drink and photo at The

Great House, which is adjacent to the river. Now extensively modernised into a hotel and bar it was formerly a public house known as The White Hart. In 1989 it was combined with a previously private house to become The Great House with an extensive riverside garden overlooking the bridge.

Before heading back to The Bull, we paid a visit to The Mill Theatre which I knew had a rather pleasant bar in which some of the mills original working parts are still to be seen in situ. Although not having tickets for the evening performance we were permitted to stay and enjoy a couple of beers. As it was not strictly a pub or inn, we agreed it wouldn't count in our final tally.

In the mill's bar we happened upon two acquaintances of mine from my village, Mike and Pat. They had driven the forty-minute journey from home to have a meal and watch a performance. They had not been aware of our trip so were keen to know all the details.

Back at The Bull we both enjoyed a fine steak with all the trimmings helped down with a bottle of red. Afterwards we chatted which some of the locals in the bar but it became very crowded and smoky and so by 10.30 we had had enough and decided to retire to our room. It had been a hard day. One of our longer days, thirteen and a half miles, in mostly very unpleasant conditions and we were more than ready for a good night's sleep.

It wasn't long before Kev had settled down in his large king-sized bed with its feather mattress - and I had crawled into my narrow, single, rickety, metal camp bed. He was soon asleep but I found it difficult to drop off, or what is more correct, I found it difficult to sleep because I did keep dropping off. I found it surprisingly difficult to stay in the bed. After rolling out for the third time I realized the reason for these involuntary ejections. My extremely slender bed was parallel to the window towards which, as mentioned before, the floor had a very distinct downward bias. Every time I turned over it was like rolling down a hill. From my lowly position I could see under the large double bed and could make out that its two 'downside' legs were propped up with blocks of wood to ensure its occupants remained horizontal.

I moved my bed into a perpendicular position, not without difficulty and not without waking my fractious companion who didn't understand the problem. I was now lying with my head nearest the window which meant that my feet were higher than my head and my pillow would not remain on the bed. Once again, my cantankerous friend was disturbed as I changed alignment, feet nearest the window this time. I did wake a few more times in the night to haul myself back up the slope as my legs seemed keen to dangle over the end of the bed.

CHAPTER 13

Dining Al Fresco

Sonning to Hurley – 12.5 miles

Thursday the 19th of August dawned bright and cheerful. The grey, damp atmosphere had retreated leaving a completely new and fresh feel to the day. Fine weather always seems to lift the spirits and we were soon up and ready and looking forward to our twelve-and-a-half-mile paddle to Hurley. As mentioned, we had planned to camp at Hurley and the last two wet days had made it seem that a daunting experience was awaiting us, but with the change in the weather we were now looking forward to the different style of accommodation. We were down for breakfast at a quarter to eight which shows how keen we were to be on the move.

There was one other customer in the breakfast room dressed in a smart dark suit which contrasted starkly with our usual canoeing garb. We exchanged pleasantries and settled down for a 'Full English'. After a minute or two the gentleman in the corner approached our table. "Excuse me," he said, "are you the two canoeists I heard about on the radio doing a pub crawl down the Thames for charity?" We told him we were, whereupon he placed a fiver on the table. "Well good luck, I wish I could join you but I've got work to do." And with that he departed before we could properly thank him.

We were halfway back to the river when one of us suddenly realised we had left our 'canoeing trainers' still sitting on the windowsill outside our bedroom window. We always tended to avoid wearing them at breakfast times in respect for the other diners. Kev went back to retrieve them while I sat on one of the blue barrels to await his return. I got to thinking back over our journey so far and how we had witnessed the gradual change of the river as it had slowly matured from a small, wild, undisciplined infant into, a not quite knowing which direction to take teenager, to a confident young adult who had ambitions and knew what it was aiming for. Now it was well into its middle age, confident, having achieved what it had set out to do. It had slowed down and was taking life easy looking forward to retirement.

It was dead on nine when we passed beneath Sonning Bridge, we were in high spirits, looking forward to Henley, one of the towns most associated with the Thames. We both know the town fairly well, it being quite near to my home, and so we were already acquainted with some of the 'stops' we would be taking.

The river glided lazily through low meadows, bordered by trees and bushes with the Chiltern Hills to its left. We paddled happily along in silence, both of us enjoying the warm sun on our backs which made a welcome change to the damp and cold of the previous few days.

The change in the weather had enticed a plethora of delicate damselflies to show off their aerial skills only inches above the water. Some as individuals but many in tandem as a prelude to mating.

There are twenty-one species of British damselflies which resemble small vividly coloured dragonflies, of which there are thirty-six British species. Often confused with one another, there are several basic differences, apart from size, which distinguishes the two types of insect. Damselflies have a slender body with a silent, weak fluttering flight, whereas the dragonfly has a stout body and a powerful flight resembling a miniature whirring helicopter. When at rest, a damselfly will fold its wings together akin to butterflies but a dragonfly at rest will always hold its wings out flat on either side, as do moths. Both have two pairs of wings resembling gauze.

Damsels and dragons both feed on other insects, more often than not taking them on the wing using their large efficient eyes to seek out and pursue them.

Damselfly

The female of both species lay their eggs in the water often walking backwards down the stems of plants until they are submerged to a depth of several inches. The eggs hatch into larvae, known as nymphs, which remain underwater living on the bottom amongst aquatic plants for up to two years. Highly carnivorous, they feed on anything they can tackle. As with the adults, the nymph of a damselfly is smaller and has a slenderer body. Another difference is the damselfly nymph has three conspicuous, feather like gills at the tail end of the body whereas the gills of the dragonfly nymph are concealed internally.

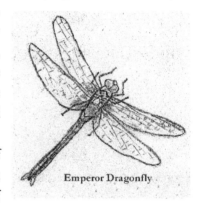
Emperor Dragonfly

When mature, the nymph of both species crawls up the stem of a plant until it's clear of the surface of the water. Their backs split open and out of the skin crawls the fully formed adult. After waiting a few minutes for its wings to dry it flies away leaving its empty nymph skin behind still clinging to the plant. Yet another of nature's miracles.

Damselflies live for a couple of weeks as flying adults. If very lucky, a dragonfly can live for up to four months in its flying stage.

We drifted past the white mansion of the famous spoon bender Yuri Geller. A regular visitor to his home was his firm friend Michael Jackson.

About a mile below Sonning, on our right, there appeared to be a smallish tributary of the Thames but on closer inspection it's clear that instead of flowing into the main river it was an outflow. It's the beginning of a backwater of the Thames called St Patrick's Stream which, after a couple of miles joins the river Loddon that flows into the Thames downstream just below Shiplake Lock. Saint Patrick's Stream is probably the only backwater of the Thames that bypasses a lock before rejoining the river.

Another half mile downstream we wound our way around two large uninhabited wooded islands before passing the village of Shiplake situated a little inland. In June 1850, the poet Alfred Tennyson married Emily Sellwood in the church at Shiplake. It was the same year he became The Poet Laureate. He wrote a poem for the vicar in lieu of the fee:-

> 'Vicar of this pleasant spot
> Where it was my chance to marry
> Happy happy be your lot
> In your vicarage by the quarry'

A contrasting literary association is that of George Orwell, the author of Animal Farm, who lived in Shiplake as a boy. One of his well-known quotes being, 'Big brother is watching you'.

Shiplake Lock was full of craft coming upstream with a downstream queue waiting to enter. We pulled over to the bankside to join the procession and await our turn. We had perfected the art of holding onto tufts of grass on the bank to keep ourselves steady, unfortunately, on this occasion, I didn't notice the young stinging nettles nestling amongst the grass.

We were instructed to enter the lock last which was much safer for us when sharing a full lock, being so much smaller and frailer than the other vessels. There was just enough room for us to squeeze in on this occasion. Even after successfully negotiating twenty-five other locks it still felt intimidating, rather like an egg sharing a box with half a dozen cricket balls.

It was now quite warm and we had worked up a good thirst but we had to be content with 'Adam's ale' from the water bottle.

Wargrave was about a mile further downstream. Unfortunately, all the pubs were inland along the high street. So, we had to bide our time until we reached Henley, a further two miles on, before our next watering hole.

Just below Shiplake lock, the other end of the backwater we passed further upstream, now the River Lodden, slips quietly into the Thames. Around this marshy area through which the little river flows, the internationally rare Lodden Lily can be found, also known as the Summer Snowflake because of its hanging bells of green tinged, white flowers. It was rediscovered a few years ago by local naturalists after being lost for over 30 years. Rather careless of them!

Lodden lily

Almost immediately a rather ugly railway bridge supported by cast iron cylinders crosses the river carrying a branch line to Henley. In the 1970's the line was reduced to a single track and one part of the twin span was removed but for some reason, the redundant cast iron supports were left in situ.

About half a mile from Shiplake we passed Wargrave which looks down on the river from slightly rising ground. The church at Wargrave was burned down in 1914, supposedly by the suffragettes, because the vicar refused to omit the word obey from the marriage service. The village has attracted several vintage celebrities to set up home in its community, amongst others were Dave Allen the comedian, the magician Paul Daniels and Vince Hill the famous singer from the 60's.

The river now weaves its way through a group of islands and passes some rather impressive wooden boat houses. This area is surprisingly noted for Brent Geese that usually haunt the seashore. It's a winter visitor spending the summer months breeding in northern Russia.

About the size of a Mallard duck, it has black, white and grey plumage and omits a deep croak.

At the beginning of August one of the oldest and largest regattas on the Thames, second only to Henley, is held annually over a weekend along this stretch of the river. The Wargrave and Shiplake Regatta has nearly one thousand competitors competing in about four hundred races over a short course of four hundred yards. The craft raced are skiffs, punts and Canadian canoes, in serious and fun events for boys, girls, gentlemen, ladies, mixed and veterans. What a pity we had just missed it. Just as well though, because as Kev pointed out we didn't have room in the canoe for a trophy. Just to prove a point we did a hundred stroke sprint.

After our workout we proceeded slowly and quietly along enjoying the warm sun. We spotted a heron standing motionless in the shallows, fishing so intently that we were able to cautiously approach to within a fairly short distance. Suddenly it struck, which resulted in an eel dangling from its spear-like bill.

Eels have always been an important source of food for both herons and humans. Once so common in the Thames they were an important staple food for the poor. They are a snake like fish normally growing to around sixty to eighty centimetres in length, rarely over a metre, and can be as thick as your wrist. Eels are carnivorous hunting mainly at night feeding on worms, snails, small frogs and fish. Adult eels can survive for a time out of water and can slither some distance over wet grass to occupy, as well as rivers, ponds, lakes and water filled ditches.

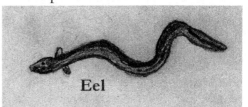
Eel

The European Eel has a fascinating life cycle. They spawn in an area of the Western Atlantic near the Bahamas known as the Saragossa Sea. After the female releases her eggs and the male has fertilised them, both the adults die.

After hatching the tiny larvae drift towards Europe in the current taking about three-hundred days. When approaching the coast, they turn into their transparent larvae stage called 'glass eels'. As they enter the estuaries and migrate upstream they change into miniature versions of an adult eel. At this stage they are known as elvers.

As the eels grow they becomes known as 'yellow eels' because of their yellow brownish colour. After spending about twenty years in freshwater they become sexually mature and at this stage they're now called 'silver eels' after the silver colour of their flanks. The mature eels now begin their long migration back to the Saragossa Sea to spawn and die.

For thousands of years men have caught eels using many varieties of methods including using funnel nets, especially adapted spears and trapping in wicker baskets. Anglers sometimes land them on a rod and line but as an eel is extremely slimy and tends to tangle the line, they are not always a welcome catch. Once extremely prevalent, the European Eel is now one of the most endangered species of our freshwater fish.

As we approached Marsh Lock we passed, on the right bank, a narrow valley with a striped lawn leading uphill, it's known as Happy Valley. It leads to a huge French Renaissance style house called Park Place. Queen Victoria nearly bought the house in 1865. Apparently, after visiting the house in disguise to look it over, she decided against it.

We floated leisurely on downstream enjoying the river after the previous day's miserable weather. Just as the fine weather had enticed out the damselflies it had also encouraged more of the boating fraternity out onto the water again, the crews all looking so much more cheerful.

Marsh Lock was full and an orderly queue of mixed craft had formed awaiting their turn. There were also quite a few folk standing or sitting around just watching and enjoying the sunshine. The lock is only a short walk along the towpath from Henley. As usual we were waved to the front of the queue by the lockkeeper to be squeezed in with the next batch to enter.

We were carefully positioned next to a beautifully presented narrow boat complete with the traditional paintings of roses and castles, shining brass and pots of bright red geraniums on the roof. It was the pride and joy of an elderly, retired couple who told us they had spent the last five years living on their boat during the summer months, exploring the Thames and canals, and hibernating in their council flat during the winter. All the artwork was of their 'own doing'.

To visit the lock by foot requires a long traverse across a wooden walkway spanning the weir stream. The reason being, a cornmill, later to become a brass foundry, once blocked the towpath.

Kayakers were 'white water' canoeing in the weir pool, fearlessly tackling the angry, turbulent water as it spewed down through the sluice gates. Some were being flipped over but they always somehow righted themselves against the raging eddies using the 'Eskimo roll' method. Unfortunately, we couldn't join in as we didn't have the time to stop, and we didn't want to appear to be showing off!

Rod Eyot, quite a large, inhabited island in mid-stream and only accessible by boat, guards the approach to Henley. As it often floods in winter all eleven homes on the island are built on stilts. Large signs instruct river traffic that a one-way system is in operation and all craft are requested, according to which direction they're travelling, to pass to the right of the island.

We now passed on our left, Mill Marsh Meadow, a large public park on which picnickers were spreading their blankets looking forward to a lazy afternoon in the sun. The River and Rowing Museum is situated in the park, opened in 1998 and built to resemble an Oxfordshire barn. Having in the past taken classes of children, I can thoroughly recommend a visit. In the car park are two splendid statues of the Olympic gold medallists, Sir Steve Redgrave and Sir

Matthew Pinsent. We contemplated on stopping but having both already visited we decided to carry on.

It happened to be my turn for the front seat so as we approached Henley my view was uninterrupted by the back of Kev's head. Henley bridge, with the church and The Angel on the Bridge pub is one of the best, well known tableaus depicting the Thames.

The five arched stone bridge replaced a wooden one which was damaged by a flood in 1774. Horace Walpole described the new bridge as the most beautiful in the world after the Ponte Santa Trinita in Florence. Over the central arch are two masks, the one facing upstream is that of Isis and the other, facing downstream, is of Old Father Thames.

The masks were sculptured by Anne Seymour Damer who was the most highly regarded sculptor of her day. She was the daughter of General Conway who, at the time, owned Park Place. She was encouraged in her work by Horace Walpole, her father's cousin. Perhaps Walpole was a little biased with his high opinion of the bridge? Anne led a sumptuous social life and became close friends with the likes of Napoleon, Lord Nelson and the famous actresses of the day, Sarah Siddons and Elizabeth Farren. Her preference for wearing men's fashion and her unconcealed relationships with women were always the favourite topic of conversation amongst the society gossips. She was reputed to be the first woman in England to wear black silk stockings.

Henley developed from an inland port in Medieval times to the world-famous town it is today. It was garrisoned by Roundhead troops for most of the Civil War because it held a key position for Cromwell's supply route, it being midway between London, the Parliamentary stronghold and Oxford, the stronghold of the King.

In the 1800's, because of its position between London and Oxford, Henley was a busy coaching town. In 1830 it was recorded that thirteen stagecoaches a day were departing from Henley destined for London or Oxford.

The well-known brewers, W.H. Brakspear and Sons Ltd., have brewed beer in Henley since 1711. The Brakspear family are distantly related to the only Englishman to become Pope. As previously mentioned, Nicholas Breakspear (note the change of spelling), became Pope Adrian IV in 1154. The brewer's traditional bunches of mistletoe and holly are still hung in the brewery yard at Christmas and left for the following year to ensure luck and prosperity. As we approached Henley, we had passed a boathouse topped with a giant bee, the brewer's logo.

The singer, Dusty Springfield, who Elton John described as 'the greatest white singer there has ever been', spent her final years in Henley. There is a memorial to her in the church. From 1971, The Beatle, George Harrison has lived in Friar Park, a one-hundred and twenty roomed Gothic mansion situated just outside the town.

We left 'the lizard' chained to a mooring post just below the bridge at 11.20 after asking a fisherman if he would kindly keep an eye on her for us. Kev checked, but he hadn't caught anything of note. We walked back a little way along the riverside road to visit the first of our Henley hostelries, The Anchor. It's true it hasn't quite got a frontage on the river but as we could easily see it as we passed by in the canoe, we decided it would count.

The interior of the Anchor seemed very dark especially after coming in from the strong sunlight. The only customer appeared to be a very old, strange looking gentleman sitting on a large upholstered armchair next to the fireplace. I bid him a good morning which he acknowledged by looking away and wheezing. The landlord, I presumed that's who he was, was sitting behind the bar straining his eyes trying to read a newspaper. He didn't greet us or ask us what we wanted so I just asked for two pints of bitter. He served us, asked for his money and then went back to his newspaper.

As our eyes became accustomed to the gloom it became apparent that the 'customer' in the chair was in fact, much to Kev's dismay, a very old boxer dog who dribbled as only boxer dogs can. Long strings of saliva were hanging from each corner of his mouth and cascading down to soak into the chair's upholstery. Every so often he looked in our direction and wheezed. After some coaxing the landlord told us the dog was called Cognac and was fourteen years old. The landlord went on to say that Cognac spent most of his time sitting upright in the chair and it was now regarded as his personal space, as nobody else ever felt inclined to sit in it!

We downed our pints and left. I'm sure I heard Cognac pass wind as we re-emerged into the sunlight. It may have been the landlord. I have subsequently been back to the Anchor and the pub is now under new management. Sadly, Cognac has passed on to the great kennel in the sky, however, in the now much brighter bar there are several photographs adorning the walls of him in his chair.

Retracing our steps, we headed for our next port of call, The Red Lion. It's situated across the road adjacent to the bridge and began life six hundred years ago as a coaching inn. Charles I stayed in 1630 and again in 1642. I wonder if he was aware that the house opposite was the birthplace of William Lenthall who was the Speaker of the House of Commons when Charles burst into the House with four hundred soldiers demanding the arrest of five MPs who he accused of treason? Lenthall refused to give them up with the now famous words, "May it please your Majesty, I have neither the eyes to see, nor the tongue to speak in this place, but as the House is pleased to direct me, whose servant I am." The five members had already fled having had prior warning.

The 18th century poet William Shenstone whilst staying at the Red Lion in room 107 is reputed to have scratched a four lined poem on the interior of a windowpane. The original pane of glass is no longer in existence but a reproduction is now in situ.

> 'Whoe'er has travelled life's dull round,
> Where'er his stages may have been,
> May sigh to think he still has found
> The warmest welcome at an inn'.

Prior to becoming George IV, the Prince Regent stayed at the Red Lion. It's reported that he ate fourteen of their lamb chops in one sitting.

The Red Lion was a distinct contrast to The Anchor. It's a large imposing red brick building which dominates its surroundings. Inside its light and spacious with dribble free upholstered furniture and a welcoming atmosphere. We felt a little out of place in such plush surroundings attired as we were in our usual canoeing garb, so we didn't take too long in downing a pint.

We re-crossed the road and after checking that 'the lizard' was still in the care of the fisherman, his keepnet was still empty, we paid a visit to the well-known Angel on the Bridge. Built in 1728, it's said to be one of the most painted and photographed pubs on the river. We sat at a table on its wooden decking which extends a few feet over the river in the shadow of the bridge. We were lucky to find a place as spaces were quickly being taken by the lunchtime trade. A very pleasant three quarters of an hour or so was passed in the warm sun chatting to some of the other customers and supping a couple more ales each and a packet of crisps. Yet again generous donations for the cause were forthcoming. It must have been about one o'clock when we bid our farewells. We still had another visit to make before leaving Henley.

After thanking the fisherman for minding the canoe, Kev was overjoyed that he had caught two small roach, we rather unsteadily got back on board to paddle the short distance to The Little White Hart. As we drifted past The Angel and under the bridge, we received cheery waves from our newly made acquaintances still sitting on the decking.

The Little White Hart, another old coaching inn, is situated just past the bridge on the left bank. We secured 'the lizard' amongst some rowing boats which were for hire and then spent an agreeable fifteen minutes or so in the pub. As we had already consumed four pints of beer each, we decided that we had had enough, so we supped a couple of whiskies.

After resuming our journey, we almost immediately past The Leander Club, Britain's oldest rowing club, founded in 1881. It has won more Olympic and World Championship gold medals than any other rowing club in the world.

We now began meandering along the mile long regatta course, the longest naturally straight stretch of river in England. I use the word meandering deliberately because I'm sorry to have to say that we didn't exactly take the direct route. Our alignment seemed to deviate at regular intervals as we zig-zagged out of Henley along the famous course. I blamed the man steering at the back, he blamed the navigator in the front. But, if the truth is to be told, the reason was that too much beverage had been consumed in too short a time on empty stomachs. But we didn't care! We did attempt a hundred stroke sprint but gave up after five.

The first official Henley regatta was held in 1889 but the seed was sown ten years earlier when the very first Oxford versus Cambridge boat race was rowed between Hambleden lock and Henley bridge, a distance of two miles. Oxford won by a hundred yards in a time of fourteen minutes. The next year Cambridge decided to stage the race in London where it has remained ever since. However, other rowing races were run over the original course and began to attract large crowds. The town decided to raise some cash for a Grand Challenge Cup for men's eights. This is still the most prestigious cup to win at the Henley Royal Regatta.

In 1856 Prince Albert came up the Thames from Windsor to watch and so it became a Royal regatta. It's a five-day event beginning on the first weekend in July and is a major world sporting venue. A must place to be seen if you're a member of the British social scene. It's definitely on our 'lottery' list.

At the end of the mile long straight is the small Temple Island which marks the start of the regatta course, so named after the miniature temple which was built on the island in the 1771 as a fishing lodge for Fawley Court. The temple can be hired for weddings and private functions.

Fawley Court, on our left bank, is hidden from the river by trees. It was the home of Parliamentarian Sir Bulstod Whitelock during the Civil War and was ransacked by the Royalists cavalry under Prince Rupert. William of Orange stayed at Fawley Court in 1688 on his way to London to accept the throne. It now belongs to an Iranian Heiress who reportedly paid thirteen million pounds for it.

Opposite Fawley Court, on the other side of the river, is the tiny village of Remenham. It consists of a Georgian farmhouse, a church dating from the 13th century, a rectory and a handful of cottages, but not a public house. Just as well!

The river now swings round a huge, graceful right-hand bend around Remenham Hill towards Hambleden Lock. On the inside of the bend a large of expanse of water meadows stretch all the way to the lock. It's a favourite haunt of walkers, joggers, cyclists and picnickers all of whom seemed to be out making the most of the sunshine. This was bad news for us as it was now becoming a priority for a 'comfort stop'. Stopping anywhere on the opposite bank was out of the question because the manicured lawn of a large white house called Greenlands swept down to the river's edge.

During the Civil War, unlike Fawley Court, the property belonged to the Royalist D'Oyley family. Unfortunately for them, during part of the hostilities, the Roundhead artillery were camped across the river in the fields opposite and used Greenlands as target practice for their field guns until it was reduced to rubble. The house was eventually rebuilt and in 1868 it became the home of William Henry Smith the newsagent, who began his empire in 1848 by opening the first railway bookstall, at Euston Station. After the Second World War, Hitler's private papers revealed that he had selected Greenlands as a future residence for himself. The house now belongs to Reading University.

A hundred yards or so from Hambleden Lock we passed the now infamous spot where, almost forty years ago, as mentioned in chapter 7, I had given Kevin his first and last fishing lesson. The incident is historically known as the 'cows and yellow cape affair'.

There were two fishermen close to the notorious spot who must have wondered why they were causing so much interest and hilarity. As predicted Kevin's enquiries featured roach. They hadn't caught any.

By now the need for a comfort stop was foremost in our thoughts. Too many people and no bushes. Consequently, we decided that the only solution was to hope that the lockkeeper would allow us to use his facilities.

As we approached Hambleden Lock, a large cruiser named 'Carician' stopped in midstream and called us over. Again, they had heard of us by way of Radio Oxford. The 'captain' proceeded to hand over two open full bottles of lager. To be frank, two empty bottles would have been more use to us at that moment. I must admit that I only pretended to take a swig from mine as I had definitely reached saturation point.

We followed 'Carician' and several other boats into the lock. Kevin immediately abandoned ship with the words, "Wait here I'll find a loo" and left me in charge of 'the lizard'. When he returned a few minutes later, I was very nearly in tears. I scrambled ashore in such haste 'the lizard' nearly capsized. Thank goodness the lock keeper had been obliging and availed us with the use of his outside latrine.

When all was calm again, we got to chatting to the captain and crew of the 'Carician'. It turned out that he was the owner of the 'Bel & The Dragon', a restaurant in Cookham, an establishment that used to be a favourite of my father's. It was always a great treat for the family to be taken there to celebrate birthdays and other special occasions. As we prepared to leave the lock the 'captain' lent over and handed me his business card. On the back he had signed and written, 'two free meals and twenty pounds from the till for UNICEF. "Just call in with my card on your way through Cookham," he called as his boat pulled smoothly away, "and give it to one of the bar staff."

The Hambleden Lock weir is, in my opinion, probably one of the widest and impressive on the river. A steel walkway takes a public footpath across the length of the weir, and it can be quite an exhilarating walk especially if the river is running fast and the sluice gates are open.

At the far end of the weir from the lock stands Hambleden Mill. A mill was recorded as being here in the Domesday Book of 1086. The present building can be traced back to the 16th century and remained in use as a flour mill until 1955. It's now been converted into luxury apartments but still retains its character and appearance of a classic mill. It's another of the most photographed and painted scenes of the Upper Thames.

A little way past the weir on the left is the site of a Roman villa. In 1912 the area was excavated and ninety-seven infant burials were found dating from the occupation of the villa. Much speculation has followed regarding this high infant mortality rate. Some have put forward the idea that it could have been the infanticide of the babies of slaves. Others have suggested that the villa was once a Roman brothel.

It was now about two-o-clock and lunch had become our priority. According to The Ordnance Survey Guide to the River Thames we would soon be passing a wooden jetty on our right at the end of a narrow lane. The jetty is sited where an old rope ferry was recorded as operating in 1785. This was the time when the commercial river boats were horse drawn and at this point the towpath switched banks, so the horses needed to cross the river. It's also the site of a bitter battle during the 1642 civil war.

The jetty belongs to The Flower Pot Inn which is just a few hundred yards up the lane in the small village of Aston. As the jetty is maintained by the pub we decided it could count as an 'official stop' – and besides we were hungry.

We found The Flower Pot at the end of Ferry Lane without any problems and spent a very pleasant three quarters of an hour eating cockles from a jar with a pile of thick fresh bread and butter, and for a change, a glass of cider. Inside, the walls are adorned with stuffed fish of every conceivable British freshwater species. Much to

Kevin's delight, a particular case held a perfect example of a pair of roach.

The Flower Pot Inn is a typical red brick Victorian pub which used to specialise in catering for the fishing and boating fraternities during the Victorian and Edwardian periods. It still retains a sign, painted on the outside wall in large, now fading letters, which reads, 'Good accommodation for fishing and boating parties.'

'The lizard' was waiting patiently at the end of the lane moored to the old landing stage. As we approached, we became aware of a considerable commotion going on in the water in the vicinity of our canoe. Four moorhens were engaged in a territorial battle in a flapping, grappling scuffle. It's a very common event as moorhens are extremely territorial and two pairs will often fight each other where the boundaries of their territories meet. It looks quite aggressive but actual damage during the tussle is rare. The battles come to an end in one of two ways. Either one bird or pair gives way and is chased off or the combatants mutually decide that they've had enough and break away to retreat slowly from each other ready to resume fighting at the slightest sign of further hostility.

A coot was watching the proceedings from a safe distance. Coots and moorhens are close relatives and are quite often mistakenly identified. They are in fact very easy to tell apart. Both appear to have prominently black plumage, the moorhen being the slightly smaller bird. The giveaway is the red shield above the red beak of the moorhen and the large white shield and white beak of the coot, giving it the appearance of having a bald patch, hence the saying, 'as bald as a coot'. Both defend their territories against their own species as described.

Moorhens spend much of their time amongst the reeds and on the bank eating plants, seeds, the lava of freshwater invertebrates, worms and molluscs. Coots are also omnivorous but spend a little more time in the water and are quite competent divers.

A coot normally has one brood of young in a year but the moorhen usually manages two or even three broods. In nearly all species of bird that have a second brood the first set are driven away from the nesting area. However, in the case of the moorhen, the first set of youngsters stay to help rear the next group of chicks, assisting in the feeding. Both species lay six eggs per brood and the chicks are able to swim within a few hours of hatching.

A pair of moorhens will set up home on the smallest of ponds but a pair of coots require a little more space. Both are very common and there are very few areas of water in the British Isles without its resident pair of coots or moorhens.

We waited a few minutes watching until the inconclusive bloodless battle was over and then continued on our way. The quantity of carbohydrates we had consumed for lunch had seemed to have counteracted the excesses of Henley and we were back to travelling in more or less a straight line. The river winds its way past two thickly wooded islands and then quietly flows along between tree lined banks and meadows, until after about a mile and a half it passes Medmenham Abbey.

The abbey was founded in 1201 and was occupied by the Cistercian Order of monks. In 1536 it was closed down as only the abbot and one monk were left in residence. The building is now a private dwelling and the ruins on show are mostly contrived but a 13th century pillar of the original building still remains.

The former Abbey is best known as the home of the notorious Hell Fire Club which met there between 1750 and 1774 for orgiastic and riotous meetings. The club was formed by Sir Francis

Dashwood, the only Chancellor of the Exchequer to admit to being drunk whilst delivering his budget speech.

The Hell Fire Club associates, which included some members of the government, met at the abbey dressed as monks calling themselves The Franciscans of Medmenham. Their motto was, 'Fayce que voudras', which translates, 'Do whatever you want'. Only 'ladies of cheerful and lively disposition' were invited. Even the gardens and grounds were said to be planted in a suitable pornographic and sacrilegious style but none of this survived the 19th century.

After passing three large islands on a wide u-bend, the river runs alongside an extensive meadow on the right bank. It belongs to a farm in Hurley and for a fee you can drive your car onto the meadow and park alongside the river. A very popular venue for families and groups for picnicking, barbecues and daytime partying. Always busy at weekends in the summer and no doubt a 'good earner' for the farmer. It was here, at the tender age of eight, that my Uncle Bill first introduced me to angling whilst on a family picnic. I remember falling in at the time and having to wear my younger and very much smaller brother's tracksuit bottoms to go home in, looking like a miniature Rudolf Nureyev.

Opposite, on the Buckinghamshire side, sitting high up on a chalky cliff sits Danesfield House. It takes its name from the Danes who built a hill fort here to protect a strategic crossing point of the river. Now a luxury hotel, the late Victorian mansion was designed in 1899 for Robert William Hudson, son of Robert 'Soapy' Hudson who invented soap powder. He was the first to use mass advertising to help sell his product. 'A little of Hudson's goes a long way'. Between 1941 and 1977 it was owned by the air ministry. In 1991 it was converted into the hotel.

A little further downstream, again on the Buckinghamshire side just before Hurley Weir, we passed one of the last of its kind remaining on the Thames. Wittington Winch as it is often referred to, is a reminder of the days when passing through a river lock was not the pleasant experience it is today.

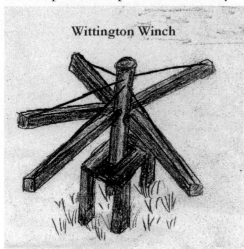
Wittington Winch

By the fifteen hundreds the river had become a vital thoroughfare for supplying building materials, grain, livestock and coal to London, but the river was then far from being 'tamed'. With the many mills along its route building dams and weirs to harness the river's power, navigation was, to say the least, not a straight forward affair but, a rite of passage along the Thames had been confirmed by the Magna Carta in 1215. Whilst the building of weirs assisted the navigators by raising water levels, they posed another problem of getting boats past the obstructions. Before today's pound locks were built the only way to traverse the many weirs and dams was by the previously mentioned flash locks. It entailed a single gate being opened to allow a torrent of water to be released to carry craft through the gap. A fairly effortless but hazardous event for boats travelling downstream. Coming upstream however was a different matter as the boats had to be hauled up against the flood of water rushing through the gate, using a massive winch or capstan anchored on the bank above the weir. The Whittington Winch is a rare example still remaining. One can only imagine the accidents which inevitably occurred. Boats capsized, cargoes lost and boatmen drowned. The impressive weirs of today are used to control water levels and the rate of flow of the river, by-passed by the adjacent pound locks.

We have The Chiltern Society to thank for the restoration and preservation of the Whittington Winch. It's now a Grade 2 listed building and described as 'a wooden capstan with metal cap on metal tie bars to five wooden arms. Part sunk into a pit with two retaining beams.'

As the river approaches Hurley Lock it divides around six wooded islands one of which was to be our campsite for the night. The weir is above the islands, so we needed to take the lock cut in order to pass through the lock and then paddle back upstream along one of the channels to our islet.

We needed to reacquaint ourselves with the lockkeeper to take possession of the key to the storeroom on the island, in which we had stowed our camping gear and fresh clothing and, we required the key to a gate which would allow us access to the village via a footbridge.

Before passing through the lock Kevin left me in charge while he went off to find 'the keeper of the keys.' I sat idly in the canoe using the now well practiced 'grasping a clump of grass method' of mooring. I got to thinking of all the other lodgings where we had dropped anchor for the night. All different, but every one comfortable, clean, warm and dry. Tonight, would be a different experience. I remembered that it was my idea, way back when planning our trip, and that it had taken some time to persuade Kev that a night under canvas would be a good idea. If you refer back to chapter three, you will be reminded of the two very different scenarios we each imagined of how the following morning would present itself after we emerged from our tent. Would I again be able to experience the perfect bacon roll?

Kev returned all smiles clutching the keys. The temporary lockkeeper, (the resident lockkeeper was on holiday and so wouldn't be joining us later in the pub as previously planned, waved us into the lock and we descended with a handful of other craft without incident. After paddling downstream for about fifty metres, we turned left to paddle back upstream along another channel towards the weir pool in search of our island. A route which we had taken before when training and reconnoitring the trip all those weeks before. As before, we ran 'the lizard' aground on the small sandy beach of our island and pulled her above the high-water mark.

Apart from a small one-man tent pitch at the far end of the island we seemed to be the only occupants. According to the experts, when marooned on a desert island the first rule is to find a freshwater supply and make a shelter. We quickly found the shower block which had a drinking water tap and unlocked the storeroom to retrieve our tent.

We decided to make camp just above the beach on a flat piece of ground which had a convenient wooden picnic table already in situ. Besides, pitching the tent here would mean we wouldn't have to carry our luggage very far from the canoe. Also, the weir pool was at the other end of the island therefore the noise of the tumbling water was only a pleasant murmur and would not, as Kev pointed out, affect our ears or our bladders during the night.

Kevin had originally provided the tent and proudly announced that it was one which was self-erecting. I was intrigued. He chose a suitable spot and explained that all he needed to do was carefully take the folded tent from its bag and toss it gently into the air and it would land assembled, then all we had to do was peg it down to make it secure. I stood back to watch.

Kev nonchalantly threw the tent up in the air and it landed with a thump still neatly folded. After five or six attempts, gradually throwing it higher and higher, he decided to give it a start by unfolding it a little. Still the same result. I will say this for my old mate - he never gives in. By this time the air was getting blue and I was in danger of disgracing myself with laughter which wasn't helping. Each time before tossing it in the air he unfolded the tent a little more. By the eleventh or so attempt it was a tangled heap of guy ropes, poles and canvas.

I felt I had to pull myself together and intervene when Kev announced that the so called 'self-erecting tent' had had its chance and was now going in the river and we would find a pub for the night. Half an hour or so later we had untangled the tent and erected it the good old fashioned way - and it was ready for occupation. It was now 4:30.

"Any minute now it's going in the river"

We collected the other bits and pieces we had left in the storeroom. Sleeping bags, air beds, cooking stove and gas bottle, frying pan and other utensils and a kettle. As well as fresh clothes for the rest of the trip. We unloaded 'the lizard' and organised the campsite as well as our distant memories of our scouting days allowed. Unfortunately, there are strict rules about not lighting fires on the island so the planned campfire singsong had to be abandoned.

We had decided weeks before that we would give pub-grub a miss on our camping night and would cater for ourselves, so we set off to find the village store. We found the footbridge to leave the island. At the far side there is a high, metal, padlocked gate with roles of barbed wire along the top, barring the way and preventing anyone getting onto the island or leaving unless they're in possession of the key. I went back to the tent to get it.

The footpath to the village takes you across the lock cut by-way-of a high wooden footbridge and then along a short hedge lined path. Hurley is a very ancient settlement; a church has existed on the site since AD333. Edward the Confessor's wife, he ruled from 1042 until his death in 1066, is said to be buried somewhere in the village in an unmarked grave. After the Norman Conquest a Benedictine Priory was established which like most other priories was dissolved by Henry VIII in 1536. The refectory remains and is now a private house but part of the cloisters are still visible. Situated in the middle of the village is Ye Olde Bell, yet another public house claiming to be the oldest in England. It dates from about 1135 and was once the guest house of the priory.

In the 1930s Ye Olde Bell was owned by Guilo Trappani who seemed to attract the 'bright young set of the day' It became known for its racy activities where one could enjoy a 'temporary honeymoon' at weekends. A variety of well-known celebrities were attracted to the establishment which include Princess Margaret. In 1933 a prominent daily newspaper ran a centre page spread reporting on nude midnight bathing at Hurley Lock.

A large tithe barn and a dovecote, both built in the 14th century, have been beautifully restored and hold a prominent position in the village.

After Henry had dissolved the priory, the land passed to Richard Lovelace who built a Tudor Manor called Ladye Place. He sailed the Spanish Main with Sir Francis Drake and the original manor house is believed to have been paid for with plundered Spanish gold.

In 1688 the third Baron Lovelace of Hurley used the vaults beneath Ladye Place with other Protestants nobles to plot the overthrow of the Catholic King James II. It was here that they signed the documents to send for William of Orange which brought about the Glorious Revolution. King William later came to Hurley after his accession to see for himself the place where his future had been planned.

Ladye Place was demolished in 1837 and replaced by an Edwardian mansion but the vaults still survive. They're said to be haunted by the ghost of a grey lady thought to be Edward the

Confessor's wife. Two secret tunnels have recently been discovered linking the vaults to Ye Olde Bell.

Hurley used to hold, and I'd like to think they still do, a festival in October on St Pyr's Day called the Hurley Marrow Wassail. St Pyr was a Welsh Abbot of the sixth century. He has been described as being an unsuitable Abbott and one of those Celtic Saints who should never have been canonised. By all accounts he liked a drink or two and one night on his way back to his cell he was so drunk that he fell into a well and drowned.

The biggest village marrow and an elected 'Marrow Queen' for the day are paraded around the village to an orchard. The 'tree bird', the marrow, is then duly sacrificed to ensure a plentiful crop of apples for the following year in order to make copious quantities of cider. The 'tree bird' is buried at the foot of a tree and toast is hung in its branches, cider is then poured onto the tree's roots. The assembled villagers then retire to the pub to drink cider to St Pyr, marrows, 'marrow queens', apple trees and anything else they can think of. The saint chosen to be associated with the Hurley Marrow Wassail was obviously thoughtfully selected.

We found the village store and for our alfresco dinner we purchased, a stick of French bread, butter, cheese, pate, tomatoes, tea and milk. Plus, bacon and rolls for breakfast. Back at camp we sat in the evening sun around the picnic table with the distant sound of the weir in the background and ate our simple fare. A refreshing change from the usual pub atmosphere and cuisine.

We were just finishing when Kev's phone rang. It was Jan calling to say she was coming over for a drink and a catch up together with Sarah, a good friend of ours and Derek and Shirley our neighbours. We were now only a half hour drive away from my home. We arranged to meet in The Rising Sun, the village pub nearest to the river at 8.

With an hour to kill we decided it would be a good time to sort out our laundry and restock our barrels with our clean attire. It would save a job in the morning, so the barrels were emptied of soiled garments and fresh tee-shirts and boxers repacked.

Kev's barrel still had the lingering smell of curry which it had previously stored in an earlier life. At one point when both barrels were empty, he tried a crafty swap when he thought I wasn't looking. But I had noticed and surreptitiously re-swapped them. For the rest of the trip, he couldn't understand why his fresh tee shirts still smelt of Balti.

Before setting off for the pub we prepared the tent for the night. Two very narrow inflatable mattresses needed to be blown up which resulted in red faces, aching cheeks, dizziness and much laughter. Sleeping bags were unrolled and made ready. There was very little room to spare and we certainly couldn't stand up in there but it looked quite inviting all the same.

As we were crossing the high wooden footbridge on our way to the village a familiar figure approached. It was my brother Chris, who knowing we were camping for the night had to come to find us and was more than ready to join the gathering at The Rising Sun.

The pub was built in 1830 and can best be described as a traditional village local favoured by walkers and boaters. Several groups of the latter, some we had become acquainted to along the way, were scattered around the bar. Much friendly banter ensued throughout the evening.

It was great to see Jan and catch up with news from home but we made it clear from the start that Kevin and I didn't want to hear about world affairs or any domestic occurrences; we wanted to stay in our 'bubble' until the end of our trip. An extremely pleasant evening passed very quickly with a fair amount of hilarity as we recounted the incidents and experiences we had shared so far with the river and its associates.

We parted company at about 11 and Jan arranged to meet us again the following evening for a meal further downstream at our overnight stop at Maidenhead. It was a dark night with only a sliver of a moon. The jollity of the evening continued as we cautiously stumbled our way back to camp without a torch. We had packed one and it was in the tent awaiting our return.

As we approached the locked gate barring our way across the narrow footbridge, I suddenly had a slight panic attack. Where was the key to the gate? Was it keeping the torch company in the tent? Of course, it wasn't because we had used it to exit the island on our way to the pub earlier in the evening! "You've got the key," I nonchalantly mentioned to Kev.

"No," he replied, "you have." I stopped and searched my pockets and eventually found it - but then immediately dropped it. We spent the next three or four minutes on our hands and knees searching amongst the grass and weeds in the dark hoping that this was not a popular dog walking route. As always laughter helped us through, and Kev eventually found the key.

The tent seemed even smaller in the dark and as we crawled in, I immediately realised that all was not well. My air bed had also diminished in size by deflating itself. By the time I had reinflated it Kevin was asleep, blithely snoring away.

CHAPTER 14

High Society & Affairs of State

Hurley to Maidenhead – 9.5 miles

I had spent an uncomfortable night. Every hour or so I felt the need to reinflate my airbed and being awake most of the night I was made aware of how damp and cold it can become in a tent at night. Kevin, on the other hand, had seldom stirred. He awoke to a fine sunny morning with a low mist hovering over the river and his mate making a brew on the primus.

After a trip to the shower-block we were ready for the bacon roll challenge. Would this morning's bacon roll taste as good as the ones I alluded to in chapter 3, cooked and consumed whilst overlooking the Llanberis Pass in Snowdonia after a similar night under canvas?

There's something about eating outside. Fish and chips sitting on a harbour wall. Ham sandwiches whilst watching a Test Match at Lords. Fresh crab sandwiches in a seaside pub garden. Hot dogs with onions at half time. A succulent steak straight off a charcoal barbecue. Freshly cooked bacon rolls on a clear radiant morning with a different vista than usual. In this case, a tranquil Thames backwater with a light, low mist quiescent over its surface with the subtle sound of a weir in the background and the call of a moorhen in the reeds by the water's edge. Yes! The bacon roll challenge had been well and truly met.

The only slight blot on the landscape was Kev's head gear. The fine, warm morning had brought forth an abundance of gnats and so he had decided to wear a transparent shower cap he had acquired from one of our overnight stops as a means of protection. He suffers greatly from mosquito and gnat attack. They always tend to home in on him ignoring everyone else in close proximity, disregarding any toxic spray he has doused himself in.

The tent came down a lot quicker that it went up, with little, if any, swearing. The camping gear and dirty washing were soon stowed away back in the store waiting for collection at a later date and all that remained to do was to return the keys to the lockkeeper. We both agreed that the experience on the island had been well worth the effort and had come as a welcome change. But I had to agree that one night under canvas was enough especially with my particular air-bed.

We refloated 'the lizard' at about 9:45; the mist had by now dispersed and Kev had discarded his shower cap. We set off downstream towards Marlow, the next riverside town awaiting our arrival. When we rejoined the main channel, we very nearly forgot to head back upstream to the lock to return the keys.

Two genial fishermen, fishing from a rowing boat anchored almost mid-stream just below the lock, summoned us over and insisted on giving us each a can of lager. It would have been rude to refuse, even at that time of the morning, so we graciously accepted their kind offer and drank their health and wished them good fishing. Kev of course verified his depth of knowledge of the sport with his usual inquiry.

We very soon passed Harleyford Manor, an unimpressive red brick house on the Buckinghamshire side of the river. It was built in 1755 for the then MP for Marlow, Sir William Clayton. His descendant, also Sir William, fought at the Battle of Waterloo and used a field nearby to graze his war horses or chargers as they were known. Hence the name of the field, Chargers Paddock. The house is now the headquarters of the Harleyford Leisure Estate and Marina. The name Harleyford perhaps suggests that once, way back in time, this was the locality of a fording point.

Almost opposite is Freebody's boatyard which is the oldest surviving boatyard in England still making and restoring traditional bespoke wooden Thames launches - stylish and elegant, synonymous with the boating scene of the middle Thames. We were lucky enough to see several of these iconic craft, with their distinctive, highly polished wooden hull and decking, and their unique sloping, chisel shaped stern gliding effortlessly on the river. It is recorded that there was a ferryman and bargeman by the name of Freebody at Hurley in the 13th century.

A few minutes later we passed beneath Temple footbridge. Built in 1989, with span of 150 feet, it is the longest wooden footbridge in Britain. It means it's now possible for walkers following the Thames Path, to cross the river here again at this point since the ferry service stopped in 1953.

The Thames Path was officially opened in 1996 after the creation of sixteen miles of new riverside paths and three new footbridges. It is now possible to walk a continuous route following the river from London to its source in Gloucestershire, a length of one hundred and eighty miles.

Temple lock soon came into view, the thirtieth of our journey down the Thames. By now the locks held little concern for us, in fact they were a pleasant interruption from the repetitive rhythm of paddling. They gave us the opportunity to relax and meet and chat to other folk. Not that we were growing tired of each other's company or running out of conversation, on the contrary, but as they say, 'a change is as good as a rest'.

Temple Lock, with its very attractive garden, had been the very first lock we had approached with great trepidation all those months before when we had first taken possession of 'the lizard' and paddled up from Marlow on a practice run. On that occasion we had elected to portage around the lock but now, being the seasoned canoeists, we thought we had become, it held no fears for us. Nonetheless, we did keep reminding each other not to become blasé about locks as they were probably the element of our journey where accidents were most likely to happen.

We shared the lock with four other vessels, two of the crews we had met the night before in the pub. We greeted each other like long lost friends. That's the effect the river bestows on its guests, a genuine feeling of camaraderie.

A hundred metres or so further downstream we passed Temple Island. In the 12th century it belonged to The Knights Templar, hence the name, who ran a flour mill on the island. They were the original builders of Bisham Abbey, just downstream.

The Knights Templar where a very powerful order of knights recognised by their white mantles with a red cross, famed for fighting in the Crusades. They were suppressed by Edward II in 1307.

There is no trace of a mill now only a modern development but in the late 18th century the island was the site of Temple Mills, producing copper. It was run by Sir Thomas Williams, known as the 'Copper King'. In those days Britain produced more than half of the worlds copper output. The opening of the Thames and Severn canal had made it possible to bring the copper by water from Swansea.

In 1848 the production changed to brown paper and continued in use until 1969. The mill once held the record of having the largest millwheel on the river.

With open fields on our left and trees to the right we paddled another half mile until we came upon Bisham Abbey sitting in stately grandeur on the right bank basking in its notoriety of Berkshire's most haunted house. We paused awhile midstream to take in one of the rivers most historic houses, fascinated by its long and troubled history.

Bisham Abbey began life way back in the 13th century when the Knights Templar built and occupied the first building, their great dining hall, built in 1260, is still in use today. In 1307, after the Templars were suppressed, Edward II used the great hall to imprison Robert the Bruce's wife and daughter.

The Earl of Salisbury bought the building in 1336 and next to it established an Augustine Priory which became one of the major religious buildings of the Thames Valley. He used the old Templars buildings as his family home.

The house remained in the ownership of the Salisbury family for several generations and six of them were buried in the priory. 'Warwick the King Maker' was also buried there in 1471 after his defeat at the Battle of Barnet.

In 1539, the then Countess of Salisbury, Margaret Pole, was arrested at Bisham by the order of Henry VIII. She was imprisoned in the Tower of London, tried and beheaded. Her only crime being that her Plantagenet ancestry gave her a possible claim to the throne. She's said to haunt the home from which she was cruelly evicted and has reportedly been seen on many occasions.

After the Dissolution of the Monasteries Henry gave the property to his ex-wife Anne of Cleves, as part of her divorce settlement. For some reason she took a dislike to the place and soon swopped it for a property owned by Sir Philip Hoby. With materials from the now abandoned priory Hoby restored and added to the house, which is very much of what we see today. The house took the name Bisham Abbey and remained in the family until 1768. It still contains much of the Hoby's furniture and portraits of the family.

Princess Elizabeth, later to become Queen Elizabeth I, was held for three years under house arrest at Bisham during the cruel reign of her sister, Bloody Mary. Whilst there she became a good friend of Elizabeth Hoby, the then lady of the house, and spent many hours sitting in the great bay window over-looking the river. When she eventually became Queen, she showed her gratitude to Lady Hoby by giving her a place at court. Elizabeth revisited Bisham as the Queen in 1597.

Lady Elizabeth Hoby was a very intelligent and proud woman who bore three sons whom she chose to educate herself at home. The youngest, William, was rather a slow learner and Lady Hoby found it very difficult to come to terms with his lack of intellect and consequently treated him harshly on the frequent occasions that he failed in his lessons. On one such occasion she was so exasperated with him she locked him in a small room at the top of the tower telling him he wouldn't be allowed out until he had completed his school work.

A little later that day lady Hoby was urgently summoned to court by the Queen. She spent a week in London and on her return, to her horror, she suddenly remembered poor William in the tower room. When the door was unlocked, he was found to be dead, slumped across his tear stained exercise book. In 1840, during major alterations to the house, a set of exercise books were found between some joists with corrections and blots believed to be tear stains on many of the pages.

It's lady Hoby's ghost which seems to be seen most often, seemingly wringing her hands in anguish for the terrible demise she caused her son. Weird noises can at times be detected as coming from behind the panelling in the hall and sobbing is also heard coming from the empty tower room.

On one occasion Lady Hoby appeared to Admiral E.H. Vansittant who had bought the estate in 1780 after the Hoby family had died out. He was the last to go to bed and was sitting in the great hall having one last drink before retiring. Hanging on the wall behind him was a large portrait of Lady Hoby. He reported that he suddenly had a feeling that someone was standing behind him. He turned to see the apparition of Lady Hoby standing staring at him and a blank picture frame hanging on the wall. The portrait is still there today, with the lady safely reframed.

Another unexplained Bisham phenomenon is said to happen at midnight on midsummer's eve. An eerie blue mist has been seen to emanate from the house, rolling across the river and then spreading out across the meadows towards Marlow.

During the First World War Bisham Abbey was used as a hospital for Belgium soldiers and in World War Two it was utilized to house evacuees and Red Cross personnel. Now it's partly a national sports centre, catering for a variety of sports, and a hotel.

Lady Elizabeth Hoby's grand tomb is one of a number of the Hoby family tombs to be found in Bisham church, just fifty or so paddles downstream. The church has a magnificent 12th century Norman tower that sits almost in the river, flood water has been known to reach the pulpit. Over the centuries the church has been greatly enlarged. Lady Hoby built the Hoby Chapel to house the family tombs and in the 19th century the church was restored and partly rebuilt.

Soon after passing the church, the elegant Marlow suspension bridge comes into view and tucked under the bridge is the Marlow Canoe Club's headquarters from whom we had borrowed our canoe. For some reason or other, it may have been our imagination, the 'lizard' seemed to have taken charge and was fairly racing along with little help from us. Was she making for home? One of us, I can't recall who, used the analogy of the way 'the lizard' was behaving, to our experiences of pony trekking.

In the past Kev and I have taken our respective schools on joint adventure weekends to Wales. One of the activities we endured, and I use that word with deliberation, was pony trekking. An unnerving and unpredictable experience with twenty or so young people taking part, none of whom, or very rarely, had had any equestrian experience.

Trekking ponies seem to me to be very astute animals, quick to ascertain whether their rider has any idea or not of how to control a horse. They very quickly get to know who is the most influential in the partnership and then take full advantage.

On the outward migration they barely seem to have the energy to put one hoof in front of the other. Stopping frequently to graze from the hedge or grass verge and no amount of cajoling makes them change their attitude.

On the homeward march however, things are very different. At the turning point the ponies' ears prick up and without any warning break into an unstoppable trot or worse, endeavouring to be the first back in the stable. It's at this point in the expedition that the cavalry break ranks, overtaking each other and even taking shortcuts with their riders in tears, screaming or falling off completely. I recall one child hanging on for dear life on the underside of his pony's neck. The pony seemed quite unconcerned and trotted for home regardless. Had our steed pricked up her ears and decided to bolt for her 'stable' under the Marlow bridge?

Before reaching the bridge, we passed on our left bank, Higginson Park. The mansion was built in the 1760s by Doctor William Battie, a mental illness specialist. He wrote the first book on the treatment of mental illness, hence the origin of the term, 'batty' for someone rather eccentric or slightly crazy. After Dr Battie had designed and built the house it soon became apparent that he had forgotten to include a staircase. It had to be added later!

The grounds of the mansion are now a public park and the house has been converted into a leisure centre. At the front of the house, facing the river, is a statue of the British Olympic rower Sir Stephen Redgrave who was born, and went to school in Marlow. He used to compete in the Marlow Regatta and then went on to win five consecutive Olympic Gold Medals from 1984 to 2000.

The poet Shelley and his wife Mary took up residence in Marlow in 1817. Whilst living there Shelley wrote The Revolt of Islam whilst his wife was writing Frankenstein. Towards the end of the First World War, the poet and Nobel Prize winner for literature T.S. Eliot also made Marlow his hometown.

Marlow bridge, the only suspension bridge crossing the non-tidal Thames, is the most appealing of bridges. It was built in 1832 by William Tierney Clark as the prototype for his much larger bridge linking Buda and Pest across the River Danube, Budapest's first permanent bridge. At the time of its completion in 1849 the Budapest bridge was the world's longest suspension bridge.

It was about 10:30 when we passed beneath Marlow bridge, we paused for a moment next to the canoe club's boathouse to remind ourselves of the day when we had had, with trepidation, our first practice in 'the lizard'. Did she know she was home? Was she drifting into the jetty on purpose? We paddled on, she still had another four days and thirty-eight miles to look after us before she could return.

Almost immediately, on our left, we passed Marlow Church which was rebuilt in 1835 to replace the original 12th century building. Inside can be found a memorial to Miles Hobart who was MP for Marlow and Speaker of the House of Commons in 1628. The monument, which was the first ever to be erected at public expense, depicts his untimely death in a coach accident on Holborn Hill in London.

It was Hobart who shut the door of the House of Commons in Blackrod's face, locking the door until the 'illegal tonnage and poundage debate' was resolved. A tradition still carried out annually during the State Opening of Parliament. Black Rod is responsible for access to, and for keeping order within the House of Lords. He or she is sent to summons the members of The House of Commons to attend the monarch's speech in The House of Lords. The doors to the chamber of The House of Commons are slammed in Black Rod's face to symbolise The Commons independence from the Sovereign. Black Rod strikes the door three times with the staff, is then admitted and issues the reigning Monarch's summons to attend the speech.

Behind Marlow church is a large three storied house once the home of Captain Morris. He was the commander of the battleship HMS Colossus during The Battle of Trafalgar.

A little away from the river is St Peters, Marlow's Roman Catholic Church. It houses the mummified, legendary 'Hand of St James' stored in a glass box, which was removed from Reading Abbey at the Dissolution and found its way to Marlow via the private chapel of Danesfield House. St James was martyred in A44 by King Herod.

On the opposite bank, next to the impressive weir, sits The Complete Angler Hotel, named after Isaac Newton's famous book written in 1653. Queen Elizabeth II visited the hotel with the president of Hungary in 1999. She took him out to lunch and it was the first time she had visited a restaurant outside of London.

We had also planned to grace The Complete Angler with our presence, however, the only access from the river seemed to be across the large, and that time, very crowded lawn. As we paddled across we became aware that the reason for the finely dressed throng was that a very 'upmarket' wedding reception was in progress, in fact, the best man's speech was well underway.

Shall we or shan't we? No, we decided, so we drank the health of the bride and groom from the 'medicinal' whisky flask whilst remaining in the canoe under the gaze of some rather quizzical looks from the lawn.

Situated across from the wedding was The Two Brewers pub where we had arranged to meet Kev's mum and dad and five of his elderly aunts and uncles. One pair had driven all the way up from Kent.

The old pub dating back to 1727 is one of the oldest in Marlow and is so called after Thomas Wethered, who was the founder of the Marlow Brewery, and Samuel Whitbread who later took over. They are depicted on either side of the pub's sign. Jerome K. Jerome wrote a part of his Three Men in a Boat book whilst staying for a while at The Two Brewers.

The fine old pub plays a part in an age-old tradition. Every third week in July one of the rivers most ancient rituals, 'swan upping', takes place and The Two Brewers is one of the traditional stops for the Swan Uppers.

In 1295 the monarch, Edward I, appointed a Royal Swan Keeper to protect and register every swan on the river. The birds were looked upon as great culinary delectations and were considered the property of the Crown. The penalties for poaching swans were severe. The Crown claimed most of the swans but some were allowed to be owned by the Dyers and the Vintner's companies for services rendered and that's still the case to this day. The Crown takes about half and the remaining are divided equally between the two companies.

The flotilla of several rowing skiffs adorned with flags with the Swan Master dressed in his finery set out from Sunbury and works its way upstream to Abingdon. The first day ends in Windsor where they drink the monarch's health. Then it's on to Marlow calling at The Two Brewers. After Marlow they stop at Sonning and finish at Abingdon.

Swans are now a protected species and not even the monarchy is permitted to eat them. Nowadays the object of the exercise is to check on the health and the number of swans on the Thames.

When a family of swans are caught the adult swan's beaks are examined and registered and then the new cygnets are marked. The Royal swans are left unmarked, the Vintner's swans have a single nick at the side of the beak and the Dyer's two nicks, one each side. A single owner of both adults claims all the cygnets. The cygnets of two different owners are divided equally. If it's an odd number of cygnets the owner of the male claims the odd one. After a final health check the family is released non the worst for their experience.

The Two Brewers is situated at the end of St Peters Street which abruptly terminates at the water's edge at the site of a wooden bridge of which there are no remains. Before the suspension bridge was built it was the only bridge in Marlow. The street used to be known as 'Duck Lane'. Not, as one would suppose, named after the feathered fowl which frequent the river, but after a ducking stool which was once positioned by the river next to the old bridge.

Ducking Stool

A ducking stool was a punishment of the Middle Ages designed strictly for women. A barbaric time when there were no laws to protect prisoners or the accused from ill-treatment. Torture was seen as a legitimate means for justice or to obtain confessions. If you were a woman accused of witchcraft, prostitution or of being a scold then the ducking stool was for you. A scold was defined as, 'a troublesome and angry woman who increases discord and becomes a public nuisance in her neighbourhood'.

The device consisted of a seat attached to the end of a free moving arm, rather like a see-saw. After the woman was strapped into the chair, it was swung over a pond or river, she was then ducked under the water. How many times and the length of immersion was decided by the operator and the crime of which she was accused. The bridge alongside Marlow's ducking stool would have made a fine grandstand from which the many spectators could watch the 'entertainment'.

As we came back across the river from The Complete Angler, we noticed some spectators standing on the wooden landing stage which stretched out into the river some eight or ten metres, they were Kev's aforementioned parents and elderly aunts and uncles. As we approached two or three became quite animated and seemed to be getting perilously close to the end of the landing stage. Thank goodness Kevin's procreators were there to shepherd them back to safety. We spent a very pleasant hour in The Two Brewers with Kev's family, enjoying a drink or two and recounting our experiences on the river to date.

It was around midday when we said farewell to Kevin's family and paddled the three or four minutes to Marlow Lock. To our surprise one of his uncles, a sprightly octogenarian, had got there ahead of us, he was standing on the lock gate with his camera poised awaiting our arrival. Unnoticed by us, he must have almost sprinted along the towpath to get there ahead of us.

We shared the lock with a full sized, seventy-one foot converted narrowboat. It was obviously the permanent residence of the young couple who were aboard as every space on the roof was taken by logs and branches to feed their wood burner, plus two old bikes, a shopping trolley, a television aerial, and a small wind turbine, which were amongst the other items of domestic flotsam competing for a place. The pair didn't seem inclined to engage in conversation with us, in fact they even seemed reluctant to converse with each other.

The river soon took us past the Longridge Canoe and Sailing Centre.

Leaving Marlow Lock

We paused for a while mid-stream reminiscing about that day way back in March when Kev did the splits and we had our first, and so far only, 'ducking' in the Thames. We carried on, feeling pleased with the progress we had made with our canoeing skills since that eventful day. We now needed to master getting in and out of the canoe without uttering 'old men's noises'!

The course of the river now takes on an almost right-angled turn to the left as it flows around the steep slopes of Winter Hill on its way to Bourne End, a couple of miles downstream. It has been said that the view from the top of Winter Hill is one of the best views over the Thames Valley. Charles Dickens described it as, 'a view as magnificent as it is extensive'.

In 1906 Kenneth Grahame lived nearby in Cookham Dean. It was here that he made up bedtime stories for his young son Alistair that were later to become The Wind in the Willows published in 1909. It's thought that the 'Wild Wood' featured in the book was inspired by the thick woodland growing on the slopes of Winter Hill, known as Quarry Wood.

Dame Nellie Melba, the opera star who died in 1931, lived in a cottage in Quarry Wood. She was the first singer to broadcast on British radio way back in June 1920. The people who lived in the vicinity of her home said her singing could often be heard wafting through the wood as she rehearsed. The Peach Melba dessert was invented and named after her by the head chef of The Savoy Hotel.

The beers we had consumed from Kev's generous family were beginning to take effect in the bladder region, so we were yet again getting anxious for a comfort stop. For the second day running we had been caught short. Private property on one side and walkers on the other. I knew things were becoming desperate when I heard my companion quietly humming an unrecognizable tune to himself. In the nick of time, we spotted a large enough gap between the ramblers on the bank with a convenient but very small bush situated about ten metres back from the river. I was first out of the canoe leaving Kev to hold on to the bank to prevent her from drifting away and sprinted for the bush. By the time I returned a large group of walkers were slowly strolling along the bank in our direction. We swopped places and Kev waited impatiently on the bank for them to pass still humming his tune. To his consternation they stopped when they reached us for a friendly chat and to pass the time of day. Kev didn't have time to pass the time of day and now seemed to be dancing to his tuneless humming. I took pity on him and between stifled laughter explained the situation to the assembly. They chuckled and apologized and continued on their way without a backward glance.

To our right, at the base of the wooded slopes of Winter Hill, we passed smart houses and chalets built at the water's edge. To our left, on the towpath side, was open meadowland strewn with walkers and families enjoying the river side. There were several shallow inlet beaches along this stretch with wading children and the launching of inflatable dinghies.

A little further downstream is the site of The Spade Oak Ferry which ceased running in 1962. As we approached, I noticed a couple sitting in folding chairs waving in our direction. It was Paul and Anne, two of my colleagues from school. We ran aground on the sandy beach adjacent to where they had position themselves. Paul knew our itinerary and had calculated our approximate time of arrival and they hadn't been waiting long. We spend an agreeable half an hour again retelling our experiences so far and sharing a flask of coffee which they had thoughtfully brought with them. After thanking them for their support we left them to finish the flask and to continue to enjoy the tranquillity of watching the river flow leisurely past.

The river now becomes quite wide as it approaches the fairly large village of Bourne End. In 1236 the village was recorded as Burnend meaning, 'end of the stream', as it is at this point the River Wye joins the Thames. On our right was the extensive open expanse of Cock Marsh, one of the few remaining areas of lowland marsh land. It's been common grazing land since the 13th century and is well known for its bird life and rare flowers and also, it's Bronze Age tumulus. Cock Marsh is now in the safe keeping of the National Trust.

The width of the river at this point makes it favourable for sailing and the Upper Thames Sailing Club were out in force. They must have been at least thirty sailing dinghies of various sizes tacking back and forth across the river spread out over about a quarter of a mile. Although there was only a moderate breeze some of them were reaching quite a fair speed.

Kev was in the stern of 'the lizard' which meant he was helmsman, so it fell to him to steer us safely through the gauntlet of sails. 'Give way to sail' is the rule and I only had to remind him two or three times and only once in somewhat urgent terms, and so we made it through without undue incident.

On the right bank, opposite Bourne End marina, is The Bounty, a quirky barn-like pub. Up until 1993 when a footbridge was added to the single-track railway bridge a little further downstream, the only way of visiting The Bounty was by way of a ferry, a small rowing boat manned by a member of the staff. You could have walked either from Cookham, a mile and a half downstream or over Winter Hill and across Cock Marsh. There are no roads leading to The Bounty and supplies still have to be ferried across the river.

It was about 1.30 when we alighted for our obligatory drink and photo. The pub has a large outdoor seating area and inside it's awash with memorabilia, curios and photographs. Years ago, Kevin used to perform with a folk group at The Bounty. He had long hair then. Did I mention it was a quirky establishment? Lunch could have been taken but we decided to claim our free meal at The Bell and Dragon in Cookham so we only stayed for 10 minutes.

We had only just set off when a somewhat large cruiser hailed us in mid-stream and called us over to pull alongside. As we drifted along, they handed down to us with the help of a child's fishing net, seventeen pounds in coins for UNICEF, some sweets and two cans of beer. How kind and generous, I wish had taken note of the vessel's name.

Continuing on our way to Cookham we passed beneath the combined rail and foot bridge. On our left were many very attractive properties most of which had lawns and gardens sweeping down to the river. We passed the time choosing the one we would each buy after our lottery numbers came up. To our right, on the towpath side, was the continuation of Cock Marsh with Winter Hill in the background.

It was dead on 2 when we reached the much modernised pub/restaurant The Ferry Inn which is situated just past the Cookham bridge. The bridge is built of iron and was erected in 1867 to replace a wooden one dating from 1840. This wooden bridge was the first crossing to be built here since the Romans left one thousand four hundred years ago. At one time there were five ferries in operation at Cookham so for some reason it must have been a very popular crossing point. I wonder why it took them so long to get around to building a bridge?

As time was getting on and we were hungry we decided to leave the canoe by The Ferry Inn and head on into the village to find The Bel and Dragon. We would postpone our drink and photo until our return after lunch.

Cookham is an attractive village laying just back from the river with a Roman and Saxon past. It's noted as being the home of the artist Sir Stanley Spencer whose best known artwork depicts biblical scenes set in Cookham. 'Christ Preaching at Cookham Regatta' is set beside The Ferry Inn, 'The Crucifixion', in the high street and 'The Resurrection', in the churchyard. The former Methodist chapel is now The Stanley Spencer Gallery where most of his works are exhibited. As we were hungry and they wanted money to enter, we just peered in through the window.

In all accounts Sir Stanley was quite an eccentric. He used an antique pram, on show in the gallery, to get his canvases, paints and other painting paraphernalia to and from his locations. Before commencing he would set up a large cardboard sign which read, 'Do Not Disturb'. Some of his canvases are enormous and as he was small in stature, he sometimes needed to place his chair on a table in order to work on them. He died in 1959 and is buried in the churchyard.

The church dates back to 1140 and has retained its Norman naive. The actress Susan George was married in Cookham church in 1984.

Cookham is said to be the haunt of several supernatural sightings. One thoroughfare is even named after the apparition which is said to appear there. Along Whiteladyes Lane, on dark nights, a phantom coach pulled by headless horses and driven by a white lady with streaming hair can be seen silently galloping down the lane.

We found The Bel and Dragon, thought to be one of the oldest coaching inns in England, in the high street and it instantly brought back many happy memories for me. Way back in the 60's my father would take the family to the Bel and Dragon to celebrate special occasions. It was and still is quite an upmarket establishment and it really was a special night out. Prawn cocktails, steak with all the trimmings, Black Forest gateau washed down with a bottle of Mateus Rose and if we were really lucky an Irish Coffee to finish. I still might have somewhere, a table lamp made from a Mateus Rose bottle.

We presented the owners business card, which he had given us in Hambleden lock, to the barman. Without the bat of an eyelid or any questions, but with a smile, he handed us two menus and a twenty-pound note from the till. We enjoyed a very satisfactory meal, even the two glasses of red wine were gratis. Since The Bel and Dragon was not in sight of the river we decided not to include it in the 'official pubs visited list', but we still took a photograph.

After a cursory glance down Whiteladyes Lane we returned to The Ferry Inn. We found four more of my colleagues awaiting our return who had also studied our itinerary and had predetermined our arrival at Cookham. Having seen the canoe, they knew we were somewhere around. After checking inside, they had presumed we had gone inland to explore. We enjoyed some beer and a catch up sitting on the pub's terrace overlooking the river. It was about 3.45 when we said our goodbyes and floated cautiously away. After the wine and three beers apiece, caution was definitely called for. We almost forgot the important photograph.

Almost immediately the river splits into four channels. We needed to carry straight on and head down the narrow, twelve-and-a-half-foot wide lock cut. To our right, two smaller natural watercourses branch away to re-join the main river further downstream. On our left, the original main course of the river winds around a half mile loop. The lock cut was built in 1832 to bypass this loop in the river. Before the cut was built, the main channel took boats past Hedsor Wharf which was an important loading point for timber, coal and paper for over five hundred years.

As luck would have it, we were halfway down the narrow cut when we met an extremely large cruiser which was travelling well over the Thames speed limit. We took evasive action by hugging well into the bank as it sped past followed by a sizable tsunami. I don't think they even noticed us. We called after them wishing them well!

After passing beneath quite a low footbridge we came to Cookham Lock. Here the river takes a right hand turn as its waters meet the high chalk cliff at Cliveden. In the 1700's this was considered to be one of the most dangerous parts of the river due to a shallow fast current and the large chalk boulders which frequently fell from the cliff. The lock was shared with several mixed craft and the usual enjoyable banter with others ensued. We then rejoined the main channel, soon to pass the confluxes of the two backwaters which had branched off before the lock cut.

This next mile long stretch of the river is known as Clifton Reach. To quote Jerome K. Jerome, 'perhaps the sweetest stretch of the river', to quote Dickens, 'Whether for the angler, the artist, the oarsman, or the simple tourist, whether for picnicking and, it has even been whispered 'spooning', to say nothing of camping out, there are few places in England to beat the Cliveden Reach at Maidenhead. Stanley Spencer wrote, 'You can't walk by the river at Cliveden Reach and not believe in God'.

On the right bank the trees on the Berkshire flood plain try to reach across the river to join the Chiltern woodlands, known as 'the hanging woods of Cliveden' They tumbledown the great chalk cliff which gave its name to this beautiful stretch of the Thames.

Perched at the top of the one-hundred-and-forty-foot cliff is the magnificent and notorious Cliveden House. A house which has had its fair share of scandal, notable incidents and jollification.

The original house was built in 1666 by the Second Duke of Buckingham in which he used to entertain his numerous mistresses.

One of his courtesan's was the Countess of Shrewsbury. Her husband, the Eleventh Earl of Shrewsbury, challenged the Duke to a duel, which took place on the terrace at Cliveden whilst she looked on. The Earl was fatally wounded by the Duke's sword, apparently much to the delight of the Countess. For this dastardly deed the Duke was banished from society which probably meant he wasn't invited to any more parties.

Frederick, Prince of Wales leased the house in 1737. It was during a party being held at Cliveden in 1741, that 'Rule Britannia' was performed in public for the first time. Whilst at Cliveden the Prince of Wales, a keen games player, became the first person to be killed, supposedly by a cricket ball. Whilst engaged in a game of cricket he was struck hard on the chest by the ball causing an abscess on the lung from which he eventually died in 1751.

In 1795 the house was destroyed by fire which was also the fate of its replacement. In 1851 the Duke of Sutherland, the new owner, commissioned Sir Charles Barry, the architect of the Houses of Parliament, to build a third house which is the one we see today.

The American billionaire William Waldorf Astor, later to become Lord Astor, bought the house in 1893 and gave it to his son as a wedding present. The Second Lord Astor and his wife Nancy, who became the first woman MP, soon established themselves by being well known for holding extravagant weekend parties at Cliveden attended by the rich and famous. Writers, artists, politicians and world leaders who frequented the gatherings became known as the 'Cliveden Set'. Winston Churchill said after attending one of the Astor's crowded parties, "Thirty dishes and no damn room to eat them." One hadn't made it until one has been invited to Cliveden!

Cliveden has had a visit from virtually every British monarch since George I in the 15th century. Queen Victoria was a frequent visitor, travelling up the river from Windsor for a 'cuppa' or to borrow some sugar. In 1938 the young Queen Elizabeth and Princess Margaret together with their mother 'called in' to meet the Kennedys who were staying with the Asters.

Joyce Grenfell, one of the best loved female entertainers of her generation, was the niece of Lady Astor. Joyce spent most of her childhood at Cliveden and it was at yet another party being held at the house where she met her husband. They were married in 1929 and lived in a cottage on the estate.

About halfway down the reach we passed Spring Cottage nestled amongst some trees on the bank of the river. It belongs to the estate and it was here in the 'swinging sixties' that John Profumo, the then Secretary of State for War 'entertained' the nineteen year old Christine Keeler. Unfortunately for John she was also 'seeing' a naval attaché from the Soviet Embassy by the name of Yevgeny Ivanov. When the affair came to light Profumo was forced to resign and it is said that the scandal, which became famously known in 1963 as 'The Profumo Affair', ultimately led to the fall of Harold Macmillan's government.

None of this would have happened if Profumo had decided to turn right instead of left. He had finished lunch with Lord Astor and upon leaving the dining room via the French doors which led on to the terrace he had the choice of turning right or left. Fate decreed that he chose left which led him past the outdoor swimming pool where his attention was caught by a young lady frolicking topless in the pool, and the rest as they say is history.

Cliveden House and the estate was given to the National Trust in 1942 by the second Viscount Astor, even so it remained the family home until 1966 but the scandal of the 'Profumo Affair' resulted in the Astors deciding to move elsewhere. Spring Cottage is now let by the Trust as a holiday home. The grounds and gardens are open to the public, but the house is a luxury hotel leased from the National Trust. A nights' stay starts at around four-hundred and ninety-five pounds per room per night, with dinner included. As we had already booked our overnight stop – we decided to give it a miss! When told Clivden was to become a hotel Harold Macmillan is reported to have said, "My dear boy, it always has been."

Cliveden's bankside was busy with picnickers and walkers enjoying the National Trust's hospitality, they had a long climb awaiting them when they decided to retreat back up the steep path to the house and car park. Three-quarters of the way down the reach we looked back to get a grand view of the house perched majestically on the cliff top gazing down on the river towards Maidenhead and Windsor.

Cliveden Reach comes to an end on the outskirts of Maidenhead but just before, we passed on our right, Islet Park House. It was here that Gerry Anderson created and produced his first 'Thunderbirds' puppet shows, which became a hugely popular TV series. As you enter the lock cut at the end of the reach leading to Boulters Lock, the main road into the town runs alongside. Creating quite a contrast to the last mile or so.

On the left, just before the lock cut, is the beginning of Britain's largest man-made river project, The Jubilee River. It was designed and built to resemble a natural meandering river complete with reed beds and is open for unpowered craft. It's a seven-mile flood relief channel to alleviate the risk of flooding to Maidenhead, Bray and Windsor from which they have suffered greatly in the past. It re-joins the Thames a mile downstream at Windsor.

Between the weir and the lock cut is Boulters Island on which are several houses. As we approached the first dwelling, we noticed an old man sitting in a deck chair at the end of his lawn, a little way back from the water's edge, contemplating the day. He appeared extremely peaceful and as we got nearer seemed oblivious to our presence. "Lovely afternoon," I called out cheerfully, but with no response.

"What a peaceful spot!" tried Kev - still nothing. I attempted to make conversation again only louder this time assuming he might have been hard of hearing.

"Have you seen many boats today?" I shouted. I noticed a middle-aged couple out walking their dog on the towpath opposite had stopped to witness this one-way discourse, with a look of amusement on their faces.

"His eyes are open," remarked Kev, "but he hasn't moved at all, perhaps he's passed away."

I was beginning to think the same. We paddled in a slow reverent manner to the end of his lawn. When we came to within a few yards we both simultaneously realised we had been attempting to converse with an extraordinary life-like, painted wooden sculpture.

Kev and I looked at each other in silence for a second or two shaking our heads in disbelief. The silence was broken by the laughter coming from the couple opposite. They kindly informed us that we weren't the first to be fooled by 'Old Charlie'. We drank his health from the 'medicinal' flask before continuing on to Boulters Lock.

Boulters Lock was made famous by the artist E.J Gregory who painted it in 1898 packed with small pleasure craft. His masterpiece is called, 'Boulters Lock- Sunday Afternoon'. For the Edwardians and the Victorians, it had become a popular venue for both boaters and families just spectating, some hoping no doubt to spot royalty or celebs passing through to visit the Astors at Cliveden.

As it's so accessible with the main road running alongside, the lock is still a very popular rendezvous. It can become very crowded with viewers sitting or loitering around, eating ice cream from the kiosk, waiting for something out of the ordinary to happen. Today was no exception. An ornate stone bridge spans the lock at the far end giving access to Boulters Island and the Boulters Lock Hotel. It also doubles as a popular viewpoint for the 'lock-watchers'.

An idea alighted on Kevin's shoulder. He suggested that because the lock was such an iconic Thames location, we should record our arrival with a photograph. He proposed that he would disembark before we reached the lock and take a picture from the bridge of me paddling triumphantly through the lock gates. I seconded his proposal, and it was agreed.

We expertly pulled over to the towpath using the 'draw stroke' and my companion made his way through the throng to the bridge.

On his prearranged wave to inform me he was ready, I pushed off from the bank into mid-stream.

As I think I've mentioned before, throughout the trip we had swapped seats each day. The person at the back of the canoe being responsible for steering and keeping on a straight course to which we had both become very efficient. Today it was my turn in the front. Now I've no doubt it's extremely easy to steer a Canadian canoe from the front using the correct fundamental methods, but I found that for some reason the fundamental methods used for steering from the back didn't seem to match those required for steering from the front.

Whatever I tried didn't prevent the back of the canoe from swinging round to become the front. As soon as I managed to straighten up again and point in the right direction; back around it came. At least the flow of the river was taking me in the right direction. Much to the delight of the watching crowd and the patiently awaiting crews of several boats already in place in the lock, 'the lizard' performed four or five graceful pirouettes as I slowly entered the lock. And there I sat facing in the wrong direction as the lock emptied and I slowly but mercifully sank from view as my audience applauded.

To save the indignity of me having to exit the lock in the manner I had entered, Kev risked life and limb by descending the lock's wet slippery steps to rejoin me in the canoe. He didn't say a word but his face had that look of constipated laughter that could uncontrollably burst forth at any moment.

Kevin somehow managed to suppress his swelling hysteria and with him back in the steering seat we expertly turned our canoe around and paddled out of the lock in complete control. He succeeded in waiting until we were well clear of the lock until he erupted. Later he confessed that because he had found my performance so hilarious, he had forgotten to use the camera!

It was about 4.30 when we visited the Boulters Lock Hotel on Boulters Island for a well-earned pint each and the photograph. It was converted in 1950 from a flour mill dating from 1726. It's quite a smart establishment so we didn't linger for very long.

We now needed to find our birth for the night, The Thames Hotel, which was situated somewhere between the lock and Maidenhead bridge. It proved easy to find. It's a modernised Victorian riverside hotel and restaurant sitting on the far side of the main road running alongside the river. The hotel once had one of the earliest telegraph facilities for the use of its aristocratic guests. It was almost 5 when we carried 'the lizard' and our luggage across the road to check in.

After leaving 'the lizard' safely at the back of the hotel by the kitchen we settled into our room for a shower and a snooze. Whilst Kev was showering the mobile rang. On answering I found it to be Three Counties Radio wanting an on-air interview with their presenter Timmy Mallet.

For several years Timmy Mallet had hosted a slightly mad and chaotic Childrens TV show but had now sunk from TV popularity. His radio presentation seemed just as mad and chaotic. He wanted to know how many pubs we had visited. Were we perpetually drunk? How many hangovers had we experienced? How many times had we capsized because we had drunk too much? How did we think our livers were holding out? Were we worried about being breathalysed on the river? What was the most we had drunk in a day? The whole interview was based around alcohol. Nothing about places visited, people we had met, any amusing incidents, money raised so far or even the weather. I was quite pleased when the interview concluded. I needed a drink!

Clean and refreshed we wandered down to the bar to await Jan as prearranged the night before. She arrived at about 7.30 pm with two more of our friends, Ann and Henry. Now it's true to say that both Anne and Henry are both very good company and enjoy a good night out especially if food and drink are involved.

We all enjoyed an extended meal in the restaurant and several bottles of wine were consumed before they left for home by taxi at around 11pm. Jan would be meeting us again in three days' time at our very last pub.

I must have fallen asleep very quickly because I don't recall hearing Kev snoring. It was good to be back in a bed after my Lilo experience of the night before.

CHAPTER 15

Soup, Chairs and a Knot

Maidenhead to Staines Bridge – 13.5 miles

Saturday 21st of August dawned hot and sunny. After a good breakfast which seemed to nullify our muzzy heads, we departed from the hotel at just past 9. We both remarked how the river seemed so smooth and glass like, there was not the slightest breath of wind to create any ripples.

Almost immediately on our left we passed the first feature of note for the day, Skindles Hotel. It began life as a coaching inn then named the Orkney Arms. In 1833, William Skindle turned it into an upmarket hotel for the fashionable upper class of the day. The railway had now brought Maidenhead within easy reach of London and once the Prince of Wales began taking Lillie Langtry to Skindles it became the place to be seen. By the 1920s and 1930s it was a well-known venue for the upper-class playboys of the time for parties and weekends away. Its notability continued and in the 60s and 70s was a popular live music venue where the Rolling Stones, the Beatles and other top bands of the day performed. Alas it later spiralled down to become a rather down- market disco club and now, as we passed, it was standing sadly empty awaiting its fate. Skindles was one of my favourite venues in the mid-60s when I exhibited myself as a 'Mod', riding my scooter with its multitude of wing mirrors and a fox tail aerial.

Just past Skindles is the striking balustraded Maidenhead Bridge built of Portland stone carrying the Great West Road over the Thames replacing an old wooden bridge in 1777.

King Charles I was allowed to meet his children for the last time before his execution in 1649 in the now non-existent Greyhound Inn on Maidenhead's high street. A plaque at the site of the inn records the harrowing meeting.

Maidenhead was a once a day's ride from London along the Great West Road on its way to Bath and for that reason it became an important overnight coaching stop. Besides which, just beyond Maidenhead was the highwayman riddled Maidenhead Thicket, not a place to travel across at night. Claude Duval, one of the most notorious highwaymen of the time, was known to prey upon travellers in this area, as was the infamous Dick Turpin. From here Turpin would ride to Sonning and stable his horse at his aunt's cottage before going into hiding in Oxfordshire. By the mid-18th century Maidenhead had become one of the busiest coaching towns in England dealing with over ninety coaches a day.

In the late Victorian and Edwardian eras Maidenhead had become the centre for Thames tourism. It gained the reputation as the place to visit for scandalous and 'wild living' for middle and upper class good-timers. There was a saying at the time which went, 'are you married or do you live in Maidenhead'?

Maidenhead has always been susceptible to flooding and over the years has suffered greatly from this phenomenon. Under the bridge there's a plaque recording the height the flood water reached during a particularly devastating flood in March 1947, almost ten feet. It reads :- 'This tablet records the grateful thanks of the people of Maidenhead for the kindness and generosity of those in all parts of the world who gave help during and after the disastrous floods of 1947.'

About a quarter of a mile further on we passed beneath Brunel's brick railway bridge comprising of two, 123-foot arches. The bridge was completed in 1839 and is reputed to have the largest brickwork spans in the world. At the time of building much doubt was expressed as to whether they would be strong enough to bear the weight of the heavy steam locomotives. Brunel had faith in his design and here it still stands today in perfect working order. It is said that under the bridge you can experience the perfect echo, so of course we couldn't resist putting it to the test, several times.

In 1844 Turner portrayed Brunel's bridge in his famous painting entitled, 'Rain, Steam and Speed'. In case you're left wondering, it depicts a steam locomotive speeding across the bridge in the rain!

For the next half a mile or so the right-hand bank is festooned with opulent dwellings dating from around the 1930s, all complete with a large, manicured garden and a cruiser moored at the end of the lawn. Several TV personalities reside along this stretch of the river - but we didn't spot any. The villas eventually merge into the village of Bray.

The tower of Bray's medieval church, made famous by Simon Alwyn who was the vicar in the 16th century, can be seen from the river protruding above some trees. By changing his religious orthodoxy between Protestant and Catholic four times during the monarchies of Henry VIII, Edward VI, Queen Mary and Elizabeth I, he managed to remain the vicar of Bray until the day he died. Not a man to let his ecclesiastic principles stand in his way! He's buried in his churchyard.

A satirical ballad was written recounting the vicar of Bray's career, the chorus of which goes :-

>'And this is law, I will remain,
>Until my dying day Sir
>That whatsoever King shall reign,
>I'll still be the vicar of Bray Sir!

Bray is also renowned for offering the opportunity, at a price, for the gastronomic experience of visiting Heston Blumenthal's, Fat Duck restaurant which is sited in the middle of the village or, Michel Roux's, Waterside Inn which is at the water's edge with moorings 'strictly for diners'. Both have three Michelin stars to their name. It was too early for lunch and besides the Waterside Inn wasn't open.

As it's strictly a restaurant it wouldn't have counted as 'pubs visited' anyway.

As we approached Bray Lock we noticed two cormorants with their wings outstretched standing motionless like a pair of black crucifixes on a half-submerged tree trunk. They're large, long necked birds with black plumage and although totally dependent on diving in water to catch fish their wings are very much less water repellent than other water birds. After each feeding session it's necessary for them to dry out their saturated wings and often several can be seen standing in a row at favourite drying spots.

Cormorant

Cormorants are strong swimmers both on and below the water and actively chase fish well below the surface. Once the fish is caught by the birds large hooked tipped bill, the cormorant returns to the surface to swallow its catch headfirst.

The bird has a powerful flight flying in a straight line low over the water but on long flights it has been observed reaching considerable heights.

Cormorants are classed as coastal birds but many have now settled inland. If on the coast they nest on cliff ledges but inland their nest sites are in trees, sometimes singly, in small groups or large colonies. The nest is an untidy heap of reeds and twigs up to a metre wide.

They have been accused of depleting fish stocks in lakes and other course fishing venues and were heavily persecuted in the last century. Many are still shot each year but in spite of that the cormorant still seems to be on the increase.

We shared Bray Lock with several other assorted craft admiring its attractive garden. Many of the lockkeepers compete each year for the accolade of the best kept lock. Judging by our experience of having visited thirty-three other locks over the last nine days, Bray had a good chance of being presented with the award.

The river was still like a mill pool and the sun was very warm on our backs as we paddled quietly along deep in our own thoughts. Whilst in the lock it had dawned on us that we only had two more overnight stays remaining until our trip was over. From now on the river would become less and less rural as it entered into its next stage of life. Below Windsor the Thames would take us through an ever-increasing urban landscape, the flanking hills, beechwoods, farmland and villages were now beginning to be left behind.

The roar of the M4 disturbed our thoughts as we passed under the concrete, New Thames Bridge which carries the motorway over the river.

A little further on we passed Monkey Island on which is situated a secluded luxury hotel. The island once belonged to the monks of Merton Abbey which was near Bray, it was then called Monks Eyot, the possible root of the modern name. In 1738 The Duke of Marlborough bought the island and built two fishing lodges upon it.

In around 1840 the two lodges on Monkey Island were merged and expanded into a hotel frequented by the rich and famous. It was here in 1991 that 'The 'Birmingham Six' chose to stay on their first night of freedom after being freed by the Court of Appeal. These were the 6 men who had spent 16 years of their life sentence in jail; convicted of the Birmingham pub bombing during 'The Troubles' in Northern Ireland. The court of appeal eventually found their convictions were unsafe. Kev and I spent the next ten minutes or so discussing where we would have spent our first night of freedom if given a choice.

We now found ourselves on slightly higher ground to our left, passing the impressive Tudor brickwork of Dorney Court. Built in 1440 it's been lived in by the Palmer family for four-hundred years. The first pineapple to be grown in England was cultivated at Dorney Court by the head gardener in 1665. It was presented to Charles II who presumably ate it. At the time, the then present owner of the house, Roger Palmer, was married to one of Charles's many mistresses.

It had now become evident since leaving Maidenhead that many of the cruisers passing us, or moored alongside the lawns of the riverbank dwellings were becoming more opulent, mirroring the riverside properties. Some of the sea going vessels probably costing as much or even more than a fair-sized house. These large boats hardly created any wash as they slipped past us, as long as they were keeping to the Thames speed limit of 3mph, whereas a small boat with an outboard motor would generate quite sizeable waves.

We now had our first glimpse of Windsor Castle about three miles away across the flat open floodplain to our left. Built in 1070 by William the Conquer and added to and improved by most of his succeeding monarchs, it's the largest inhabited castle in the world.

To our right we passed the back of Bray Studios which are now used mostly for TV productions. It began life as a house built in 1750 for a publisher named Jacob Tonson. In 1951 the then derelict Down Place as it was called, was bought by Hammer Films where they made amongst other films, The Curse of Frankenstein, Horror of Dracula and the Mummy's Shroud, which after about eighty previous horror films, was the last to be made at Bray studios in 1966.

A little further on is Oakley Court, an atmospheric grand Victorian mansion built in the Gothic style which since 1981 has been another luxury hotel. In 1919 it was bought by Ernest Olivier, a friend of General de Gaulle. During the Second World War de Gaulle was a frequent visitor as the house was being used as the secret headquarters of the French Resistance.

After Olivier's death in 1965 Oakley Court was left uninhabited but was put to good use by the next-door studios. It was a ready-made spooky location for their particular genre. It was also St Trinian's School, Tommy Steele's home in Half a Sixpence and featured in The Rocky Horror Show.

The river now takes quite a sharp left as it begins to skirt around the Windsor Racecourse. Unfortunately, there wasn't a meeting on today otherwise we would have had frequent close-up views of the racing as we paddled by.

Just before Boveney Lock is, in my opinion, a building which is the opposite end of the spectrum to the grand Oakley Court. It's the small, now unused and lonely 12th century church of St Mary Magdalene. It can only be reached by footpath as it's so close to the river. Built of chalk and flint and still only lit by candles, it was built for the use of the bargemen and bargees working on the Thames. It's looked after by the charity, The Friends of Friendless Churches, which, Kev pointed out, now means that it isn't friendless.

There was just enough room for us in the lock amongst four capacious cruises which towered over us. I don't think anyone else knew we were in the lock apart from the lock keeper. Drink was being taken and had definitely already been taken for some time on one of the vessels. The crew of eight were speaking in very loud voices in order to make themselves heard above Santana who was performing via their more than adequate sound system.

Just downstream from Boveney lock is a bathing spot known by the scholars of Eton College, which is just across the fields. Nicknamed by the boys 'Athens', it was their custom to leap off the bank naked into the river. An old Etonian rule states that if a boat of females is approaching, the boys either have to jump into the water for the sake of modesty or hide behind the screens which were provided. Kevin and I were tempted for a second or two to re-enact this old custom but the water was rather cold, so we resisted.

The Thames bends around the end of the racecourse and then takes a sharp left-hand turn. A boat coming the other way at first sight seemed to be the venue for a mobile fancy dress party, but as it drew closer it was evident that the revellers on board where a troupe of male Morris dancers. They were a jovial crew and we stopped mid-stream for a chat. They informed us that they were on their way to Maidenhead to perform in four different alehouses during the afternoon. As Morris dancers tend to be avid beer drinkers, they were quite taken by our quest to partake of a drink in every pub we passed. After a whip-round they gave us a generous donation and then continued on their merry way.

We soon passed under the modern concrete road bridge carrying the Windsor bypass over the river and then almost immediately a wrought-iron railway bridge. It was built in 1849 and is said to be the oldest bridge in the world built of wrought iron still in use.

The soaring battlements of Windsor Castle now dominated the view. It towers over the river from a chalky outcrop which sits on a plain of thick clay, which suggest to some that the mound could have been man-made. It's known that there has been a fortress of sorts here since pre-Roman times. The castle was first built of wood by William the Conqueror in 1070 but in 1170 Henry II extensively rebuilt it in stone.

It's reported to be the Queen's favourite home. If she's in residence the Royal Standard is flown from the top of the Round Tower. The Royal Standard is quartered, showing three yellow lions on a red background in the top left and bottom right quarter. The bottom left quarter, depicts a yellow harp on a blue background and on the top right quarter, is a lion rampant with a yellow background. The flag flying today was the Union Jack, so she was elsewhere.

Windsor is a mecca for tourists and attracts thousands of visitors a year from all over the world and today was certainly no exception. On this warm Saturday morning the river was littered with a multitude of pleasure craft of all types and sizes, from small rowing boats hired by the hour to large passenger boats ferrying people back and forth along the river for an hour's pleasure cruise. People lined the bank feeding the abundant wildfowl, having picnics or just strolling along enjoying the sun and the character and atmosphere of Windsor.

There was also a multitude of Mute Swans. They must have been in their hundreds. Once gracing the tables of medieval banquets,

I don't imagine there would have been quite so many in this particular vicinity in years past, they are now of course a protected species.

There is a legend that the Mute Swan was first brought to England by Richard I on his return from the Crusades in around 1192. However, ornithologists believe that there is evidence that swans were present in England dating back as far as ten-thousand years ago.

Britain has three species of wild swan. The Mute Swan, which is by far the most prevalent, can be seen on lakes, ponds and rivers all year round. The Whooper Swan and the Berwick Swan are both winter visitors. The latter two are smaller and have quite distinctive calls whereas, as its name suggests, the Mute Swan is almost silent apart from an angry hiss when provoked. The Whooper and the Berwick have yellow bills with a black tip, the Mute has an orange to red bill with a black tip and a black knob over the nostrils, which is more pronounced in the male.

Mute Swan

The Mute Swan must be the most easily identifiable British bird with its pure white plumage and long graceful 'S' shaped neck. It never ceases to amaze me how they remain so clean and immaculate looking whilst living in a wet and often muddy environment.

Swans use their long necks to feed on underwater plants. If its neck is not quite long enough to reach the aquatic food in deeper water, it 'up-ends' ducklike. It also swallows grit and fine gravel for roughage which has led to many a swan's untimely death. As well as the grit and gravel they may have taken in lead shot and fishing hooks which have been discarded by careless anglers. The use of lead shot and weights have now been forbidden throughout English and Welsh waters.

When a swan is between two and four years of age it will look for a mate. When paired up they are not gregarious and go in search for an isolated nest site where they will aggressively defend their territory. The male known as the cob, and the female, the pen, tend to mate for life and return annually to their territory to breed. Unlike ducks, the male stays with his mate helping to raise the cygnets.

They remain together as a family until the cygnet's plumage changes from grey to white. They are then driven away by the parents and fly off to join a flock of other non-breeders which congregate in such localities as Windsor. These delinquent juveniles have a couple of years enjoying the singles life before settling down with a mate. Windsor can be likened to a holiday club in Ibiza for adolescent swans.

Being such a large bird, an adult swan is too heavy for a standing position take off. It has to run on land or the surface of the water rather like a plane, to get airborne. Whilst flying its powerful wing beats make a loud rhythmic whistling noise. When it comes into land on water it has to use its large, webbed feet as water skis, as it surfs to a stop with its wings outstretched as airbrakes.

We threaded our way through the throng of swans, ducks and pleasure boats to pass beneath the arched Windsor Bridge under the ever watch full eyes of the Castle. There has been a crossing point here for over eight-hundred years, but the present bridge was built in 1822 with three cast iron arches supported by two large granite pillars mid-stream. Since 1970 the bridge, which links Windsor to Eton, has been for pedestrian use only.

Eton is a village with only one main street, but it is dominated by Eton College. The College was originally founded for twenty-four poor scholars by Henry VII in 1440. He gave a large amount of land and other benefits including the right to eat swans on the Thames. Today there are still places for seventy 'King's Scholars', known as Collegers, who attend Eton on scholarships, but the majority of the boys pay full fees, they are known as Oppidans and usually have 'family money' as the fees are extremely high. These boys number around one thousand two hundred but do not live within the original college buildings but in large boarding houses situated in the village, some accommodating as many as fifty boys at a time. The boys, all between the ages of thirteen to eighteen, are required to wear as part of the school uniform, a black tailcoat, worn in mourning for George III.

Over its long history, up to the time we passed by, Eton College has educated nineteen Prime Ministers. The Victoria Cross has been awarded to thirteen old Etonians. It was at The Battle of the Somme that a platoon was led into battle across no-man's land led by an Etonian kicking a football. The Duke of Wellington was educated at Eton as was Prince William and Prince Harry and the list goes on of well-known alumni. Fictitious old Etonians include Tarzan, Bertie Wooster and James Bond.

On the celebrated playing fields of Eton, the main sports in which the boys participate are rugby and cricket but there is a more bizarre and brutal game which is unique to Eton. The Eton Wall Game, first played in 1766. As far as I can gather it's a mixture of football, rugby and mixed martial arts with ten players per side and very few rules, although there are two umpires. Players are not allowed to handle the ball and no 'sneaking', 'knuckling' or 'furking' are permitted?

The game is played against the base of a wall one-hundred and ten metres in length along a five-metre-wide pitch. The object is to score a goal at your opponents end of the wall. One goal is a door, it's known as the Good Calx. The other goal used to be an ancient elm tree but since its demise it's now a chalk line, known as the Bad Calx. The duration of the game is about fifty-five minutes with teams changing ends at half time after a five-minute break.

From what I've read the game consists of one great scrum, known as a 'bully', from which the ball hardly ever appears. Many injuries occur during a game, but no substitutes are allowed.

An annual Saint David's Day match is played between the Collegers and the Oppidans. It begins after the Oppidans have thrown their caps over the wall, which is owned by the Collegers, and they then climb over to retrieve them in defiance. The last time a goal was scored was in 1909.

A few hundred metres down-stream from the bridge is the 'Donkey House' situated just below the castle. It's Windsor's only riverside pub and one of its oldest. It's actually called The Boatman but is known locally as the Donkey House as it once stabled the donkeys which worked by the river.

It was 11.20 am when we left 'the lizard' safely chained to the pub jetty under the watchful eye of another friendly fisherman who hadn't caught any roach. As it had been a very warm morning and we had worked up a good thirst, we downed a pint each before wandering up to the town.

The name Windsor is thought to be derived from the Anglo-Saxon word 'Wyndesore' meaning, winding shore, which I suppose makes sense since Windsor is built along a prolonged curving bend in the river. Shakespeare wrote his play The Merry Wives of Windsor whilst staying in the town. It also has a soup, a chair and a perfect knot for a tie named after it. The high street was near the start and part of the 1908 Olympic marathon course. This was the race in which Dorando Pietri was immortalized in a flickering black and white film which shows him staggering, drunken like on rubbery legs in first place towards the finishing line. Just three or four metres from the finish he almost collapses and is helped over the line, only to be disqualified for being assisted.

The high street was swarming with tourists, so after admiring the castle from close up for a few minutes we retraced our steps to the sanctuary of the tranquil environment we had become used to. On our way back we crossed the bridge to visit the Hogs Head pub by the river on the Eton side. Another pint was leisurely downed before we returned to the Donkey House for lunch.

We managed to find a table on the terrace overlooking the river and enjoyed prawn sandwiches washed down with cider. We soon got chatting to other customers sitting in our vicinity, a fair number were American visitors. They wanted us to relate all we knew about the River Thames, Windsor Castle and the Queen. Another couple of pints of cider, generously donated, helped to loosen our tongues and it was nearly 2pm when we eventually bade farewell to our 'cousins from across the water'. Yet more unasked-for generous offerings were added to the fund. Our guardian of the canoe was still fishing but much to my companion's disappointment the keepnet, although holding several other species, was still bereft of his favourite fish.

A few minutes downstream brought us to Romney Lock. There was quite a backlog of boats waiting to enter but as usual we were called forward to jump the queue and got squeezed in amongst more 'gin palaces'. From the lock there's a fine view of the magnificent old buildings of Eton college. The lock's history goes back to the 1400's when the records tell there was a flash lock here called Bullokeslok . It was converted into a pound lock in 1795. Kev brought my attention to a notice on the lock side which stated that it was twenty-three miles to Teddington lock, our ultimate destination. I felt a sense of panic rise up inside me as I realised the end of our trip was very near, but fortunately, we still had a couple of days left.

Nearby is, J Suttons, Traditional Oar and Scull Makers, who make the oars for the Oxford and Cambridge crews. They also made the oars for Sir Steve Redgrave when he won his Olympic gold medals.

We left the lock and passed another long queue of boats coming up stream waiting to enter. We estimated that those towards the far end wouldn't be through the lock for at least another forty-five minutes.

We glided around a long sweeping right hand with another fine view of the Eton playing fields to our left, and then under yet another railway bridge, this one carrying the Waterloo to Windsor line. It's called Black Potts Bridge. The area around here has been known as Black Potts for at least three-hundred years but nobody seems to know why. A little further down-stream the Jubilee River, the flood relief channel which begins just above Maidenhead, re-joins the Thames.

For the next mile the right-hand bank is lined with Sycamore and Chestnut trees, the boundary of the extensive Home Park, Her Majesty's back garden. It's only a small corner of the four thousand, eight hundred acres of Windsor Great Park. At regular intervals black sign boards with white script informed us that no mooring was allowed. We wondered how long it would be before security arrived if anyone ignored the signs. Not very long we suspected.

We soon passed beneath the Victoria Road Bridge linking Windsor to the village of Datchet. It was rebuilt in concrete after suffering damage in 1967. Datchet's history is extremely old, older in fact than Windsor Castle by thousands of years. Evidence has been found of occupation going way back to the Bronze and Iron Ages.

The first person to own a motor car in Britain lived in Datchet. His name was the Honourable Evelyn Ellis who lived in a riverside home which is no longer in existence as it burnt down. His car, a Panhard-Levassour powered by a three and a half horse powered Daimler engine was made in Paris. It was shipped over to England and then on by rail to Mitcheldever railway station in Hampshire. On the 6th of July 1895 Ellis collected his car and drove it back to his home in Datchet, the first ever 'horseless carriage' journey in Britain. According to a newspaper report the fifty-six-mile journey took five hours and thirty-two minutes at an average speed of 9.84 mph. Ellis went on to be one of the founders of the RAC. His original car is in the Science Museum.

The Thames was extremely busy with boat traffic, mostly all very friendly. We suspected that this amount of boating activity would now be the norm as the river flowed ever nearer to London. This proved to be correct.

To our right we had a splendid view of the castle across Home Park. We passed the former Royal Boathouse which up until 1953 housed the royal barge, it's now kept at the National Maritime Museum at Greenwich. We also caught a glimpse of the white,

Frogmore House situated in the park. Its name derives from the preponderance of frogs which used to live in this once low-lying marshy area. The original house was built in 1680 and has been lived in over the years by many royals. It was enlarged and modernised in 1792 by Queen Charlotte. It became a great favourite of Queen Victoria, so much so that on her death she was buried, along with Prince Albert, in a specially built mausoleum standing on the west side of the house. They had both planned to have a mausoleum and within four days of Albert's death in 1861, the Queen had chosen the site. Victoria joined him in 1901. Our present Queen spent part of her honeymoon at Frogmore. At the time we passed by it was uninhabited but was used by the royal family to host private and official gatherings.

After looping around the Home Park, the river takes a gentle left-hand turn leaving the park behind and then passes under the Albert Bridge. The road which crosses the bridge runs through Datchet and then re-crosses the river via the Victoria Bridge under which we had passed upstream. Well before these two bridges were built, both designed by Prince Albert, there was a ferry crossing almost midway between them further up-stream linking Windsor to Datchet. This ferry was later replaced by a wooden bridge in 1706 but in 1811 it was decided it needed rebuilding because it had become unstable.

An argument ensued between Buckinghamshire and Berkshire as to who should pay for the replacement bridge because their boundaries met in the middle of the river. It was eventually decided that both counties were responsible for the rebuilding of the bridge. Buckinghamshire agreed to build their half and Berkshire their half and they would meet in the middle. The result was a 'hideous monstrosity', as Berkshire had built their half in iron and Bucks, in order to reduce costs, had used wood for their half of the bridge.

The bridge was eventually removed in 1847 as part of the Windsor Improvement Act which resulted in Prince Albert's two bridges being built. The old original bridge which replaced the ferry is the only bridge to have been built as a main crossing over the Thames that was completely demolished and not rebuilt.

A weir on our left barred us from following the river's natural course which takes a mile long meander before rejoining its original bearing. In 1822, when time meant money to the Thames bargemen, the cut was built thus eliminating the mile long loop. The island it created is known as Ham Island, now a nature reserve. There are a few dwellings on the island, the inhabitants use a private footbridge spanning the cut to access their homes.

At the end of the short cut, Old Windsor Lock was congested but as before the lockkeeper allowed us to jump the queue. Whilst in the lock we as usual engaged in conversation with the crews of the boats which surrounded us. By the time we departed we had accrued a fair amount of money for UNICEF and four cans of lager and a bag of toffees for us.

After the lock we soon passed a small island known as Friday Island. So named because it's supposed to resemble the footprint of Man Friday, which Robinson Crusoe found in the sand.

Dr Julius Grant once lived in the cottage on the island. He was a forensic scientist and it was he who proved in 1984, that the Hitler Diaries were, after all, fake. Dr Grant, who died in 1991, also analysed Tutankhamun's mummy wrapping and what's more, was involved in the development of Marmite.

I was weaned on Marmite. On each day on my return from school, my mother would have the top of a crusty loaf spread with a generous layer of butter and Marmite waiting for me. Have you tried a mashed banana and Marmite sandwich, scrambled eggs with Marmite or a poached egg on toast with Marmite? Trust me! My fellow traveller refuses point blank to try any of the above.

Old Windsor, on our left bank, as the name suggests is older than Windsor but now the 9th century village and the site of Edward the Confessor's Saxon Royal Palace have been consumed by suburban houses. William The Conqueror lived for a while in the wooden palace at the side of the river but he soon built his stronger castle three miles up-stream.

Sir Elton John has a house in Old Windsor and the golfer Nick Faldo is his near neighbour. In the 13th century church is an effigy of the author and diplomat, Sir Charles Murray who in 1850 brought the first hippopotamus to England. The hippo, named Obaysch, was from Egypt and went to live in London Zoo. Murray became very fond of Ogaysch and went to the zoo nearly every day to visit him.

It had become a hot cloudless afternoon and we felt in need of an excuse to stop but there seemed to be a shortage of alehouses in the vicinity. As we approached Wraysbury we were hopeful but to no avail. We passed Honey Pot Cottage where the actress Beryl Reid lived until her death in 1996, together with her large family of stray cats.

At last, half a mile further on the welcome sight of The Bells of Ouzeley came into view. It was by now 3.25. Jerome K Jerome described the establishment in his book as, 'a picturesque inn where a very good glass of ale may be drunk'. The ale didn't disappoint.

The Bells of Ouzeley has a long and varied history. The original building was built in the 13th century and brewed beer to supply Windsor Castle, it was also used as accommodation for bargemen and other river navigators. In 1936 it burnt down and unfortunately was rebuilt in the Mock Tudor style as it appears today.

The pub is named after a legend dating back to Henry VIII reign. Reputedly in 1538, during the dissolution of the monasteries, some monks were fleeing from Henry's agents. The monks had come from the now long disappeared Osney Abbey near Oxford. They had travelled down the Thames by barge carrying with them five large bells of repute which they were hoping to save from the Abbey. The story goes that the barge ran aground in the shallows by the inn. The barge capsized and the bells were swallowed up by the thick mud never to be found again. The pub was renamed The Bells of Ouzeley, a corruption of the name Osney.

According to newspaper reports at the time, on the 16th of June 1944 a V1 flying rocket, known as a 'doodlebug', exploded in the pub garden. Two bodies and four severely wounded were recovered from the damaged building.

As Kev walked ahead of me across the lawn to order our beers my attention was drawn to the back of his legs. They appeared to be very pale in colour. Having been exposed to the elements for the past nine days we had developed quite a healthy tan. We had worn shorts almost every day and the front of our legs had been very much exposed to the sun but being in a seated position the backs of our legs had remained in the dark. I pointed this out to Kev and of course on inspection, mine were the same. It's surprising how two middle-aged men can feel so self-conscious about such a trivial phenomenon!

It being such a hot afternoon and not knowing how long it would before be our next stop, we thought it best to have a couple of pints each. It was getting on for four o'clock when we took our leave and walked back across the crowded lawn, the backs of our legs shimmering in the sunlight.

The Thames now took us into Surrey, the sixth county it had visited. Since leaving Cricklade we had passed through Gloucestershire, Wiltshire, Oxfordshire, Buckinghamshire and Berkshire. After passing the town of Wraysbury it was now becoming very much a suburban river with houses and bungalows crowding down on each bank almost to the water's edge. But after about a mile the river becomes rural again for just a while, as it passes Magna Carta Island and Runnymede.

The small Magna Carta Island, known as the 'Birthplace of Democracy', was to our left. As every schoolboy and girl knows, on the 15th of June 1215 King John was summoned by his rebellious barons, who had tired of his inept rule, to travel from Windsor Castle to meet them at Runnymede to agree to their demands. The island was then owned by the nearby St Mary's Priory. The barrens had forty-nine grievances drawn up which needed to be addressed. The

Magna Carta or, Great Charter, is England's earliest constitutional document.

The charter he was being forced to sign was supposed to limit his powers and proposed the equality of all men before the law. Clause thirty-nine states that, 'No man shall be taken, imprisoned, outlawed, banished or in any way destroyed, nor will we proceed against or prosecute him, except by lawful judgement of his equals and by the law of the land'.

Other parts of the charter standardised weights and measures. Clause twenty-three deals with the right of navigation on the Thames and states that all fish weirs on the Thames were to be removed as they were a hindrance to trade and transport.

King John had no choice but to sign the Great Charter, however later that year, civil war broke out between John and the barons and John ignored his obligations under the charter. After he died in 1216 his son Henry III voluntarily reissued Magna Carta, with some changes, and it formally became English law in 1225.

Just past the island, a little way back from the river, are the diminutive remains of St Mary's Priory. The priory was built next to the Ankerwycke Yew. The tree is still standing and is reputed to be about two-thousand years old. Henry VIII is said to have wooed Anne Boleyn in its shade when she lived nearby in Staines.

To our right on the south bank a wooded ridge looks down on the river. On the slopes which cover one-hundred and ten acres, owned by The National Trust and known as Coopers Hill, are three memorials, situated well apart. We didn't stop because we had visited them before, but they are well worth mentioning.

The first is the memorial to the Magna Carta. In the centre of some oak trees there's a small Greek style temple housing a granite stone on which is inscribed, 'To commemorate Magna Carta symbol of freedom under law'.

Fifty metres or so away, hidden in the trees is the entrance to the J.F Kennedy memorial. In 1963 this acre of England what is given to the USA in memory of their assassinated president. A plaque reads,

'This acre of English ground was given to the USA by the people of Britain in memory of JFK, President of the USA 1961-1963, who died by an assassin's hand ....'

At the summit of Coopers Hill is the Commonwealth Air Forces Memorial. In the immaculate gardens is a set of cloisters consisting of many stone pillars on which are the names of 20,455 airmen and women who were lost over Britain and Europe during World War Two and who have no known graves. A tall tower with a spiral staircase to the top gives a breath-taking view of the Thames, Windsor Castle and the meadows of Runnymede.

The water meadows of Runnymede cover one-hundred and eighty-eight acres and have been maintained by the National Trust since 1929. They stretched for about a quarter of a mile alongside the river on our right. Unfortunately, the busy A308 runs fairly close to the bank, separating the river from this 'area of outstanding natural beauty'.

The name Runnymede is derived from the Anglo-Saxon 'runieg' meaning regular meeting and 'mede' meaning meadow. The council of the Anglo-Saxon Kings known as the 'Witan' was held at times at Runnymede. The very far off forerunner of today's parliament.

Many people had gathered at Runnymede on this hot Saturday. It's a very popular spot for family picnics and general get togethers. Part of the meadow had also been claimed by a large flock of Canada Geese grazing on the grass. Whilst feeding they make quite a mess and many a picnic blanket has come to grief, which tends to keep the two parties well apart.

The Canada Goose was introduced to Britain in the 17th century from North America as an ornamental waterfowl. Charles II kept them on his lake in St

Canada Goose

James's Park and large landowners soon followed suit. By the 1950s the geese had begun to spread, colonising gravel pits, parks and reservoirs and are now very abundant along the Thames. It's not a migrating bird as are many of the other wild species of geese in Britain.

It's a large handsome bird with a long black neck and chest with white cheeks. The upper parts of the body are grey with much lighter underparts. It's the most 'musical' of the geese with a far carrying 'honk'.

The river now takes an almost right angle turn away from the meadows and then virtually, almost immediately sweeps right to continue on its way to London. From now on it will be an almost completely urban scene on both banks. We had now been part of, and experienced all of, the River Thames's phases of life. From a narrow, young, energetic, untamed and at times lonely stream to a wide, languid, mature and now very busy river.

Many of the gardens of the bungalows and new housing on both banks were occupied with families and fisherman enjoying this sunny Saturday. The river was extremely busy and as the song goes 'There were big boats and wee boats and all kinds of craft…messing about on the river'. We took our time idly paddling amongst them, the mile or so to Bell Weir Lock, acknowledging the frequent waves from the riverside dwellers.

When we arrived, the lock didn't even have room for us so we waited patiently in the queue joining in with some jovial banter with other waiting crews. Kev's day was made when a young fishmen proudly showed us the five roach in his keepnet. By the time it was our turn for the lock, several cans of beer and lager, more sweets and about seven pounds in small change for UNICEF had been donated.

A few years back the lockkeeper at Bell Weir Lock retrieved a bag of rubbish from the river. On closer inspection some papers included in the rubbish were found to be a full set of floor plans for the Bank of England. They were very quickly collected by the constabulary without delay.

Just after leaving the lock, we entered a twilight world of what seemed like tall concrete tree trunks covered in graffiti. We were passing under the substantial bridge carrying the M25.

When we emerged from the gloom the glare from the sun reflecting off the water took us by surprise. In order to give our eyes time to adjust we pulled into the side and each partook of one of the kindly donated lagers. Somewhat refreshed and our eyes now fully functional we continued on our way.

We soon passed the quite large and long Holm Island that hides the secluded and much smaller Hollyhock Island on which there used to be a small house, pulled down in the 1930's, called The Nest. It was the secret hideaway of Edward and Mrs Simpson.

Somewhere around this area of the now commuter town of Staines, we should have passed the London Stone which stands by the river. It's one of a number of boundary stones, placed in 1285, that stand beside the rivers Medway and Thames which marked the City of London's limit of jurisdiction over the rivers fishing rights. The City greatly increased its revenue by charging duties on those licenced to fish. Before the locks were built this particular stone also marked the upper limit of the tidal river. We looked out for it but we must have missed it. I've found out since that the stone we were looking for was only a replica, the original is housed in The Old Town Hall's Art Centre in Staines!

Staines was originally a Roman town with a Roman bridge, one of the first to be built across the Thames. It's thought that Julius Caesar forded the Thames at this point when he first invaded Britain. The Roman bridge was later replaced by a Saxon bridge and that was replaced by a Norman bridge. In 1832 the present three arched white granite structure was built.

The Staines market hall once stood on the site of the present town hall. It was here in 1603 that Sir Walter Raleigh, the great explorer and favourite of Queen Elizabeth I, was tried and condemned for treason for plotting against James I after Elizabeth's death. The trial took place outside of London to avoid the plague.

For some reason Raleigh was spared the death penalty and was imprisoned in The Tower of London. In 1616 he was released by James in order to lead an expedition to find gold in South America with strict orders not to upset the Spanish who were also exploiting the native Americans.

Against the King's orders Raleigh's men attacked a Spanish fort. When he returned to England in 1618 Raleigh was executed to appease Spain.

Raleigh has the dubious honour of supposedly introducing tobacco to England after observing the indigenous population of Virginia smoking the weed.

In 1862, Frederick Walton, the inventor of linoleum opened his first linoleum factory in Staines. It soon became a very popular floor covering and was distributed all over the world. The Staines factory closed in 1969.

Just below Staines Bridge the River Colne adds its water to the Thames and almost opposite is The Swan, our over-night stopover.

The Swan has its own moorings, so we chained and locked 'the lizard' to the landing stage and booked in, it was around five o-clock: It's a fine 16th century inn, beautifully situated overlooking the river. The establishment is named from the swan upping ceremony previously mentioned. The flotilla traditionally stops here on the second day for their lunch. Samuel Pepys, the famous diarist, was a regular visitor.

The terrace was bathed in the late afternoon sun so before finding our room we relaxed in two very comfortable chairs and supped a beer watching the river flow past.

A group of Mallard ducks were busying themselves

Ducks Dabbling

feeding from the riverbed, up-ending with heads down and tails in the air.

> 'All along the backwater,
> Through the rushes tall,
> Ducks are a dabbling,
> Up tails all!
>
> 'Ducks' tails, drakes' tails,
> Yellow feet a-quiver,
> Yellow bills all out of sight
> Busy in the river!'

Kenneth Grahame
from the Wind In The Willows.

Mallards are probably the most common, widespread and best-known duck on the river and need little introduction. The colourful male has an easy life as once courtship and mating are over he has little to do with his mate and family. The dapple brown female is left to incubate the seven to eleven eggs and then look after the ducklings. The young can run, swim and feed themselves as soon as they leave the nest, after only a few hours of hatching. Perhaps only about three or four will survive to the flying stage after about six weeks if they are lucky. They fall prey to pike, rats, seagulls and other predators. Wet cold spells of weather also take their toll. The Thames has an ample population of Mallards and on every day of our trip we must have seen several.

Mallard Drake

It was such a pleasant spot that we hadn't realised how quickly the time had passed. Kev's wife Kate and their eldest son Richard had arranged to meet us for a meal and a catch-up so we had to hurriedly adjourn to our room for a quick shower and a change of attire.

We returned to the terrace to await their arrival from Coventry. We decided that we fancied a different cuisine tonight and so suggested to them that we should seek out an Indian restaurant for a curry. It was agreed and we soon found an establishment to our liking.

A very pleasant evening was spent chatting and eating and retelling our adventures until it was time to head back to the Swan for a night cap in the bar. Kate and Richard were spending the night with an old friend of Kate's at Twickenham. It wasn't worth their while returning all the way back to Coventry as they would be part of the welcoming party to meet us the day after next, at our last pub at Teddington.

Kev and I returned to our very comfortable room at about 11pm. We hung our trainers out of the window for the penultimate time and settled down to sleep with the faint aroma emanating from Kevin's open blue barrel, reminiscent of our evening meal.

CHAPTER 16

As Green Turns to Grey

Staines to Sunbury Lock – 9.5 miles

Under overcast skies but with no precipitation and after yet another substantial breakfast, we departed from The Swan at 9:30. From now on a grassy towpath beside the river would become a scarcity, for we were now entering serious urban sprawl where concrete and brick ruled. Never-the-less it was still the river we had got to know and it continued to hold its charm for us, but now in a different way. A peaceful corridor through the bustle and hyper activities of a suburban existence.

We soon passed beneath the Staines railway bridge. It has quite a striking appearance because in 1965 it was painted with yellow stripes to prevent swans from flying into it.

The banks along this stretch are occupied by a diverse style of dwellings made up of bungalows, chalets and houseboats. Some of the houseboats were quite unconventional and of indeterminate age and it's a wonder how a number of them managed to stay afloat. This seemingly haphazard settlement continued along both sides for about a mile and a half until we reached Penton Hook Lock.

The lock was opened in 1815 to cut out a half mile loop in the river which turns back on itself to almost complete a circle. Before the lock was built rivercraft had to navigate this half mile loop in order to travel just 20 yards (18m). Before its creation, barges would often attempt to break through the narrow neck of land during spells of high water. Although very hazardous, when successfully achieved it would have saved a great deal of time.

We shared the lock with three large cruisers which were travelling in convoy. They had been up as far as Oxford and were now returning to their moorings at Richmond. They had intended to have gone further upstream but one of their craft proved too large to pass under the notoriously low Osney Bridge. We shared some of our river experience with each other before we parted company but not before we had accepted yet another generous donation.

The bungalows and houseboats continued for about another half mile or so until they merged with the village of Laleham. The name means 'village by willows', which were very evident along the bank forming a barrier between the village and the river.

Laleham village and manor has been owned by the Lucan family since the Earl of Lucan bought it in 1803. The third Earl Lucan, who led the charge of the light brigade in 1854, is buried in the churchyard. The seventh Lord Lucan, who mysteriously disappeared in November 1974, was the patron of the church and the golf club president, he isn't buried in the churchyard, as far as we know!

The poet, Matthew Arnold, who described Oxford as, 'the city with its dreaming spires', also has his resting place in Laleham churchyard. His father, Thomas Arnold, was a renowned headmaster of Rugby School and was immortalised in the book, 'Tom Brown's School Days'.

The sun had burnt away the low cloud and was now making itself felt, so much so that we needed to don our caps and sunglasses. We also felt in need of a 'watering hole' but alas there were none to be seen in the vicinity.

The urban landscape had come to a brief end as we passed Laleham Park on our left , formerly the grounds of Laleham House but it's now a public park and campsite. Somewhere in the park is the site of Chertsey Abbey, built in AD666, once one of the greatest Abbeys in England. During the Reformation it was completely dismantled and the Benedictine community moved to Bisham. Very little remains on the site as much of the stone was shipped downstream and used for extending Hampton Court Palace. Shrewd recycling and money saving by Henry VIII.

The river was still very busy with craft travelling in both directions, mostly in the large cruiser category. It became apparent that as we got closer to London the boats were becoming even more opulent and capacious. We found it safer to stay close to the bank out of harm's way.

We now passed beneath the concrete M3 bridge, the hum of the traffic blocking out all other more pleasurable noises, to emerge just above Chertsey lock. This part of the river was once referred to as Laleham Gulls. It was an area of shallow water causing many difficulties for the barges and other river traffic. Back in the 16th and 17th centuries it was easily fordable. Chertsey lock and weir were built in 1813 to rectify this hazardous area.

There was a long queue waiting to enter the lock, so as was now the norm, we paddled to the front to make ourselves known and hopefully be called through with the first wave of craft. However, it soon became apparent that our tried and tested method of holding tussocks of grass to secure ourselves to the bank whilst waiting, was now going to be impossible as there was no grass or vegetation of any sort to grasp.

Whilst we were hovering around Kev noticed what at first looked like a child's water slide situated just to the left of the lock gates. The top being at water level before descending into the weir-pool. On closer inspection it proved to be a chute for canoes, allowing them to bypass the lock by sliding down into a safe area of the weir pool. It was equipped with rollers which enabled a canoe to glide effortlessly down if the water level was too low. We decided to put it to use.

Not having encountered one before we were unsure whether or not to disembark and lead 'the lizard' carefully down the slide with the mooring rope, which seemed a little wimpish, or, stay on board and just go for it. As there was a fair amount of water cascading down the chute we decided on the latter.

We paddled back almost to midstream in order to gain some extra momentum. We paused for several seconds in the style of a long jumper revving themselves up before their sprint to the take off point. This needed to be successful as we had become aware that we had gained an audience. Accurate steering would be essential as the chute was only just a little wider than the width of the canoe.

Kev was in the steering seat at the rear. "On my command, ramming speed" he ordered. "Ok then" I dubiously replied. "Go!" shouted Kevin. We went for it – and his aim was spot on! As we entered the chute at already a fair pace, the descending surge of water, the rollers and gravity took charge. As I was at the front, I was the first to become aware that the incline was far steeper than our first impression.

We shot down the chute at a rate of knots to be deposited in a calm corner of the weir pool. I was drenched as the front of 'the lizard' dived briefly below the surface. The sudden unexpected baptism of cold water momentarily took my breath away, but the laughter and applause from the onlookers quickly restored my equilibrium. Another lesson learned - but great entertainment! After a few minutes spent bailing out, we paddled out of the weir pool and continued on our course downstream, whilst the warm sun began to dry out my T-shirt and shorts.

Most of the locks from now on proved to have canoe chutes installed to allow canoeists to by-pass the locks. We decided however, to continue to go through the locks as usual because utilizing the chutes would have meant missing out on the craic and banter we shared with other fellow lock users and the lockkeepers.

Just before Chertsey's stone bridge, which featured in Charles Dickens's book Oliver Twist, we saw the welcome site of The Boathouse pub. It looked fairly new, built to resemble a large wooden boat house with plenty of tables on a patio leading down to the water's edge. Seated at one the tables were two females who as we approached waved enthusiastically in our direction.

We soon realised that one of the said females was Kev's wife Kate, with her friend Rachel with whom she had stayed the night. Kate had reasoned that The Boathouse would be the first of our days stops and had approximated our time of arrival to within twenty minutes.

It was around 11:30 when we left having spent about three-quarters of an hour chatting and consuming a couple of pints. We bid farewell to Kate until tomorrow when we would meet again at our last pub.

Duly refreshed we resumed our expedition downstream past Chertsey, one of the oldest market towns in England. It also boasts to have arguably the oldest cricket club in England, founded in 1737. In the 18th century it was one of the strongest clubs in the country and in 1778 it beat a Rest of England team by more than an innings.

At the time when Chertsey Cricket Club was first formed the game was played with only two stumps at each end. Each pair of stumps was bridged with a single bale, which had to be dislodged by the ball in order for the batsman to be bowled out. Chertsey had a bowler amongst their ranks by the name of Edward 'Lumpy' Stevens who is regarded as crickets first great bowler. He is reputed to have been extremely accurate and on incessant occasions would beat the batsmen. However, the ball would pass between the two stumps leaving the bale in place, thus the batsmen remained in.

As you can imagine 'Lumpy' became extremely irritated and complained frequently to the Cricket Association. In 1775 they eventually agreed that a middle stump with two small bales should be added. From then on 'Lumpy's wicket haul rapidly multiplied.

The considerably sized curfew bell, once the property of Chertsey Abbey, now hangs in the Church of St Peter in Chertsey. The bell plays a major part in a romantic historical story.

During the Wars of the Roses a Lancastrian soldier was captured by the Yorkists, thrown into jail at Chertsey and condemned to die at the sounding of the curfew bell. However, he was pardoned by the King, but the messenger with a reprieve from London was seen waiting for the ferry on the opposite bank with only a few minutes to curfew. The soldier's lover, Blanche Heriot, realised that the reprieve wouldn't be delivered on time so she flung herself on to the clapper of the curfew bell thus preventing it from sounding. A bronze statue of Blanche can be seen by Chertsey bridge. The curfew Bell is still rung at 8pm each night from Michaelmas (29th September) until Lady Day (25th March).

In the seventies, Keith Moon, the eccentric but very talented drummer of the rock band The Who, lived in Chertsey.

The urban landscape was again temporarily replaced by the one hundred and seventy-five acres of one of the great flood plain meadows of the Thames known as Chertsey Meads. A public area popular with dog walkers and families where four hundred plant and one hundred and eight bird species have been found.

Before the flow of the river was regulated by the weirs and locks, the river along this stretch running past Chertsey Meads was only 1.3 metres deep which enabled cattle to be herded across to the meadows to graze. During the great flood in 1947 the river is said to have become three miles wide at this point.

Urbanisation soon returned as we approached Weybridge, and Shepperton lock. Before the lock the river divides around the substantial Pharaoh's Island. It was given to Lord Nelson after the successful Battle of the Nile in 1798. He used it as a fishing retreat but it's now a settlement of large private dwellings only accessible by boat.

Shepperton means, 'shepherd's habitation' but the assembled flock we were about to meet were definitely not of that ilk. As we rounded the far end of the island, the point of which was colonised by a cluster of willows, we noticed beneath the trees a flotilla of six small motorboats each with the crew of one. They were milling around each other in a haphazard way which resembled the dodgem cars at a fairground. When they spotted us, they abandoned their frolicking and surrounded 'the lizard'.

Five of the craft were controlled, and I use that word loosely, by females, the other by a solitary male. Drink had been and still was being taken. One lady had probably taken a few more than the others and we were in fear of her ramming us.

The assembly turned out to be an amiable group of work mates from a local estate agent on their annual summer outing. They forced us to drink wine and eat crisps and were genuinely interested in our trip, giving a generous donation to the cause.

We spent a good twenty minutes in the company of these gregarious associates who were messing about on the water like a flock of unruly ducks, before we managed to bid farewell. At one point we had to persuade one of their number that it wouldn't be a good idea to clamber into our canoe. It was to be the nearest we came to being kidnapped by an Amazonian tribe of female warriors.

A few minutes after tearing ourselves away from our estate agent friends, we came upon The Thames Court Inn built in the 1920's, it has an interesting history. It started life as the private residence of the Dutch Ambassador, but then became a select private members club in the 1950's, later to become an inn. Inside it's embellished with fine hand painted delft tiling, a legacy from its Dutch occupancy.

We sat in the garden and soon got chatting to the owner of a beautifully painted traditional narrowboat moored next to 'the lizard'. He was now retired and having lost his wife a few years back had decided to sell up and buy the narrowboat on which he now lived, passing his time cruising up and down the Thames and other inland waterways, frequently meeting old friends and making new ones.

As it was just past midday, we decided to join him for lunch. In convivial company time passes quickly and more food and drink seem to be consumed than is normally necessary. An hour and a half later our newfound friend retreated to his boat for a nap, while we rather unsteadily resumed our places in the canoe and set off on the few hundred yards downstream to Shepperton Lock.

Ignoring the canoe chute, we joined the front of the queue. We sat quietly waiting for the lock to open using a convenient set of steel steps descending from a concrete wall into the water to steady ourselves. The wine, the beer, the steaks and the sun were taking effect and I was feeling rather drowsy.

I was just nodding off when we were called into the lock. I think Kev, who was sitting behind me, had also dozed off as I had to rouse him a couple of times before I caught his full attention. We were placed in the lock alongside a small cruiser whose crew consisted of four middle aged chaps out on the river on this fine sunny afternoon determined to enjoy themselves. Yet again drink was being taken and they were very eager for us to join them and promptly offered us a can of lager each. To be honest it was the last thing either of us wanted but it would have been churlish to have refused, so we accepted their kind offer and drunk their health.

Almost immediately after vacating the lock we passed on our right the confluence of the River Wey and the River Thames, marked by a pleasant iron bridge. The town of Weybridge is built alongside the River Wey, which is navigable for twenty miles to Godalming, with thirteen locks. It was one of the first man made navigations in Britain. Three hundred and fifty years ago the Wey was impassable until Richard Western, a wealthy landowner spent a great deal of his own money transforming the river into a navigable highway by copying the lock and canal system, then widespread in the Netherlands.

Weybridge was once only a very small village, just a place where a bridge crossed a river, but it rapidly grew after Henry VIII built Oaklands Palace at Weybridge in 1538 for his fourth wife, Anne of Cleves. Later the palace became the favourite home of James I. In its garden he established The Kings Silk Works where silkworms were kept to provide silk for weaving.

When Charles was executed at the end of the civil war in 1651, much of the palace was demolished, however, quite a large dwelling remained which between 1790 and 1827 was owned by Prince

Frederick. He is better known as the Grand Old Duke of York who marched ten thousand men up a hill and then back down again. Oaklands is now a hotel, the chimneys of which can be seen from the Thames protruding over the treetops.

Just after the River Wey joins the Thames the towpath swaps banks and there was quite a queue on both sides waiting to make the crossing via the Shepperton Ferry which still provides a service for pedestrians. There's been a ferry here since the reign of Henry VII and it has been in continuous operation for over five hundred years.

The river now traverses around D'Oyly Carte Island named after Richard D'Oyly Carte who bought it in 1887. He built a house on the island and used it as a country retreat for him and his family. He was host to many famous people amongst whom were William Gilbert and Arthur Sullivan. Whilst staying on the island they wrote the song 'Tit Willow', which is featured in their comic opera The Mikado. The inspiration for the song supposedly came from the willow trees at nearby Shepperton which could be seen from the island. Richard established the D'Oyly Carte Opera Company, a luxury hotel empire, amongst others, The Savoy, and also built two of London's theatres.

After the island the Thames divides, the natural course taking a looping three-mile route past Shepperton with its renowned film studios. The film director John Boorman lived in Shepperton, one of his notable films being 'Deliverance'. A very apt film for us!

The natural course of the river is still navigable although quite shallow in places. I wish now we had taken the original course, perhaps a more interesting route, instead we took the straight three quarters of a mile Desborough Cut which was created in the 1935 to yet again make it quicker and easier for the working barges and boats of the era.

The cut is named after Lord Desborough who was head of the Thames Conservancy at the time it was built, a post he held for 32 years. In all accounts he was quite an extraordinary sportsman. Twice he swam the Niagara rapids, the second time to prove to

Paddling Our Own Canoe

sceptics that he had indeed done it the first time. He was a member of the Oxford boat race crew in 1877 when the race was declared a dead heat, and also the following year when Oxford won. He rowed across the English Channel on three occasions and climbed the Matterhorn. He was also the amateur punting champion. In 1908 he was president of the London Olympics. In all he served on one hundred and fifteen committees. Where on earth did he get the time and the energy?

When the cut was completed, it created a man-made island of one hundred and twelve acres now known as Desborough Island. It's almost uninhabited, much of it being open space for public use having access via two bridges. A part of it is left as site for nature conservation.

As we paddled along the cut, the island to our left was obscured by hawthorn, oak and sycamore trees. On the right a road ran close to the water's edge.

About halfway along the cut we spotted, what we thought at first glance to be a small otter, but when it reappeared I was able to identify it as being a mink. The American mink was introduced in Britain early in the 20th century to be bred in captivity on fur farms. They proved to be expert escapees and many were also given their freedom by rogue animal welfare groups. The mink quickly started to breed in the wild and are now widespread in mainland Britain. They seem to have little fear of humans, being active at all hours of the day even when people are in evidence.

For most of the year they are solitary animals having their own territory which they patrol and fiercely defend from other

Mink

mink. They live near water, rivers, canals, lakes and marshes and are good swimmers and climbers. The mink will have several dens within its territory, perhaps in a hollow log, a hole in the bank, and even in an abandoned nest of a large bird. Their diet consists of anything they can handle, from a mouse to a rabbit. They take fish and birds such as moorhens, coots and ducks.

The American mink has been blamed as one of the main reasons for the depletion of the water vole and have been known to devastate the population of waterfowl in an area. They have now been officially classed as a pest.

Having rejoined the natural course of the river at the end of the cut, we passed beneath the low, metal, and it's fair to say, very ugly Walton Bridge and the resumption of suburbia. It's the fifth bridge to be built on this site, the first constructed in 1747. It was a timber latticework construction once described as 'the most beautiful wooden arch in the world'. In the Dulwich Picture Gallery, there's a painting by Canaletto depicting the bridge. The second bridge, constructed of brick and stone in 1788, must have been equally attractive as it was painted by J.M.W. Turner.

Before the first bridge there was an ancient ford on the site. This is another spot where Julius Caesar is reputed to have forded the Thames with his invading army in 64BC. Nearby, the Engine River adds its water to the Thames.

Walton on Thames, on our right bank, is where Julie Andrews was born in 1935.

'Lumpy' Stevens is buried in the church yard.

Things were becoming desperate on board 'the lizard' as both Kevin and I were feeling the effects of the earlier beverages. A 'pump out' was becoming a necessity.

As usual in these situations, the paddling became more urgent and conversation ceased.

As luck would have it, not one but two pubs, almost side by side, came into view in the nick of time. The paddling increased to 'ramming speed'.

The staff and customers of The Anglers first became aware of our arrival when we burst into the bar and Kev, hopping from foot to foot, enquired in a distressed manner the direction of their facilities. Duly relieved we returned to the bar and apologised for our earlier abrupt entrance and hasty disappearance.

The Anglers holds the dubious record of being the fiftieth pub visited on our trip.

It was our original intention to attempt to reach that magical number, but having succeeded we decided there was no point in passing any other remaining hostelries without stopping. The landlord bought us both a pint in way of celebration.

The pub has existed since the mid-18th century but has been extensively modernised.

The weir at Teddington now marks the tidal reach of the river but before it was built, in 1811, the tide would reach as far upstream as Walton. The foreshore in front of The Anglers was then a popular venue for fishermen.

After a pint apiece and the all-important photograph we adjourned next door to The Swan. The present premises were built in the 1900's on the site of a previous inn dating from 1760. It gets its name from the swan upping tradition, the 'uppers' always stopping at the swan on their way to Staines.

In 1909 Jerome Kern, the American composer of over seven hundred songs including, 'Smoke Gets In Your Eyes', 'The Way You Look Tonight' and appropriately, 'Old Man River', stopped at The Swan whilst cruising on the Thames. He fell in love with the landlord's daughter, and they subsequently married in St Mary's church in Walton. When in England the couple always stayed at the Swan.

In 1915 Kern was due to return to The Swan from New York on board The Lusitania to be reunited with his wife. Luckily for him he overslept, having stayed up late playing poker and missed the boat. His friend Charles Frohman, an America theatre manager and producer who was on board, died when the ship was sunk by a German U-boat.

Another couple of pints later we said farewell yet to more new acquaintances and continued on our way. It was now three o'clock with the hot Sunday afternoon sun smiling down upon us without a cloud in the sky to impede its vigour.

The river was busy with an accumulation of craft of various types and sizes from small rubber inflatables to obese cruisers. At one point we found ourselves amongst a flotilla of paddle boarders, some kneeling, some standing, but all with a fixed look of concentration on their faces. We kept a lookout for our estate agent friends, but to no avail. I wondered if they managed to return their hired boats safely and unscathed from whence they came and were able to reclaim all of their deposit?

It's a fairly straight stretch of about a mile to Sunbury lock, often used for regattas. The first Thames Punting Club Regatta was held along this course in 1891.

Both banks were congested by a concentration of houses of little interest and the now familiar houseboats.

Before the Lock we needed to stop at The Weir Hotel, a classic Victorian pub built in 1830. Its large riverside terrace was crowded with all tables taken so we sat on the lawn with the other revellers. There was a great atmosphere and we could have stayed well into the evening but we tore ourselves away after about an hour before it got too 'messy' and moved on.

The lock approach was heaving with the longest queue of boats awaiting entry that we had come across so far. We decided to give the lock a miss this time and take the canoe chute route instead to hurry proceedings along. As we were now aware of the procedure, we slid down into a calm corner of the weir pool in a more sedate manner than previously.

Sunbury weir has the highest volume and speed of water on the Thames and for that reason it's very popular with free-style kayakers. They were out in force today, paddling fearlessly into the white, turbulent mainstream of water as it tumbled angrily into the weir pool. Some capsized but resolutely regained an upright position by expertly executing an 'eskimo-roll' and then heading straight back into action to test their skills again in the raging waters.

We sat and watched the kayakers for three or four minutes admiring their fearless skill, but decided not to join in as the sun was too hot, Kev had his watch on, we might have lost our sunglasses and we both needed the toilet. We could have come up with many more excuses but those will do for now!

Sunbury dates well back in time, evidence of Bronze Age settlements have been found in the area. It was recorded in the Domesday Book as a village. In the 1660's the wool merchants of London moved out of the city and made it the 'in' place to live. Charles Dickens used the churchyard of St Mary's Church as a setting in his book Oliver Twist. Bill Sykes and Oliver slept under a yew tree in the churchyard on their way to Shepperton to commit the burglary which went badly awry.

Sunbury seems to be a Mecca for singers and musicians. Eddie Calvert the jazz trumpeter, Adam Faith, David Gilmour from Pink Floyd, Tom Jones and Dickie Valentine have all lived there at one time or another.

We re-joined the main course of the river and paddled past the extensive queue of vessels awaiting their turn to enter the lock to go upstream. After a few minutes we came upon The Phoenix, it was about four o'clock. It's a very pleasant pub that has its own landing stage and terrace overlooking the river both of which we made good use of for half an hour.

The Phoenix was originally two cottages which were knocked into one in around 1818. It's said to be haunted by an old woman who took her own life in one of the original dwellings.

After using their facilities, which again were urgently needed, we found a spot on the terrace and relaxed, each with a cider. Luckily as it turned out, we fell into conversation with an amiable young couple, recently married and still at the holding hands and looking into each other's eyes stage. During the course of our conversation, we happened to mention that we were booked in at The Flower Pot for the night and asked them if they knew of its whereabouts. They instructed us to go back towards the weir bypassing the lock, to find The Flower Pot just past The Magpie. Somehow, we had passed them both unnoticed. We knew our berth for the night was somewhere below Surbiton lock but we could have been way down stream before realising we had in advertently passed by!

After thanking them for their valuable information and wishing them all the best for the future, we retraced our steps back upstream towards the weir. We soon had The Magpie in sight, it wasn't like us to have missed a hostelry, for by now we had become very adept at spotting pubs and inns, even from a distance. But to be fair to us The Magpie was quite a small unassuming place and The Flower Pot, we later found, was back off the river at the top of its very long, narrow garden. We moored 'the lizard' at the end of The Magpie's pocket-sized garden terrace and supped another cider in the warm late afternoon sun.

The Magpie is one of the oldest pubs in Sunbury dating back to about 1729. In 1889 a group of music hall stars, led by two comedians, Jo Elvin and Jack Lotto, met at The Magpie and formed The Grand Order of Water Rats. Still going strong, it's a charitable organisation formed to help show business colleagues who are less fortunate and in need of support. The first 'King Rat', elected in 1890, was a music hall singer of comic songs by the name of Harry Freeman.

Jo Elvin, Jack Lotto and Richard Thornton, a music hall owner, were regular drinkers at The Magpie. Thornton, an avid supporter of the 'sport of kings', owned a trotting pony named Magpie which he regularly raced. After one particular race, held in heavy rain, the horse was described as looking like a drowned rat, hence the title was conceived, The Grand Order of Water Rats.

For quite a while we both sat quietly, deep in our own thoughts, which when I broke the silence proved to be similar. "Do you realise," I said to my old mate, "this time tomorrow we will have probably gone our separate ways."

"That's just what I was thinking," he replied.

It was a strange feeling of a mixture of sadness and a sense of achievement and elation. Nothing more was said for a further few minutes as we both re-immersed ourselves back into our own thoughts. The melancholy mood persisted as we proceeded to move a little further upstream to The Flower Pot, our eleventh and last overnight mooring. However, our sombre state of mind soon left us and our spirits rose after a couple of verses of 'messing about with the lizard'.

We needed to find safe anchorage for 'the lizard' as it became apparent that The Flower Pot did not have a landing stage or moorings. We spotted Wilson's Boatyard a little further on and decided to ask if they would mind an extra boat for the night. They were very obliging. She spent the night in the company of two beautifully handmade small wooden canoes dating back to the 1920s. We were told there were originally three such craft called, 'Daddy Bear', 'Mummy Bear' and 'Baby Bear'. 'Baby bear' was requisitioned by the Navy for a clandestine mission during World War 2 but sadly never returned.

It was 5.15 and still very warm as we walked back along the towpath with our barrels and the other bits and pieces to The Flower Pot. It's another of Sunbury's old pubs, once a coaching inn dating back to the 1700's, now tastefully modernised inside and very comfortable. We were shown to our room and after a shower and change of attire we retreated back downstairs to the bar, to decide how we were to spend our last night.

The curry we had had the night before had made another pleasant change from pub grub so we chose to explore Sunbury to see what it had to offer on its gastronomic scene. We found several very inviting restaurants but, in the end, decided to go oriental and settled for a 'Chinese'.

It was around 10pm when we arrived back at The Flower Pot and adjourned back to the bar for a nightcap. There was a lively crowd in, but unlike our usual practice we didn't join the throng but sat away in our own corner and reminisced with laughter and nostalgia over the past eleven days.

Midnight was about to strike when we retired to our room. After the ritual of hanging the trainers out of the window for the last time, we settled down to sleep. Tomorrow was to be a short paddle of only eight miles but we were determined to savour every inch of the way.

CHAPTER 17

Parting Is Such Sweet Sorrow

Sunbury to Teddington Lock – 8 miles

Monday 24th August began as a warm sunny day with a blue, cloudless sky and a slight breeze, perfect for paddling a canoe.

The landlady of The Flower Pot very generously made no charge for our substantial breakfast. During the trip we had met some very benevolent folk who in different ways had donated to the cause. Our faith in human nature had risen considerably.

It was 9am when we were reunited with 'the lizard' and paddled away from the boatyard for the last chapter of our journey. We passed The Magpie and The Phoenix for the second time but despite habits dying hard, it was too early to stop.

Some fine Georgian houses line the riverbank at Sunbury, one of them by the name of Monksbridge has a colourful history. In the 1920s the liberal MP, William Dudley Ward, lived there with his wife Freda. At the time she was the mistress of the Prince of Wales before he met Wallis Simpson. The Prince, whose nickname was 'teddy', had a large topiary teddy bear created in the garden on the river bank as a 'thank you' to Freda, which is still to be seen to this day.

In the 1950s Monksbridge was converted into a nightclub called Le Club de Clio where actress Diana Dors was frequently amongst the clientele. In the 80's the property became the home of Pink Floyd rock band member, David Gilmour . The name of their album, The Wall, is said to have been inspired by the wall around the tennis court.

The river wasn't as busy as the weekend, but there were still plenty of boats to look out for and many opportunities to sing the Hawaii Five-0 theme as we rode their wakes. The Thames was now separating Middlesex from Surrey, Surrey being on the right bank with Middlesex on the left.

After passing Sunbury Court Island with its impeccable array of chalets and bungalows, the opposite side is taken by a large area of reservoirs which stretched for almost three quarters of a mile along the Surrey bank. A seemingly endless, Victorian built high brick wall separates the reservoirs from the river which somewhat restricts the view. We employed the 'hundred stroke ramming speed' method to get past as quickly as possible. This somewhat boring stretch comes to an end as the river divides around Platt's Island.

The island has a history of naval boat building. A boat builder, who occupied the island by the name of Thorneycroft, was awarded a contract by the Admiralty to construct motor torpedo boats and landing craft during both world wars. Thorneycroft's boat building business on Platts island came to an end in the mid- 1960s.

We had only been going for 45 minutes but we decided to pull over by the Hampton ferry to stretch our legs and also to kill a bit of time. The plan was to arrive at Teddington lock at 5pm where the welcoming committee had planned to assemble to witness the end of our adventure. As we only had eight miles to cover on our last day, we didn't want the anti-climax of arriving ahead of the said committee.

The Hampton ferry has been in service since 1514 and is one of the oldest ferries on the Thames still in use. For a reasonable charge the ferry will take adults, children, dogs, bicycles and pushchairs back and forth across the river between Hurst Park and Hampton.

Hurst Park, on the Surrey bank, was once a prominent sporting venue. In 1723 one of the first organised competitive cricket matches was played here between The Gentlemen of London and The Gentlemen of Surrey. After the game both teams took tea at Hampton Court as the guests of the Prince of Wales.

Another 'first' took place at Hurst Park. In 1758 one of the earliest recorded golf matches was played between John Hume and The Reverent Alexander Carlisle.

The park was also the place to go and watch bare knuckle fights. The contests were banned at this venue in 1816 after one of the combatants was beaten to death by his opponent. It then became a racecourse until 1960. Alas, most of Hurst Park is now covered by a housing estate.

We left our canoe under the watchful eye of a young fisherman who, much to Kev's joy, had caught three Roach which he proudly showed to us in his keepnet. They were a metallic blueish silvery colour with red fins and red eyes all about twenty centimetres long. On average a Roach will grow to be between twenty to thirty centimetres and weigh around a pound, although the British record is a whopping four pounds four ounces.

They're a very common fish widely distributed in lakes and rivers and are easily caught by anglers. As they tend to swim in shoals, if you catch one you are likely to catch a few more. The Roach is an unfussy omnivore feeding on insects and their larvae, crustaceans and vegetable matter and so they take almost any bait presented to them. They in turn have many natural predators such as Pike, Perch, Eels and fish-eating birds and mammals.

We spent twenty minutes or so wandering around Hampton. It's a pleasant enough place with a diverse mix of properties from several eras, ranging from period cottages to more recently built developments, clustered around its dominant church. The village is yet another setting for Dickens. Bill Sykes and Oliver called at an inn in Hampton on their way to the burglary at Shepperton. In Dickens novel, Our Mutual Friend, Mortimer Lightwood and Eugene Wrayburn spent their summer vacation in a cottage in the village.

Two notable guitarists of contrasting styles are associated with Hampton, Brian May, the rock guitarist with Queen, was born in the village and Julian Bream, the famous classical player also grew up there.

In 1754 David Garrick, the actor, playwright, theatre manager and producer bought Hampton House. In the garden, Garrick had a white classical temple built as a tribute to William Shakespeare in which he placed a bust of the bard sculptured by Roubiliac, once described as 'probably the most accomplished sculptor ever to have worked in England'. The bust is no longer in situ but can be seen in the British Museum. Later we had a fine view of the temple from the river as we passed by.

Whilst ambling around Hampton we came upon an off-licence and an idea alighted on Kev's shoulder. He suggested we bought a bottle of Champagne to drink as a way of celebration when we arrived at Teddington. The motion was carried and he went inside to emerge a few minutes later clutching a bottle of Cava. He rightly made the point that a bottle of Champagne would be a wasteful extravagance. Moreover, our allotted kitty, brought with us for daily expenses was getting low and we didn't know how many more 'stops' we'd need to make.

When we returned to our canoe guardian, he eagerly reported that he had caught four more Roach since our departure. I made a mental note to one day explain to Kev that other than Roach there are Perch, Carp, Dace, Tench, Barbel, Gudgeon, Pike, Trout, Eel, Bream, Chub, Pope, Bleak, Bullhead, Rudd, Ruff, Catfish and Minnows available to be caught in the Thames.

After stowing our precious bottle of Cava carefully away we set off again passing the impressive Garrick's Temple amongst some trees sitting on the lawn of Hampton House. Just downstream from the temple, on the same side, we passed a strikingly elegant and well-maintained houseboat by the name of Astoria. It dates from 1913 when it was built for the impresario Fred Karno. Since then, it's had various owners but in 1986 it was bought by David Gilmour of Pink Floyd who turned it into a recording studio.

Just before Moseley lock, we passed Tags Island, one of the largest islands on this stretch of the Thames, named after Tom Tag, a successful boat builder who built a hotel on the island in 1872. It became another of the 'in' places to visit and attracted the famous and the well-heeled set of the day. The Prince of Wales entertained Lily Langtry and Alice Keppel there, and Sarah Bernhardt, the French actress, stayed for a while at the hotel. J.M. Barrie of Peter Pan fame rented one of the hotel's houseboats.

In 1912 the lease was bought by the aforementioned Fred Karno, who at the same time had his luxurious houseboat, the Astoria, built. The hotel was converted into a music hall and casino which he named Karsino, which at its most popular period rivalled Skindles Hotel in Maidenhead.

Karno became one of the great comedy music hall slapstick comedians and impresarios and has been credited as discovering Max Miller, Charlie Chaplin, Will Hey, Stan Laurel and Flanagan and Allen. They were known as 'Karno's Army'. He has also been credited as the inventor of the 'custard pie in the face' gag.

In 1926 Fred Karno was declared bankrupt and the hotel went into steady decline. It was eventually demolished in 1971 and the island became the property of the 'upper-class' houseboat community whose houseboats now encircle it.

Opposite tags island, on the Middlesex bank, is a genuine Swiss chalet. It was shipped from Switzerland in 1899 and reassembled as a garden feature for a now demolished house. The five-storey chalet is now an extremely luxurious riverside home.

At the downstream end of Tags Island is a densely forested island called Ash Island which is also surrounded by grandiose houseboats.

Kev came up with a new source of amusement as a diversion to paddling. 'The pie in the face game'. Between us we had to compile our top ten living celebrities who we would like to be the recipient of a pie in the face, delivered personally. We had to form our own list first and then compare and between us agree with the final ten. It was surprising how many we quickly agreed upon. The top of our list needed no discussion. The majority were TV presenters with a few MPs making up the number. The final top ten could be disclosed for a sum of money!

At one point the game was interrupted by a call from Radio Oxford. It was to be their last contact with us and they wanted to record a potted report, to be aired in the morning, of how we had fared during our twelve days on the river. Kev did the honours whilst I did my best to put him off by impersonating the noise of ducks in the background.

Just before Moseley lock the river begins a long, left-hand bend around Bushy Park and Hampton Court Palace. The area was created in the 16th century as a hunting park for the palace. Covering around one thousand six hundred acres it's the second largest of London's eight Royal Parks, the largest being Richmond Park.

Teddington Hockey Club, arguably the worlds' oldest surviving hockey club, has its home in Bushy Park. Some say that it was from here in around 1871 that the rules of the modern game were established.

During the Second World War part of Bushy Park was utilised as the European headquarters for the US air-force. General Eisenhower used it as his base when planning the D-Day landings.

It was 10.25 when we reached Moseley lock with its impressive weir, it's the second largest lock on the Thames second only to Teddington, which was only four and a half miles downstream. We still had plenty of time so decided to leave the canoe at the lock and become tourists for a couple of hours. The plan was to follow in the footsteps of J. K. Jerome's 'Three Men in a Boat' by visiting the Hampton Court maze.

We crossed the river by way of Hampton Court Bridge. It was like entering another world, one we would soon be permanently rejoining. The road was bumper to bumper with traffic in both directions and the pavements were teeming with pedestrians. We threaded our way through the throng, our river water perfumed trainers leaving a scented trail in our wake.

The first bridge on this site was built in 1753 replacing, as was the norm, an ancient ferry. It was of a wooden construction reminiscent in appearance of the Chinoiserie style of the bridge depicted on Chinese Willow Pattern plates. It only lasted twenty years needing to be replaced by a more substantial structure. The present bridge was opened in 1933 and was designed to blend in with the palace.

We found the maze in the grounds of Hampton Court quite easily and confidently entered. At this particular time of the day, we seemed to be the only ones attempting the challenge. The maze was commissioned by William III in 1690 and was originally planted with hornbeam later to be replaced by yew. It's the oldest surviving hedge maze in the UK and covers one-third of an acre and has half a mile of pathways. The average time to reach the centre is twenty minutes. Average of course meaning that some people complete the challenge much quicker than twenty minutes and others a lot longer. Kevin informed me that he had a foolproof system that never failed when negotiating mazes.

After my intrepid pal and I had passed the same discarded crisp packet for the third time I began to question Kev's fool proof system. However, I kept my thoughts to myself and dutifully followed my determined leader in silence. We strode on ever hoping that around the next bend we would come upon the wooden bench which marks the centre of the maze. Kev was obviously getting more and more frustrated, and I was finding it harder and harder to suppress the laughter I felt bubbling to the surface. At yet another dead end, my silence got to him. "Well say something!" he demanded.

I don't think it helped when I replied in a deadpan voice. "I wonder what time they close?"

Kev gave me a long thoughtful stare before declaring that he had given up and suggested we go back to the exit. I agreed and asked him which way was the exit. The look of despair on his face was the trigger which prevented me from holding back my restrained laughter any longer. For a second or two Kev remained silent then he too saw the funny side of the farcical situation and also relaxed into laughter.

After a moment or two a state of calm was restored and we began, as far as we vaguely knew, to retrace our steps. Up to now we seemed to have had the maze to ourselves but as we rounded yet another bend, after passing the said discarded crisp packet again, we stumbled upon an obviously well-acquainted young couple sitting on a bench. We had achieved our objective and reached the centre of the maze. It had only taken us thirty-nine minutes!

We eventually found our way back after passing the crisp packet twice more. We met a few other intrepid souls near the exit who were just beginning their quest and we couldn't help the smug look of success on our faces as we wished them good luck. I asked Kev why he hadn't offered them his foolproof system, but he ignored my question.

In spite of the extra quarter of a mile or so we had trekked around the maze we were enjoying the exercise, so we decided to extend our walk even further by seeking out the royal tennis court which is situated around the back of the palace.

Hampton Court Palace is an incredibly substantial building, part Tudor and part Baroque. Once a Knight Hospitaller house bought by Cardinal Wolsey in 1514 who began to extensively extend it. He wanted it to be the largest and grandest house in England. Henry VIII became rather jealous of the grand property and in 1526 'persuaded' Wolsey to give the then incomplete house to him as a present. Henry finished the job at great cost but it became his favourite royal palace requiring five hundred servants to run it. Five of his six wives were in residence here. Not at the same time! It's been extended over its five-hundred-year history by several kings and queens who made it their home. The palace was first opened to the public by Queen Victoria in 1838.

The greatest changes to Hampton Court were made by William and Mary who wanted to rebuild and extend the palace in the Baroque style. In 1689 they commissioned Christopher Wren to design and oversee the work which included demolishing the old building. But Mary died in 1694 and William lost interest. The work stopped, leaving thank goodness, half of the Tudor palace still intact but with a fine Baroque extension.

Finding the tennis court was a lot easier than finding the centre of the maze! It was built by Wolsey in 1526 and it's the oldest surviving Real Tennis court in England.

Real Tennis from which the modern game is derived is itself a derivation from an earlier ball game played in France in the 12th century when the ball was hit with the hand. By the 16th century a racket was being used. It's always played indoors, and the construction of a court is complex and difficult as it resembles a mediaeval courtyard. Real Tennis became particularly popular in France and in 1596 there were two-hundred and fifty courts in Paris alone. There are now only forty-eight active courts in the world, over half in Britain.

It seems to me to be a mixture of Squash and Lawn Tennis. It's played with solid cloth covered balls which have the consistency of a cricket ball. Pear-shaped, gut strung wooden rackets are used to strike the ball over a net into your opponent's half of the court. You may play the ball off the walls in the same way as in the game of Squash. The game of Real Tennis has the longest line of consecutive world champions of any sport, dating from 1760.

A mens singles match was in progress, so we were able to actually watch a game being played. It looked a great game to play and we decided to add it to our bucket list. Henry VIII enjoyed playing and it was here whilst in the middle of a match that he was informed of the successful completion of Ann Boleyn's execution, further downriver at the Tower of London. He wasn't going to let the trivial matter of his wife losing her head get in the way of a game of tennis.

We felt we had been away from the river for long enough, nevertheless we had enjoyed our brief deviation. Retracing our steps back across the bridge we stopped halfway to look down on Old Father Thames as he flowed proudly below us. We had been with him as he had grown from being not much more than a stream, where we first launched 'the lizard' at Cricklade, to now being a fully grown majestic river.

Before we rejoined 'the lizard' back at Molesey Lock, we visited our first pub of the day, The Streets of London, situated adjacent to the bridge. It's a large Victorian building with an attractive water side terrace. We enjoyed a pint each as we sat watching the river effortlessly slip past.

The time was 12.20 when we paddled off again after thanking the lock keeper for the safe keeping of the canoe and our belongings. After passing The Streets of London and emerging from under the bridge we noticed, on our right, the tributary of the River Mole from where the town of Molesey gets its name. Yet another river adding its water to the prestigious Thames. There is a theory that the river Mole was thus named because it vanishes underground on several occasions along its course as it flows from Gatwick Airport to its confluence with the Thames.

We hadn't travelled for more than ten minutes when we came upon The Fox On The River. It has an inviting large riverside patio with an impressive view of Hampton Court Park across the river with Hampton Court Palace in the distance. It seemed a good venue for lunch. After another beer and a very acceptable round of prawn sandwiches each we set off again. It was now 1.25 and we still had time to kill.

Luckily, five minutes later, Ye Olde Swan at Thames Ditton hove in to view. It's a large pub which dates back to the 13th century, once used as a hunting lodge by Henry VIII. Now of course much altered but still retaining character and very welcoming.

During the 18th century the area around Thames Ditton was notorious as a favourite haunt of highwaymen, in particular along the road leading to Portsmouth.

Beside the terrace of the pub is an attractive suspension bridge which links Ditton Island to the village of Thames Ditton on the Surry bank. Upon the island are a number of quality built wooden houses and bungalows each with their own gardens and moorings. Every dwelling is built on brick piles to avoid flooding.

Opposite the island, on the Middlesex bank, is an attractive red brick house built in 1700. It's situated in Hampton Court Park and was designed as a summer house for William of Orange by Christopher Wren. The young Queen Victoria was a regular visitor often staying there when it later belonged to her father Prince Edward.

Whilst we sat on the terrace supping another beer, a 'just past middle age' couple sitting eating lunch at an adjacent table engaged us in conversation. They had seen us arrive and were intrigued as to what we were up to. It transpired that he was the president of the Royal Canoe Club. Founded in 1866, it's the oldest canoe club in the world. In the same year it was founded Edward VII became Commodore of the club and in 1870, by command of Queen Victoria, it became the Royal Canoe Club.

The president and his wife showed a great deal of interest in our expedition and wanted to know all the details, especially the planning side of things. We eventually bade farewell to our esteemed and cordial new acquaintances and feeling a little self-conscious under their watchful gaze, re-embarked and hopefully paddled away in a manner resembling a degree of proficiency.

The river continues its long, left curve around Hampton Court Park and Bushy Park to head off in a northerly direction. On our right we passed the Victorian built suburb of Surbiton, famous for being the setting of the 70's sitcom The Good Life.

The first Briton in space, Helen Sharman lived in Surbiton, she was the first woman astronaut to visit the Mer space station. On the 18th of May 1991 she flew with two male Soviet cosmonauts on board the Soyuz TM-12 and docked with the space station on 20th May. Helen spent almost eight days in space before returning to Earth.

After only another ten minutes or so paddling we were required to stop again, at a pub named Hart's Boatyard. It's large and contemporary, more restaurant than pub, built to resemble a wooden warehouse, but the beer and toilet facilities were good. We stayed for about twenty minutes and nearly forgot the important photographic evidence of our visit.

We were now approaching the ancient market town of Kingston-upon-Thames. Its history goes way back to Roman times when the Romans used this shallow part of the river as a fording point. A settlement soon grew, as often happened where there was a fording point. Over the years the Saxons built a number of wooden bridges here and up until 1729 Kingston was the first bridge upstream from London Bridge.

Way back in AD838 long before any bridges were built on this site, King Egbert, the great grandfather of Alfred the Great, held a great council under a tree on the banks of the river to discuss with his 'counsellors' important matters of state, the earliest beginnings of a parliament. Between the years of AD902 to AD979 it is believed that the first seven Saxon kings of England were crowned at Kingston. The coronation stone or 'kings stone', the earliest throne of England, on which they were crowned, is exhibited outside of Kingston's Guildhall.

Since the 13th century a market has been regularly held in the old market square in the town. In 1628 Charles I declared that no other markets were allowed to be held within a seven mile radius of the town.

Donald Campbell, the only person to simultaneously hold the world water and land speed records was born in Kingston. As was John Cleland, the author of Fanny Hill.

On checking our Ordnance Survey Map of the River Thames, we realised that we had approximately only two and a half miles left of our journey. Where had the last 133 miles, 43 locks, 58 pubs and 12 days gone? I felt a strange feeling of panic as the reality dawned on me that our adventure would very soon be coming to an end. I wanted time to standstill. I didn't want to reach Teddington where our bubble would burst.

The huge expanse of Bushy Park and Hampton Court Park were still on our left with the urban sprawl of Kingston threatening to spill over into the river on our right. Two extremes separated by the river.

Half a mile further along this long wide stretch we came upon The Ram, a traditional pub with a large riverside garden. Now being in a permanent built-up area, pubs seemed to be cropping up more frequently, all needing our custom. As we didn't know how many more stops would be required between here and Teddington we decided this one should only be a fleeting visit. An Irish Whiskey each and we were away again in fifteen minutes. It was now 3.30 and the afternoon was slipping by.

The Hogsmill River joins the Thames at this point after flowing through Kingston. In the town the Clattern bridge crosses the Hogsmill. Built in 1175, it's one of the oldest bridges in Britain still carrying modern traffic.

A few minutes later as we approached Kingston Bridge yet another hostelry craved our attention, The Bishop Out of Residence. Nestled at the foot of the bridge, it's a fairly modern pub opened in 1979. The name refers to a previous house on the site owned by the Bishop of Winchester in the 14th century. After the Bishop died in 1404 the house was occupied by a brewer who is said to have entertained Henry V here in 1414. It became a rather unpleasant smelling tannery in 1663 and remained as a tannery up until 1963. Nothing now remains of the original building.

In olden times almost every town had at least one tannery. Ancient methods of preparing animal hides for leather goods involved using human urine and animal faeces, commonly dog and pigeon. These combined with the smell of rotting flesh made tanning an odoriferous trade. Nowadays chromium sulphate does the job in a less effluvious way.

We secured our canoe at the base of the 'Bishops' patio. We were well below eye level and needed to clamber precariously out of 'the lizard' and up and over the wall. Again, our sudden appearance startled another young family who up till then had been enjoying the peaceful scene before them. A good half an hour was spent chatting to the family over a beer. The two young boys aged about ten and twelve seemed completely taken with the idea of canoeing on the river. As we left dad was under considerable pressure to agreeing to buying them a canoe. I hope he did!

The present five arched Richmond bridge, built of Portland Stone, was built in 1828. The first, built of wood, replaced a Roman ford in the 12th century. Before the first bridge was built this was the lowest point downstream where livestock could wade across safely.

The last recorded public use of a ducking stool in Britain took place in 1745 by Kingston Bridge. The 27th of April edition of the London Evening Post reported that, 'a woman that keeps the Queens Head, in Surrey, was ordered by the court to be ducked for scolding and was accordingly placed in the chair and was ducked in the River Thames under Kingston Bridge in the presence of two thousand or three thousand people'.

Jerome K Jerome's three men in a boat began their 1889 fictitious journey to Oxford from Kingston Bridge. It became one of the most popular books of the time, selling two million copies within the author's lifetime. The book was credited at the time with the huge rise in the craze for leisure boating on the Thames. Already a popular pastime, it was intended to be a travel guide for boating, but it turned into a delightful sequence of comic anecdotes and situations as the three men and a dog rowed up to Oxford and part of the way back.

A little further downstream, after passing beneath Kingston railway bridge, we became conscious of the solid urbanisation pressing in from both sides of the river. Urbanisation means more people needing more sustenance which in turn means more alehouses by the river. So only five minutes later we came upon The Boaters Inn. Another very decent watering hole with its obligatory water-side terrace. Another pint each was downed amongst a lively crowd from whom we had to tear ourselves away as it was now well past 4. Less than one hour to go!

We began to encounter a growing amount of sailing and rowing activity along this stretch. Judging by the number of sailing and rowing clubs we were passing we guessed the weekends must be pretty hectic.

By now the alcohol consumption from the six pubs already visited today had had the effect of replacing our melancholy mood to one of blissful high spirits. There were plenty of motor craft making suitable wash for our Hawaii Five-O game, between verses of 'messing about with the lizard'. We very nearly came to grief as we were cutting across a particularly good set of waves whilst singing the theme tune at the tops of our voices, but not noticing another cruiser bearing down on us. In the nick of time, we were able to take evasive action. That would have been a very sorry end to twelve wonderful days. It did have the effect of calming us down, but only a little.

We knew we had at least one more pub to add to our list, The Tide End Cottage, at the very end of our trip at Teddington lock. Kev was already well acquainted with it as it was one off his regular haunts when he was a student at the nearby Strawberry Hill College, training to be a PE teacher. As well as Kev, other well-known celebs have been known to frequent 'The Cottage' because almost next door is the former Warner Brothers film studios.

Warner Brothers bought the studios in 1931 making several films on the site. It's now mainly used for producing TV programmes. Opportunity Knocks, The Benny Hill Show, The Tommy Cooper Show, This Is Your Life, Minder, Pop Idol and The Office are just some of the television productions which have been filmed at Teddington studios, (but now demolished since we passed that way).

Noël Coward was born in Teddington in 1899 and as a child sung in the church choir.

The National Physical Laboratory is situated at Teddington and it was here that Barnes Wallis developed his bouncing bomb made famous by the film The Dam Busters. To perfect his idea, he utilised the giant water tanks originally used for designing ships, now unfortunately demolished.

As we approached our final destination, we could see about a quarter mile away the iron girder footbridge spanning the lock cut which links Teddington to Ham. As we drew closer, we could make out a group of people wildly waving their arms in the air. It was the reception committee made up of Jan, Kate, Kev's youngest son Johnny and Sarah and Lorraine, two of my colleagues from school. We in return waved our paddles enthusiastically in the air as a saluting gesture nearly causing a capsize. Now that would have been a dramatic ending.

It was 5 minutes to 5, nearly perfect timing, as we passed beneath the footbridge amongst cheers and photographs. Several complete strangers joined in the waving and cheering. We called up to the committee to meet us at The Tide End Cottage at the other side of the lock, our last lock, our forty-fourth, the first being St John's Lock way back upriver with its statue of Old Father Thames.

Teddington lock, is the first or last lock on the Thames depending of course in which way you're travelling. It separates the tidal from the non-tidal waters and is the longest lock on the river. There are actually three locks. A small skiff lock, known as a coffin lock, a conventional launch lock and a large six-hundred-and-fifty-foot barge lock. A wide dramatic weir makes up the complex. From where we had set off we had witnessed the shallow tiny river, no more than five metres wide, grow to the mighty Thames which tumbled over the Teddington weir at a rate of about six hundred million litres per day in the summer, but rising to around fifty-four billion litres at peak flow in the winter. From here the river continues to grow in size and will flow another sixty-eight miles before it reaches its destination, the North Sea. To quote Shakespeare:

> 'The River Thames, that by our own door doth pass
> His first beginnings is but small and shallow
> Yet keeping on course, grows to the sea.'

It was from Teddington in 1940 that the flotilla of little ships assembled before bravely sailing across the channel to Dunkirk to assist in the evacuation of our troops, code named Operation Dynamo. The Tides End Cottage was used as the headquarters to coordinate the 'little ships' epic mission.

We went through the conventional lock with a large private launch, two smaller holiday hire boats and a narrowboat. As usual we got chatting to the crews who were all are very interested to hear of our adventure. It felt odd telling them that this was the end of our story.

Before we paddled out of his lock, the lockkeeper came over to us. As had been the norm with every lockkeeper he had known all about us before we arrived. He gave us a donation, congratulated us on the completion of our successful voyage and wished us a safe journey home.

We paddled round to the slipway which led down from the pub. The 'committee' had assembled at the top together with quite a few of the general public who gave us another round of applause; it was quite emotional. Before we disembarked, we retrieved our bottle of 'champagne' from its safe haven and took it in turns to drink the health of each other and to 'the lizard' until the bottle was empty.

The slipway afforded us the luxury of being able to step out of the canoe in a dignified way, not having to scramble out and up a bank or wall or onto a jetty as so often in the past. Just as well as our alcohol intake for the day had been well above average.

We all adjourned to The Tide End Cottage for a sandwich and one last beer. Our sixty-second Thames side pub. It dates from around 1820 and is situated at the end of a row of cottages. It was formerly numbers six and eight, the two semi-detached cottages were combined to create the public house.

Seated around a large circular outside table the 'committee' were eager to hear every segment of our adventure. There was far too much to tell in the time available, so I rashly said that I would write a book to recount our trip in detail. So here it is, twenty odd years later. Fortunately, we had kept a daily log.

At one point Kate complained of a pungent smell coming from beneath the table. Our Thames water sodden trainers were without ceremony, immediately consigned to an adjacent litter bin. They had served us well, being hung outside of our bedroom windows each night to ward off evil spirits.

The End of the Journey

It was getting on for 6.30 when Kevin and I decided the time had come for the inevitable task we had been putting off. We wandered down to the water's edge where, as usual, 'the lizard' was patiently awaiting our return. We carried her up to the pub car park and proceeded to transfer all of our baggage to the appropriate cars. Kev only took his curry infused blue barrel with his clothes, together with his paddle and 'nookie'. As I had an estate, I took all the rest, to be sorted out at a later date.

Our canoe now sat empty except for three plastic pint glasses, an empty bottle of Cava, a plastic wine glass, two empty cans of lager and some sweet wrappers. Every picture tells a story. These remaining items joined our trainers in the bin and 'the lizard' had to suffer the indignity of being strapped to the roof of my car.

We had the last photo taken outside of The Tide End Cottage and then didn't linger long over our goodbyes. Kev was coming down next weekend to help me take the canoe back to her home under Marlow bridge and to collect the rest of his belongings. We also needed to evaluate how much we could expect to have made for UNICEF and our respected schools after all the pledges per pub had been collected, plus, the contributions we had been given along the way.

Our last port of call

It was getting on for 7pm when we went our separate ways. Kev back to Warwickshire driven by Kate and me and 'the lizard' back to Buckinghamshire driven by Jan. An overwhelming feeling of fatigue swept over me and I felt more tired than ever I had over the last twelve days. I sat back and let my mind wander back over the days we had spent paddling our canoe down the Thames.

During our one-hundred- and five-and-a-half-mile journey we had accompanied the River Thames whilst it flowed through delightful quiet rural landscapes, picturesque villages, historic towns and bustling suburbia as it grew from a small country stream into a majestic waterway. The Thames has influenced the lives and history of the people who lived by its banks. They in turn have influenced the river, its shape, its look and even its course.

Populated since the Stone Age, the Thames Valley has always been an important part of English history. The Romans first named the river Temesis, they were the first to recognise the rivers strategic and cultural importance. Their fortifications, settlements and villas were scattered along the whole length of the river which flows for two-hundred and fifteen miles from its source to the North Sea. Warring armies have fought over important bridges and crossing points. Castles, palaces, monasteries and abbeys were built on its banks. Its power was harnessed to drive mills up to the early 19th century and it was used as a main highway and trading route. Barges laden with coal, stone, cheese and cloth navigated between Lechlade and London. In the late 13th century, the major cargo was wool, England's main product. In the Middle Ages milling and fishing were the two major industries along the river.

The Thames had always held an abundance of fish but by the 18th century the variety and quantity had been greatly diminished by pollution. The river is now very much cleaner and the fish stocks have increased back to a healthy level. Thanks to Kev's meticulous field study during our trip, we have unequivocal evidence that roach are being caught on a regular basis.

The pursuit of leisure now dominates the Thames, although the first recorded pleasure trip was way back in 1555 when a boat taking paying customers was charted from Abington to Oxford to watch the burning of the martyrs, Latimer and Ridley. Paddlers, punters, rowers, scullers, sailors, cruiser owners, holidaymakers, fishermen and women, walkers, picnickers, campers and swimmers are all drawn together by the camaraderie the river brings. Nearly everyone involved with the river are friendly and amicable as if all belonging to one harmonic fraternity bonded together by the magnetic Thames. I'm sure there are exceptions, but we didn't meet any.

We had met many characters and made new acquaintances along the way both on and off the water. The lockkeepers had kept a protective eye on us, the Thames grapevine keeping them informed of our progress. The locks were probably where mishaps were most likely to happen but we had survived all forty-four of them unscathed. The locks had provided us with a welcome break from paddling and afforded the opportunity to chatter and mingle with other river users.

The sixty-two pubs and inns we had visited had also been a break from paddling and a chance to socialise. All very diverse, some with an interesting history and even the odd ghost. Some of the 'overnight' publicans had been very generous giving us free board and lodging. Of course, all the pubs had the same added attraction to offer, the proximity of the river.

Our one overnight camping stop on the island at Hurley had been a great success even taking into account my air bed dysfunction. Our simple evening meal and the bacon rolls for breakfast had made a refreshing change from our usual cuisine.

Despite the majority of our diet consisting of pub grub and fried breakfasts with more than enough intake of alcohol and, it has to be said, feeling a little under the weather on the occasional mornings, my fitness level now felt very high. It just goes to prove what is said about regular exercise.

We had been privy to the rivers ever changing character during bright sunny and warm days and during dull, grey wet and cold ones. I had even conducted a live local radio interview in mid-stream during a violent overhead storm whilst Kevin bailed out the torrential rain rapidly collecting in the canoe.

It was easy to comprehend how the Thames with all its varied moods, features, and picturesque vistas had inspired and continues to inspire artists, authors, playwrights, poets and composers. Two of my favourite works of fiction have always been The Wind in the

Willows and Three Men in a Boat. The latter was unconsciously probably the origin of the idea for our trip. I now felt a greater affinity to both books and resolved to read them again.

The rich and the famous have always been attracted to the Thames and we had seen much evidence of this fact. Magnificent houses both old and new, mansions, villas and luxurious boat houses are strung along the river's length. Not to mention the 'gin palaces' and other expensive craft which are a necessary accessory to living in style on the banks of the river. All intermingled with more modest dwellings and boats of all sorts of designs, age and condition - but all sharing the same environment.

During the whole length of our journey, I felt we had been the guests of the true inhabitants of the river, the wildlife and the plants. There is a large diversity of flora and fauna above, beside and in the river and we had been lucky to come into contact with a fair few of the many species which have made the river their home. Being in a canoe, which is quiet and low in the water, we were able to approach fairly close to creatures before disturbing them. An abundance of wild flowers, especially in the upper reaches above Oxford, have made claim to their unique habitats on the banks, in the shallows and below the water. Many species of bushes and trees also claim their space along the water's edge providing shelter, food, and nesting material.

If I had to choose my favourite part of the Thames it would be the peace and seclusion of the upper reaches, but every section had its attractions. The Thames is not a mighty river compared with many others worldwide, but what it lacks in size it makes up for in historic interest beauty and diversity.

We had begun our trip as canoe novices but now after twelve days negotiating forty-four locks and paddling beneath approximately seventy-six bridges, I felt quite proficient and confident at paddling a canoe. I had spent the last twelve days in close proximity with my old friend and they had been the most carefree of days. All we had to worry about was arriving at our night's lodging before dark. As the furthest we had needed to travel in one day was eighteen miles, and that was on the first day, we had little to worry about. In spite of the hardship of having to frequently stop and consume alcohol I'm proud to say that not once did we fall in, but what I consider more important is, that not once did we fall out.

Epilogue

After a few weeks, when all pledges had been collected, Kev and I were able to present a cheque for £2,010 to a UNICEF representative in person. In addition, we were also able to give £500 to each of our school's PTAs – the money raised by our pupils' parents, a separate sponsorship from UNICEF.

A month or two later Kev and I followed the Thames back from Cricklade on foot to its official source in Gloucestershire. It was a walk of twelve miles to a meadow near Cirencester named Trewsbury Mead. A pile of stones beneath an old ash tree marks the spot where during periods of heavy rain a spring struggles to break the surface. A simple stone has this inscription upon it.

The Conservation of the River Thames
1857-1974
This stone was placed here to mark the source of the River Thames.

The source of Old Father Thames

Elizabeth I is said to have visited this remote spot in 1592 to look at, "the very first trickle of my fine Thames."

We passed only one pub along the way, The White Hart Inn at Ashton Keynes. A pint each and a photograph were taken.

During several expeditions over the following year, we walked both sides of the river from Teddington lock through central London to the Thames Barrier. As was now the custom, all pubs along the way were visited and photographs taken. Perhaps that could be the subject of another book, if you can wait that long.

Over the twenty years it's taken me to complete this book, Jan and I have married and my stepdaughters have produced three grandchildren. We've moved house twice and we've owned eight different cars.

I took early retirement from teaching on reaching sixty. I lost my dear mum at the age of ninety-one and I lost my faithful dog Barney who reached the grand old age of seventeen years. The terrible events of 9/11 occurred, we've lived through the great Brexit debate and have seen the comings and goings of five prime ministers. Prince Philip, the Duke of Edinburgh has passed away and sadly also Great Britian's longest reigning monarch, Queen Elizabeth II. We have endured the COVID-19 pandemic which resulted in me actually finishing this book to help pass the time during the forced lockdowns. If it hadn't been for the virus perhaps Paddling Our Own Canoe would have remained unfinished.

A great deal of water has passed beneath the bridge for us all since those twelve carefree days, and numerous changes will have occurred along the river. Some of the pubs may have changed their names and regrettably, some may have ceased to exist, but whenever my old pal and I get together on a 'Men Behaving Badly' day, conversation inevitably still drifts towards that summer of 1999 when we paddled our own canoe down the River Thames.

The Author

Phil Waterton was born in 1949 in a small village amongst the Chiltern Hills in Buckinghamshire. He worked as a teacher until taking early retirement at age 60. He then fell into his second career as a tutor on TV and Film sets, working on over 60 productions, including many major films with international stars.

Covid lockdown gave him the opportunity to complete *Paddling Our Own Canoe*. Just in the nick of time it seems, as a new challenge had arisen. He had begun to lose his eyesight rather rapidly due to problems with the optic nerves, for which there is no treatment, and he is now registered as severely sight impaired. He also had an operation for prostate cancer, diagnosed during his experience of sight loss.

He says: "It occurs to me that life is somewhat like travelling down a river, not knowing what lies around the next bend, but having to meet the challenge, overcome it and travel on".

Printed in Great Britain
by Amazon